ABE SAPIEN™

CREATED BY
MIKE MIGNOLA

A DARKNESS
SO GREAT

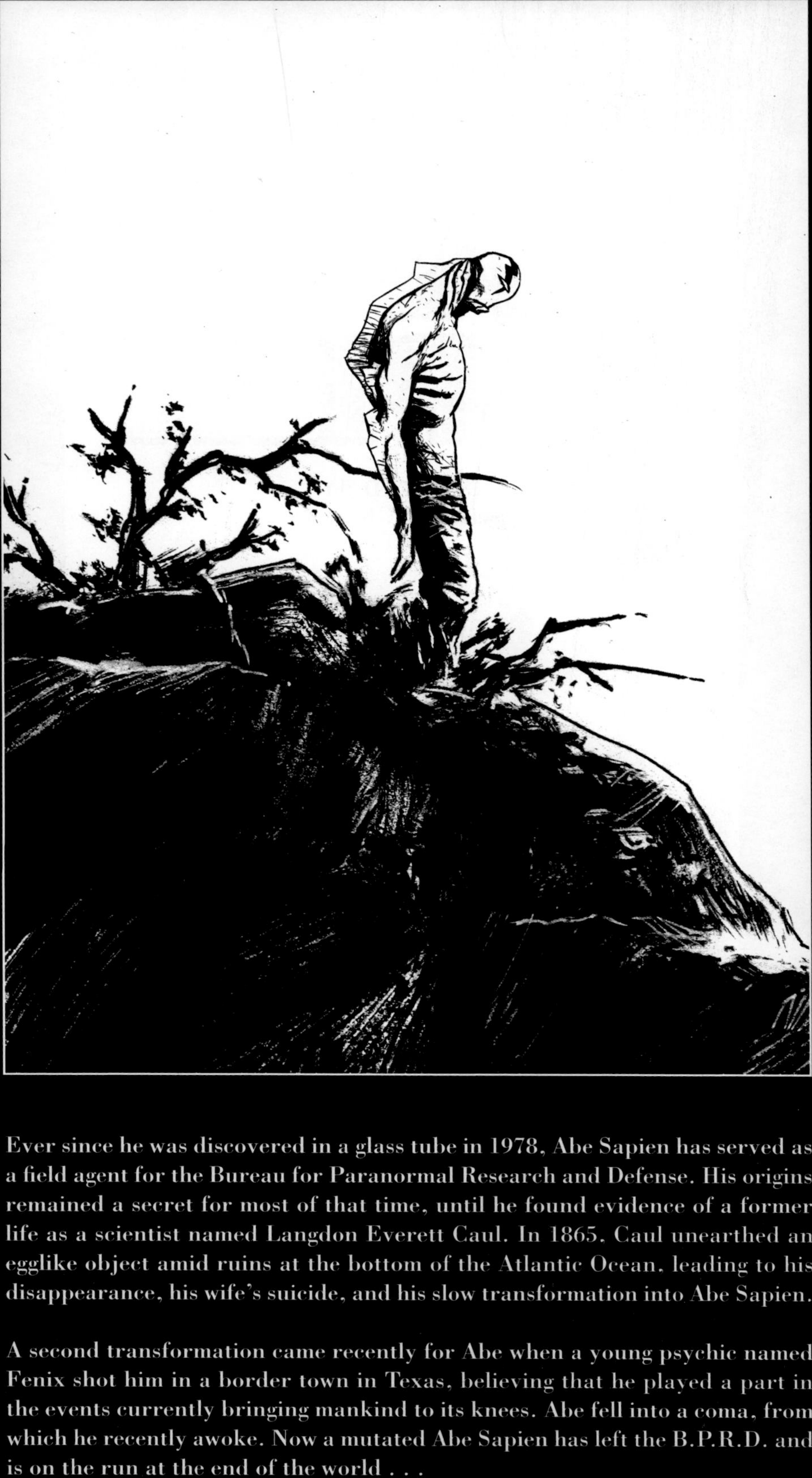

Ever since he was discovered in a glass tube in 1978, Abe Sapien has served as a field agent for the Bureau for Paranormal Research and Defense. His origins remained a secret for most of that time, until he found evidence of a former life as a scientist named Langdon Everett Caul. In 1865, Caul unearthed an egglike object amid ruins at the bottom of the Atlantic Ocean, leading to his disappearance, his wife's suicide, and his slow transformation into Abe Sapien.

A second transformation came recently for Abe when a young psychic named Fenix shot him in a border town in Texas, believing that he played a part in the events currently bringing mankind to its knees. Abe fell into a coma, from which he recently awoke. Now a mutated Abe Sapien has left the B.P.R.D. and is on the run at the end of the world . . .

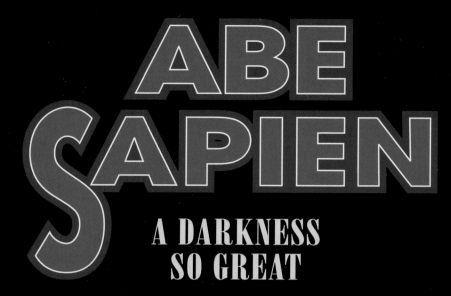

ABE SAPIEN

A DARKNESS SO GREAT

STORY BY
Mike Mignola and Scott Allie

Grace, Megan, and *Abe*

ART BY
Max Fiumara

Dayana and *Arbogast*

ART BY
Sebastián Fiumara

COLORS BY
Dave Stewart

LETTERS BY
Clem Robins

PAGE 7 BY
R. Sikoryak

COVER ART BY
Max and Sebastián Fiumara with Dave Stewart

SERIES COVERS BY
Max Fiumara with Dave Stewart

EDITOR **Scott Allie**
ASSISTANT EDITOR **Shantel LaRocque**
COLLECTION DESIGNER **Rick DeLucco**
PUBLISHER **Mike Richardson**

DARK HORSE BOOKS

Neil Hankerson *executive vice president*
Tom Weddle *chief financial officer*
Randy Stradley *vice president of publishing*
Michael Martens *vice president of book trade sales*
Scott Allie *editor in chief*
Matt Parkinson *vice president of marketing*
David Scroggy *vice president of product development*
Dale LaFountain *vice president of information technology*
Darlene Vogel *senior director of print, design, and production*
Ken Lizzi *general counsel*
Davey Estrada *editorial director*
Chris Warner *senior books editor*
Diana Schutz *executive editor*
Cary Grazzini *director of print and development*
Lia Ribacchi *art director*
Cara Niece *director of scheduling*
Mark Bernardi *director of digital publishing*

Published by Dark Horse Books
A division of Dark Horse Comics, Inc.
10956 SE Main Street
Milwaukie, OR 97222

First edition: July 2015
ISBN 978-1-61655-656-3

1 3 5 7 9 10 8 6 4 2
Printed in China

This volume collects *Abe Sapien* #18–#22.

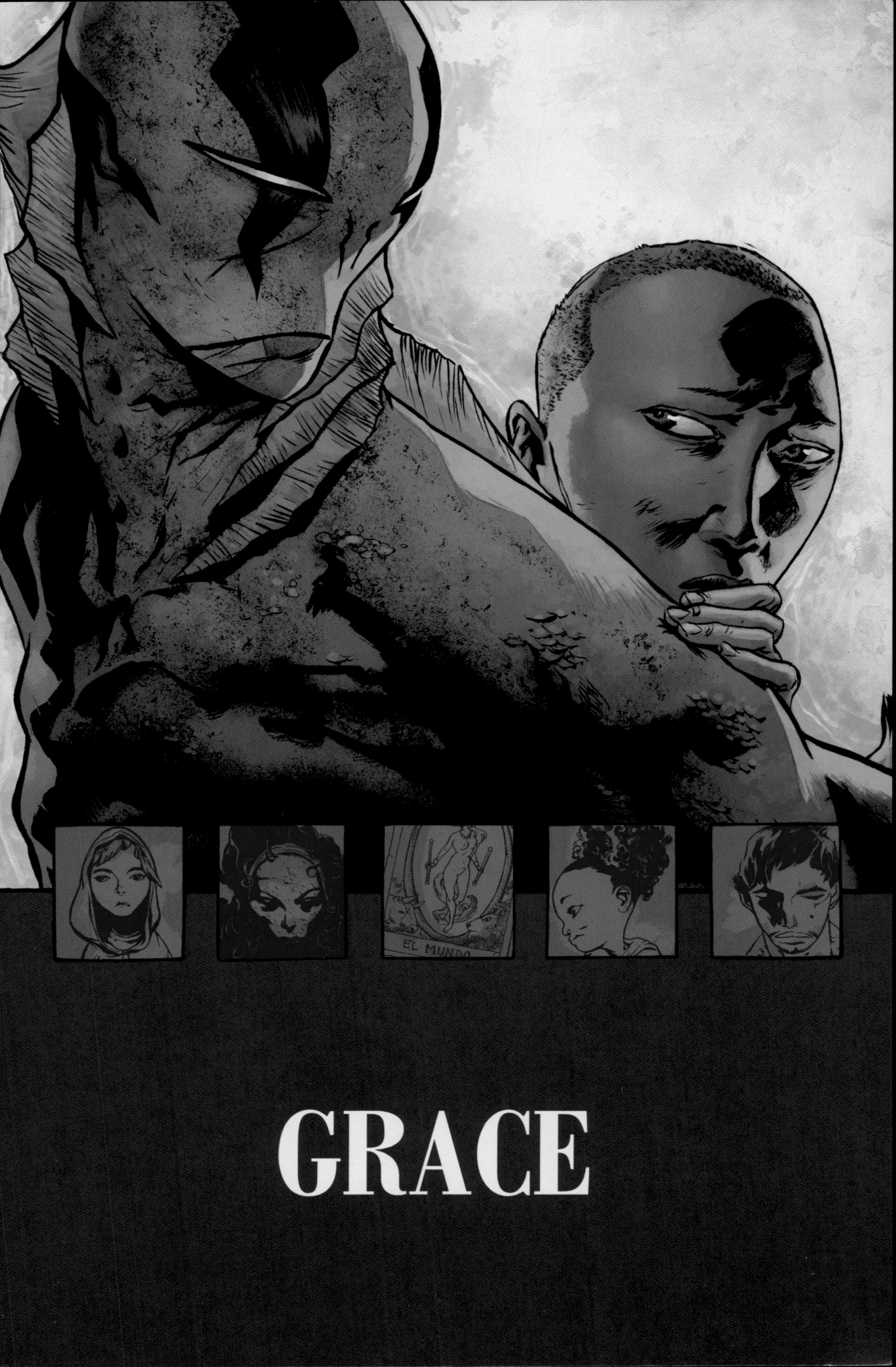
EL MUNDO

GRACE

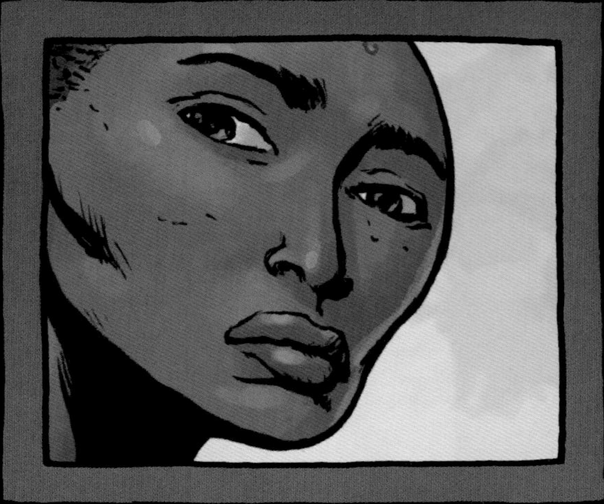

After losing her family in Gallup, New Mexico, Grace was held prisoner in an abandoned house by a delusional man. She was rescued by Abe Sapien and followed him through Arizona into Texas, never revealing the extent of her tragedy. Now traveling with a small Santa Muerte cult, Grace hopes to find peace along the Texas Gulf Coast.

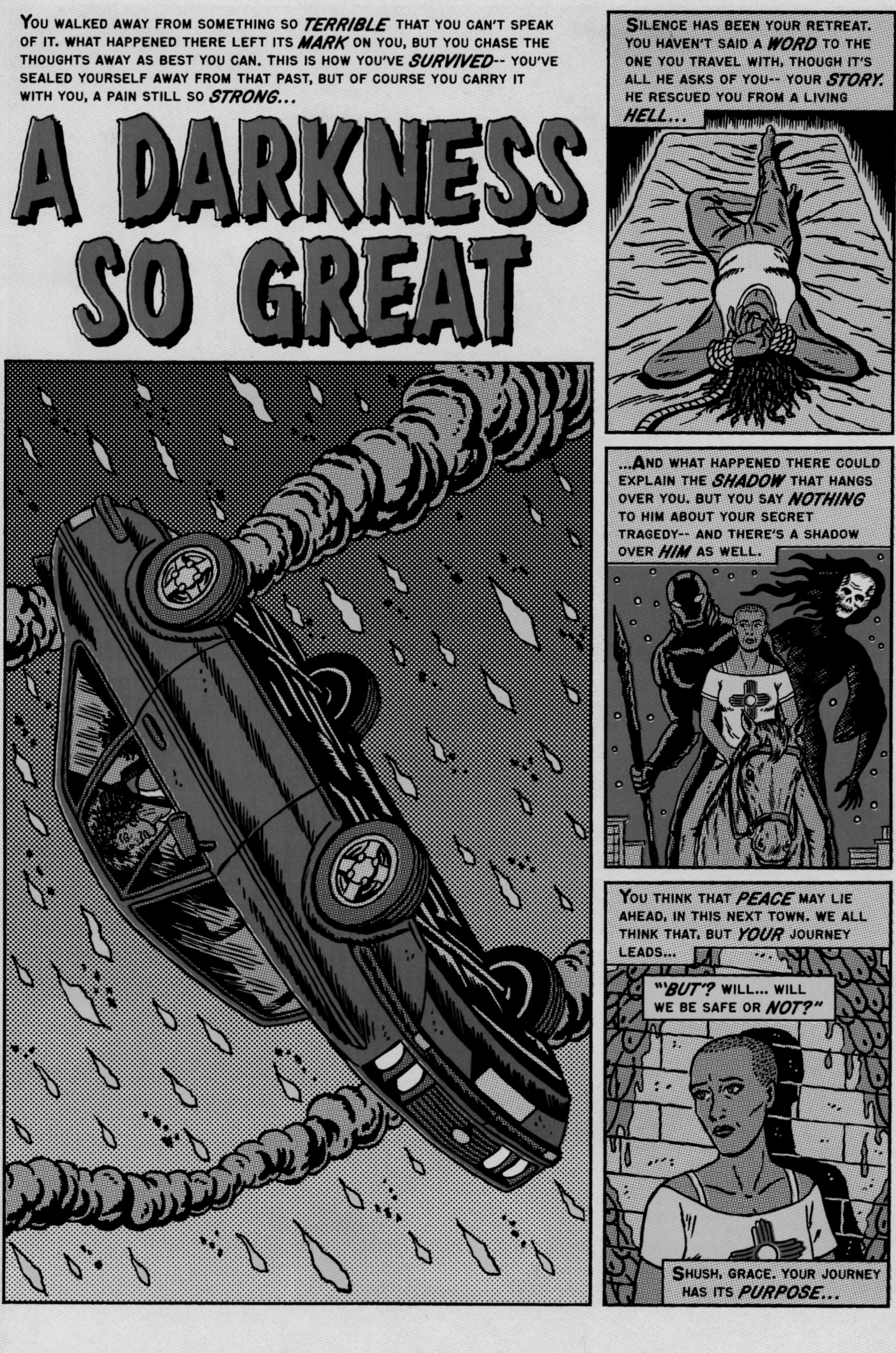
You walked away from something so TERRIBLE that you can't speak of it. What happened there left its MARK on you, but you chase the thoughts away as best you can. This is how you've SURVIVED-- you've sealed yourself away from that past, but of course you carry it with you, a pain still so STRONG...
A DARKNESS SO GREAT
Silence has been your retreat. You haven't said a WORD to the one you travel with, though it's all he asks of you-- your STORY. He rescued you from a living HELL...
...And what happened there could explain the SHADOW that hangs over you. But you say NOTHING to him about your secret tragedy-- and there's a shadow over HIM as well.
You think that PEACE may lie ahead, in this next town. We all think that, but YOUR journey leads...
"BUT'? Will... will we be safe or NOT?"
Shush, Grace. Your journey has its PURPOSE...

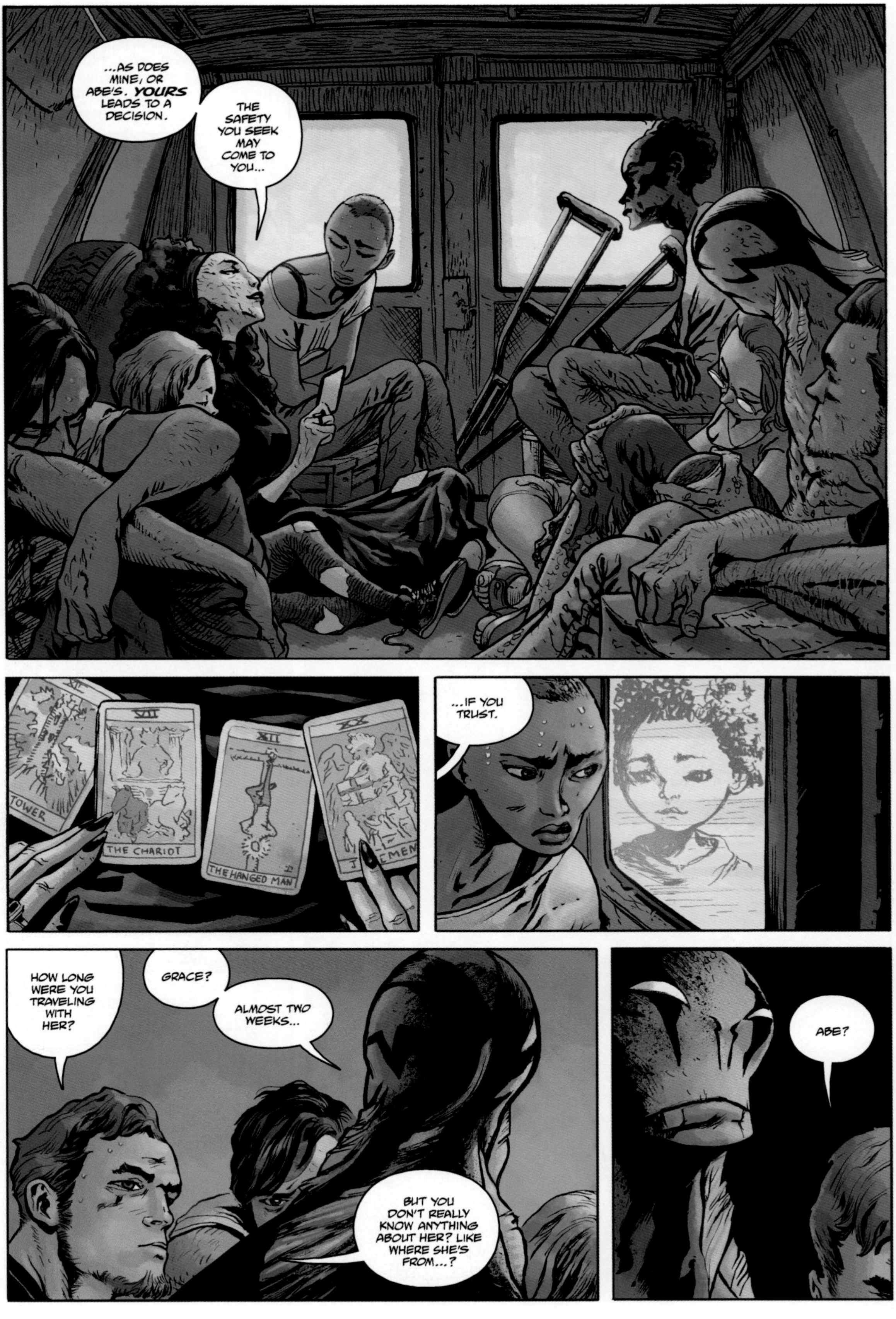
...AS DOES MINE, OR ABE'S. YOURS LEADS TO A DECISION.
THE SAFETY YOU SEEK MAY COME TO YOU...
TOWER
THE CHARIOT
THE HANGED MAN
...IF YOU TRUST.
HOW LONG WERE YOU TRAVELING WITH HER?
GRACE?
ALMOST TWO WEEKS...
BUT YOU DON'T REALLY KNOW ANYTHING ABOUT HER? LIKE WHERE SHE'S FROM...?
ABE?

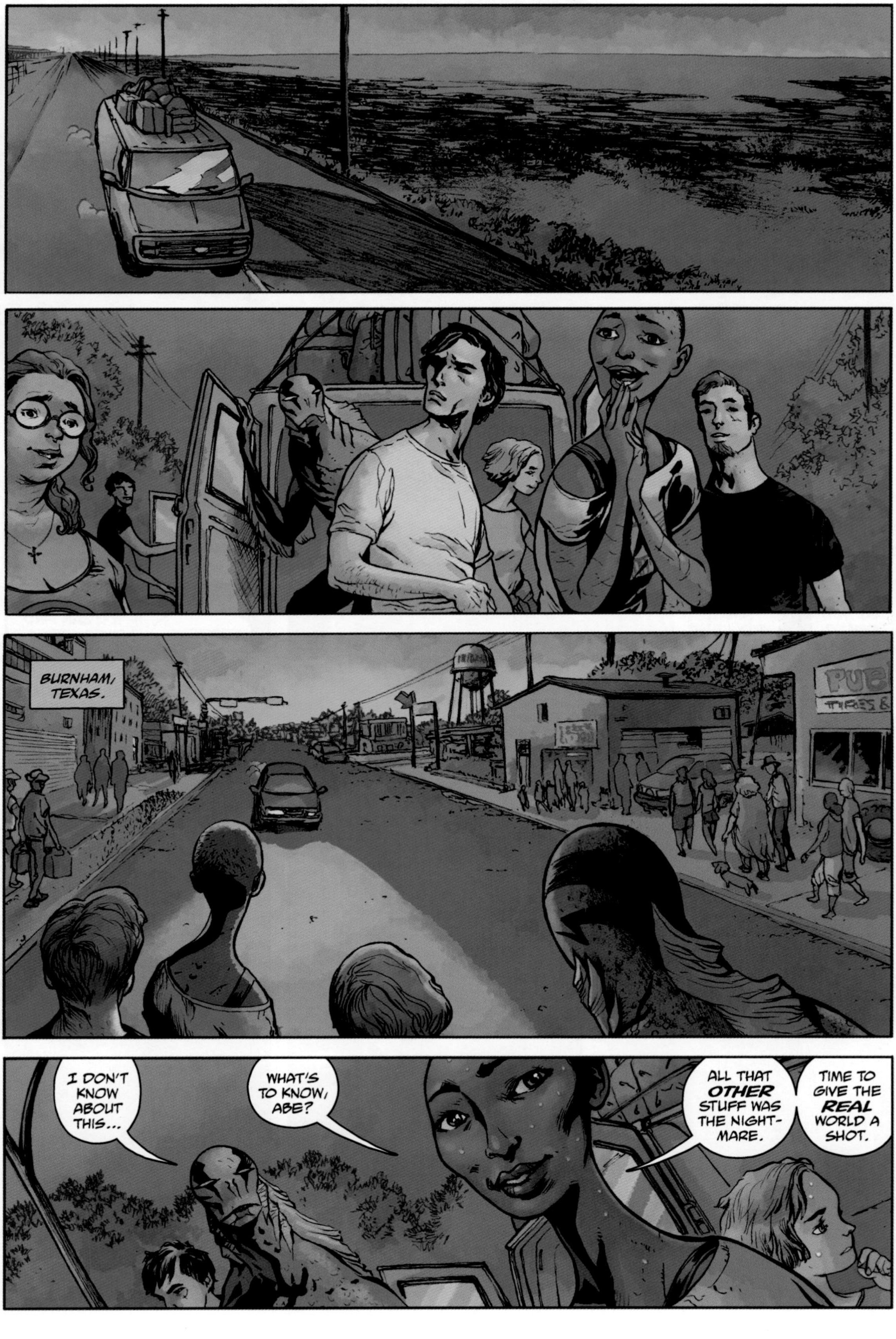
BURNHAM, TEXAS.
I DON'T KNOW ABOUT THIS...
WHAT'S TO KNOW, ABE?
ALL THAT OTHER STUFF WAS THE NIGHT-MARE.
TIME TO GIVE THE REAL WORLD A SHOT.

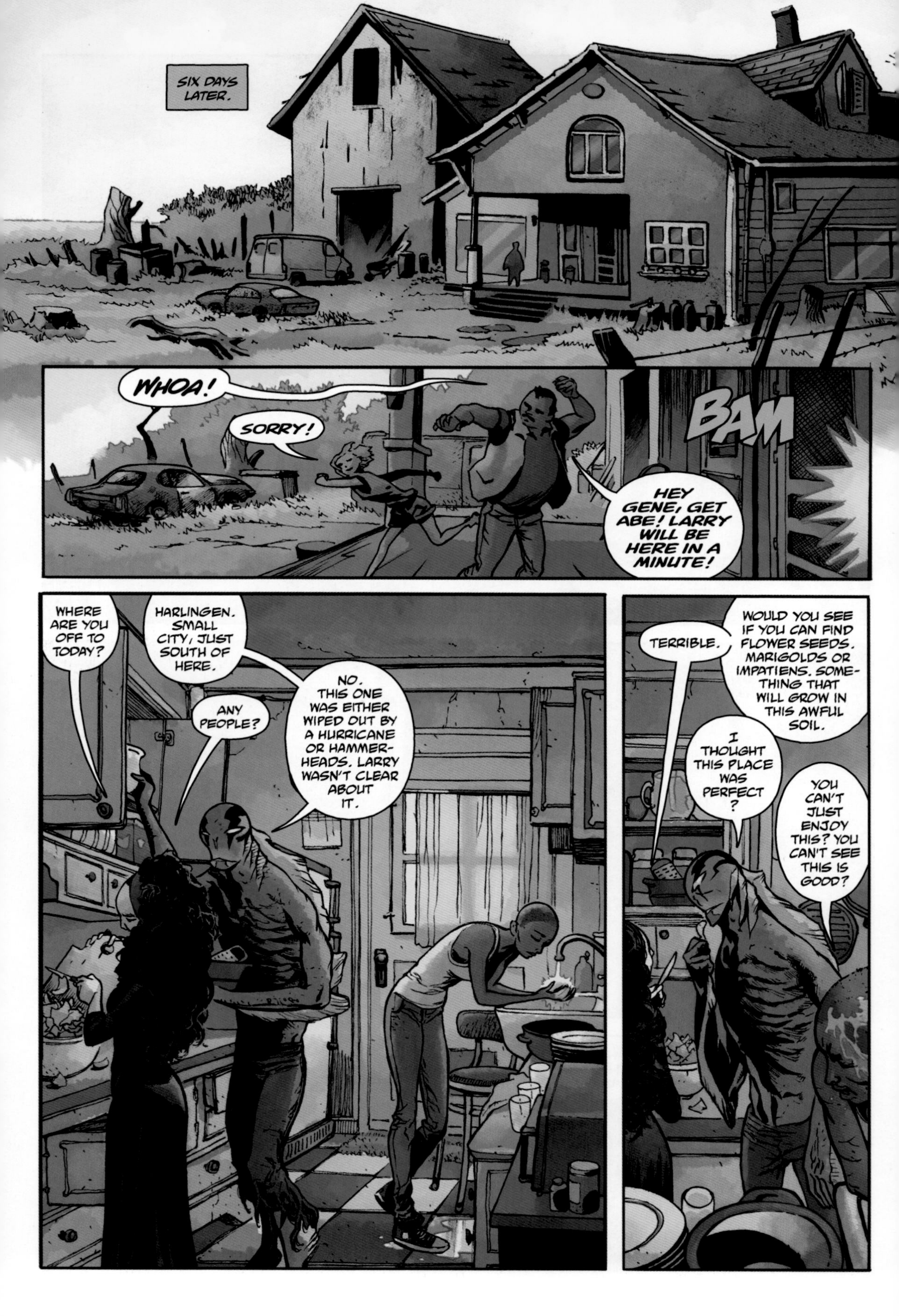
SIX DAYS LATER.
WHOA!
SORRY!
BAM
HEY GENE, GET ABE! LARRY WILL BE HERE IN A MINUTE!
WHERE ARE YOU OFF TO TODAY?
HARLINGEN. SMALL CITY, JUST SOUTH OF HERE.
ANY PEOPLE?
NO. THIS ONE WAS EITHER WIPED OUT BY A HURRICANE OR HAMMER-HEADS. LARRY WASN'T CLEAR ABOUT IT.
TERRIBLE.
WOULD YOU SEE IF YOU CAN FIND FLOWER SEEDS. MARIGOLDS OR IMPATIENS. SOME-THING THAT WILL GROW IN THIS AWFUL SOIL.
I THOUGHT THIS PLACE WAS PERFECT?
YOU CAN'T JUST ENJOY THIS? YOU CAN'T SEE THIS IS GOOD?

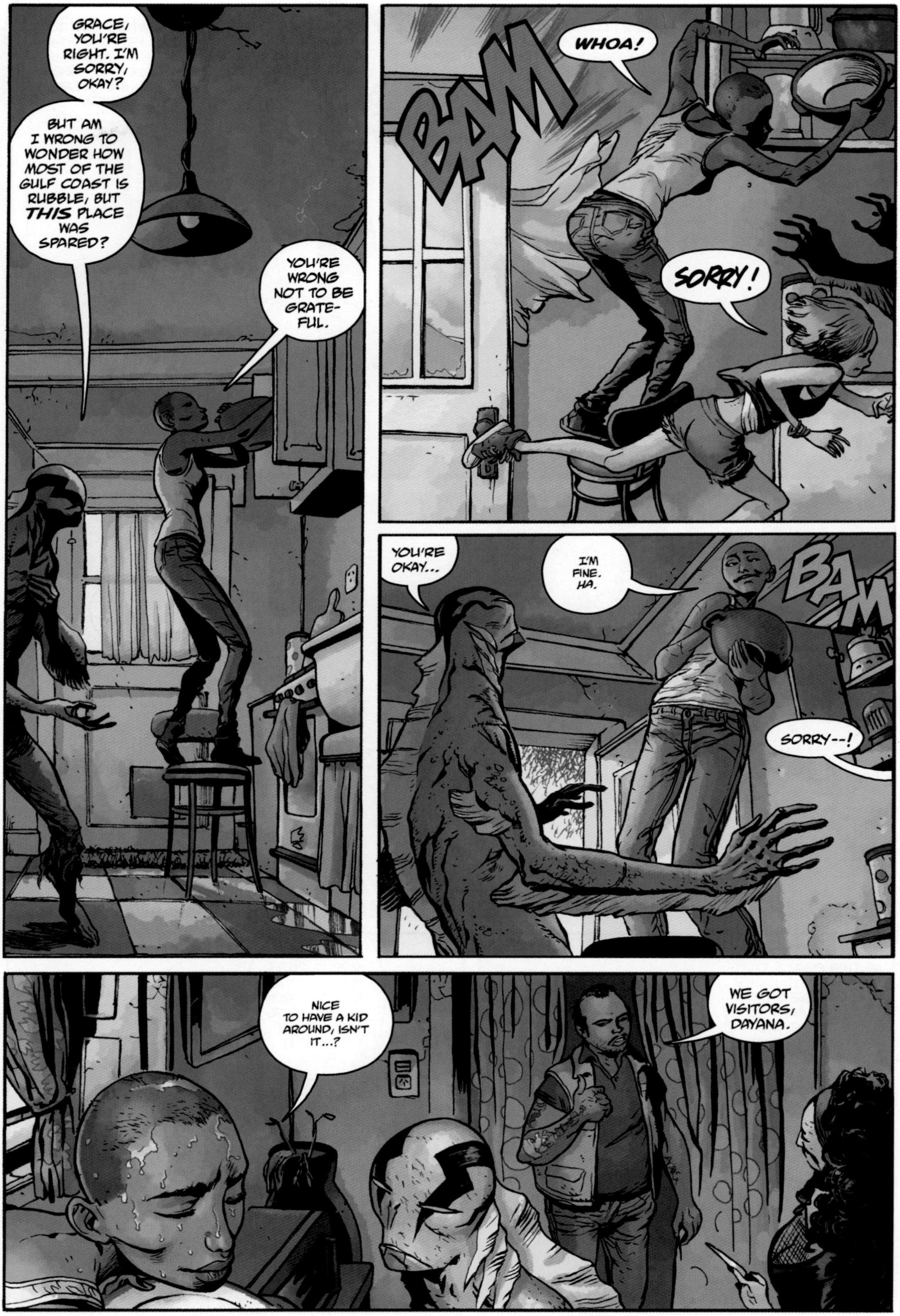
GRACE, YOU'RE RIGHT. I'M SORRY, OKAY?
BUT AM I WRONG TO WONDER HOW MOST OF THE GULF COAST IS RUBBLE, BUT THIS PLACE WAS SPARED?
YOU'RE WRONG NOT TO BE GRATE-FUL.
BAM
WHOA!
SORRY!
YOU'RE OKAY...
I'M FINE. HA.
BAM
SORRY--!
NICE TO HAVE A KID AROUND, ISN'T IT...?
WE GOT VISITORS, DAYANA.

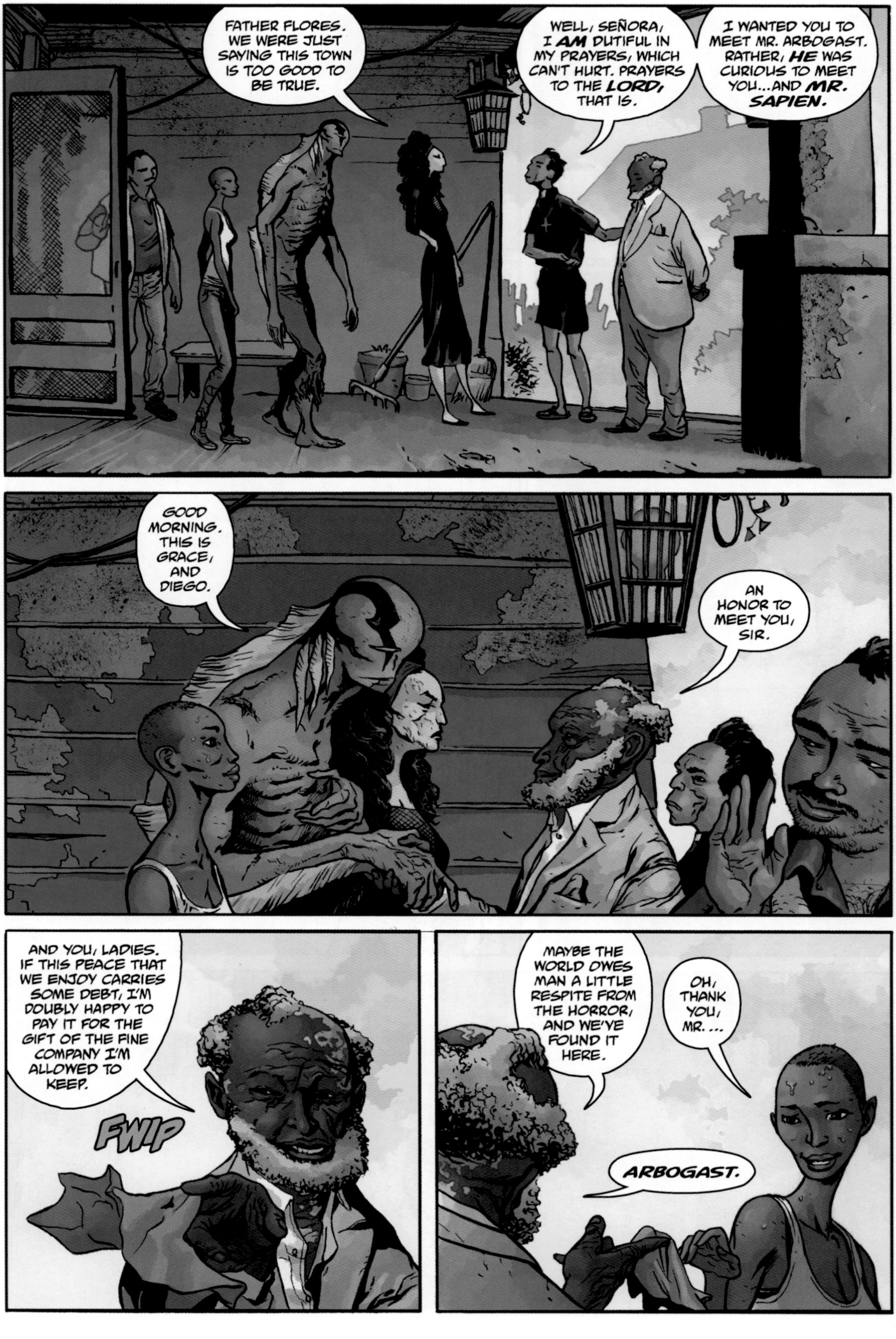
FATHER FLORES. WE WERE JUST SAYING THIS TOWN IS TOO GOOD TO BE TRUE.
WELL, SEÑORA, I AM DUTIFUL IN MY PRAYERS, WHICH CAN'T HURT. PRAYERS TO THE LORD, THAT IS.
I WANTED YOU TO MEET MR. ARBOGAST. RATHER, HE WAS CURIOUS TO MEET YOU...AND MR. SAPIEN.
GOOD MORNING. THIS IS GRACE, AND DIEGO.
AN HONOR TO MEET YOU, SIR.
AND YOU, LADIES. IF THIS PEACE THAT WE ENJOY CARRIES SOME DEBT, I'M DOUBLY HAPPY TO PAY IT FOR THE GIFT OF THE FINE COMPANY I'M ALLOWED TO KEEP.
FWIP
MAYBE THE WORLD OWES MAN A LITTLE RESPITE FROM THE HORROR, AND WE'VE FOUND IT HERE.
OH, THANK YOU, MR. ...
ARBOGAST.

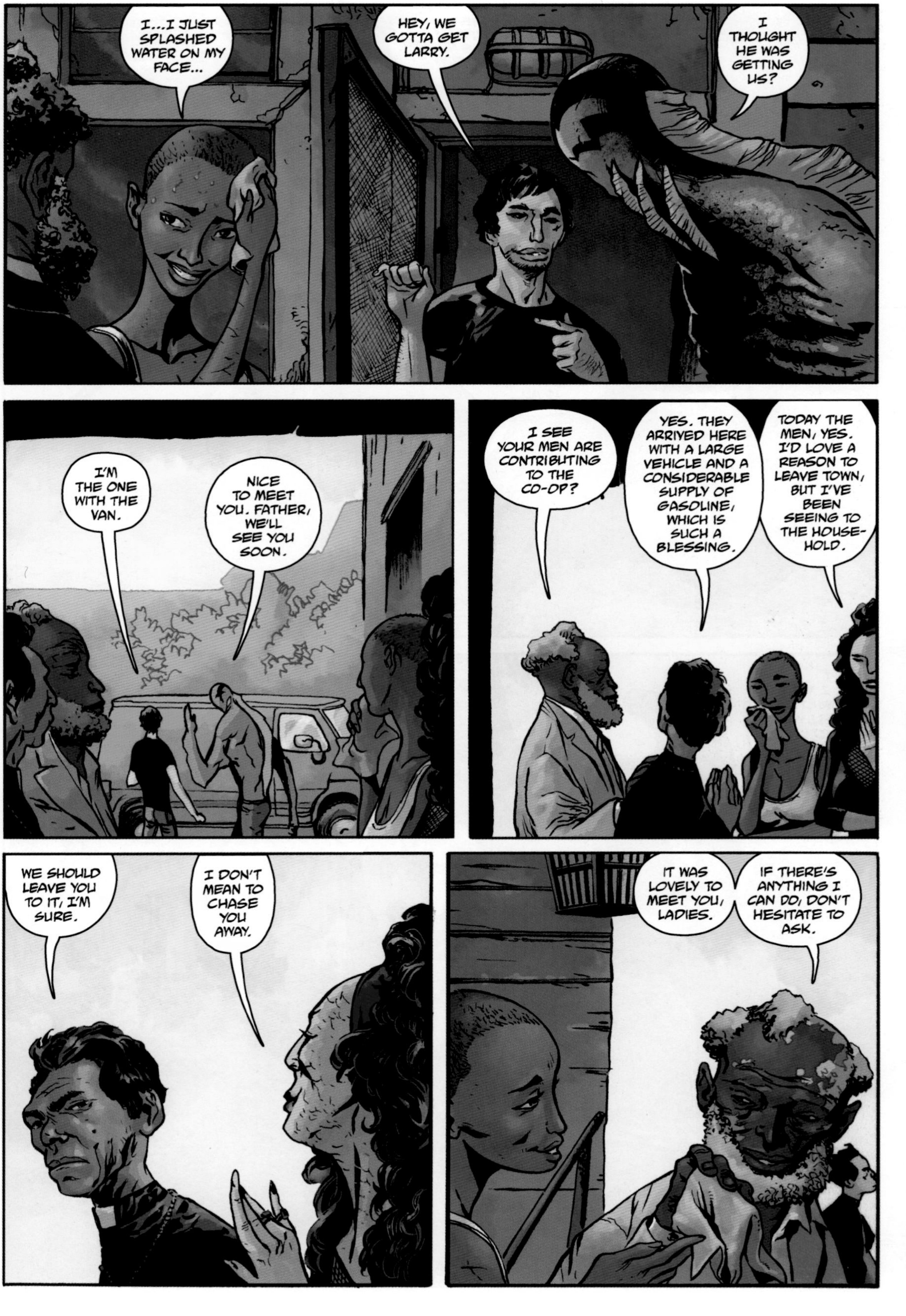

I...I JUST SPLASHED WATER ON MY FACE...
HEY, WE GOTTA GET LARRY.
I THOUGHT HE WAS GETTING US?
I'M THE ONE WITH THE VAN.
NICE TO MEET YOU, FATHER, WE'LL SEE YOU SOON.
I SEE YOUR MEN ARE CONTRIBUTING TO THE CO-OP?
YES. THEY ARRIVED HERE WITH A LARGE VEHICLE AND A CONSIDERABLE SUPPLY OF GASOLINE, WHICH IS SUCH A BLESSING.
TODAY THE MEN, YES. I'D LOVE A REASON TO LEAVE TOWN, BUT I'VE BEEN SEEING TO THE HOUSEHOLD.
WE SHOULD LEAVE YOU TO IT, I'M SURE.
I DON'T MEAN TO CHASE YOU AWAY.
IT WAS LOVELY TO MEET YOU, LADIES.
IF THERE'S ANYTHING I CAN DO, DON'T HESITATE TO ASK.

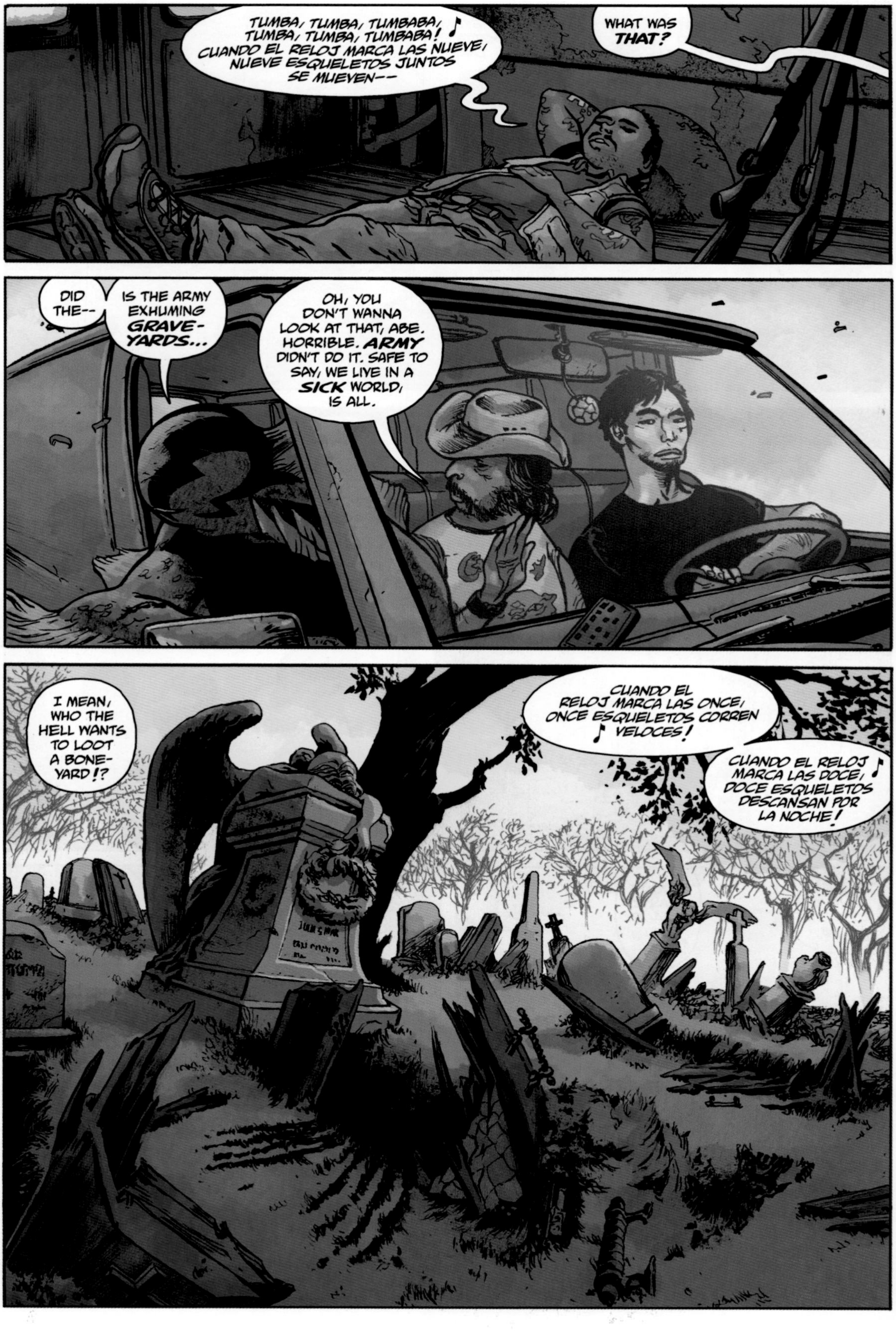
TUMBA, TUMBA, TUMBABA, ♪
TUMBA, TUMBA, TUMBABA! CUANDO EL RELOJ MARCA LAS NUEVE, NUEVE ESQUELETOS JUNTOS SE MUEVEN--
WHAT WAS THAT?
DID THE--
IS THE ARMY EXHUMING GRAVE-YARDS...
OH, YOU DON'T WANNA LOOK AT THAT, ABE. HORRIBLE. ARMY DIDN'T DO IT. SAFE TO SAY, WE LIVE IN A SICK WORLD, IS ALL.
I MEAN, WHO THE HELL WANTS TO LOOT A BONE-YARD!?
CUANDO EL RELOJ MARCA LAS ONCE, ONCE ESQUELETOS CORREN ♪ VELOCES!
CUANDO EL RELOJ ♪ MARCA LAS DOCE, DOCE ESQUELETOS DESCANSAN POR LA NOCHE!

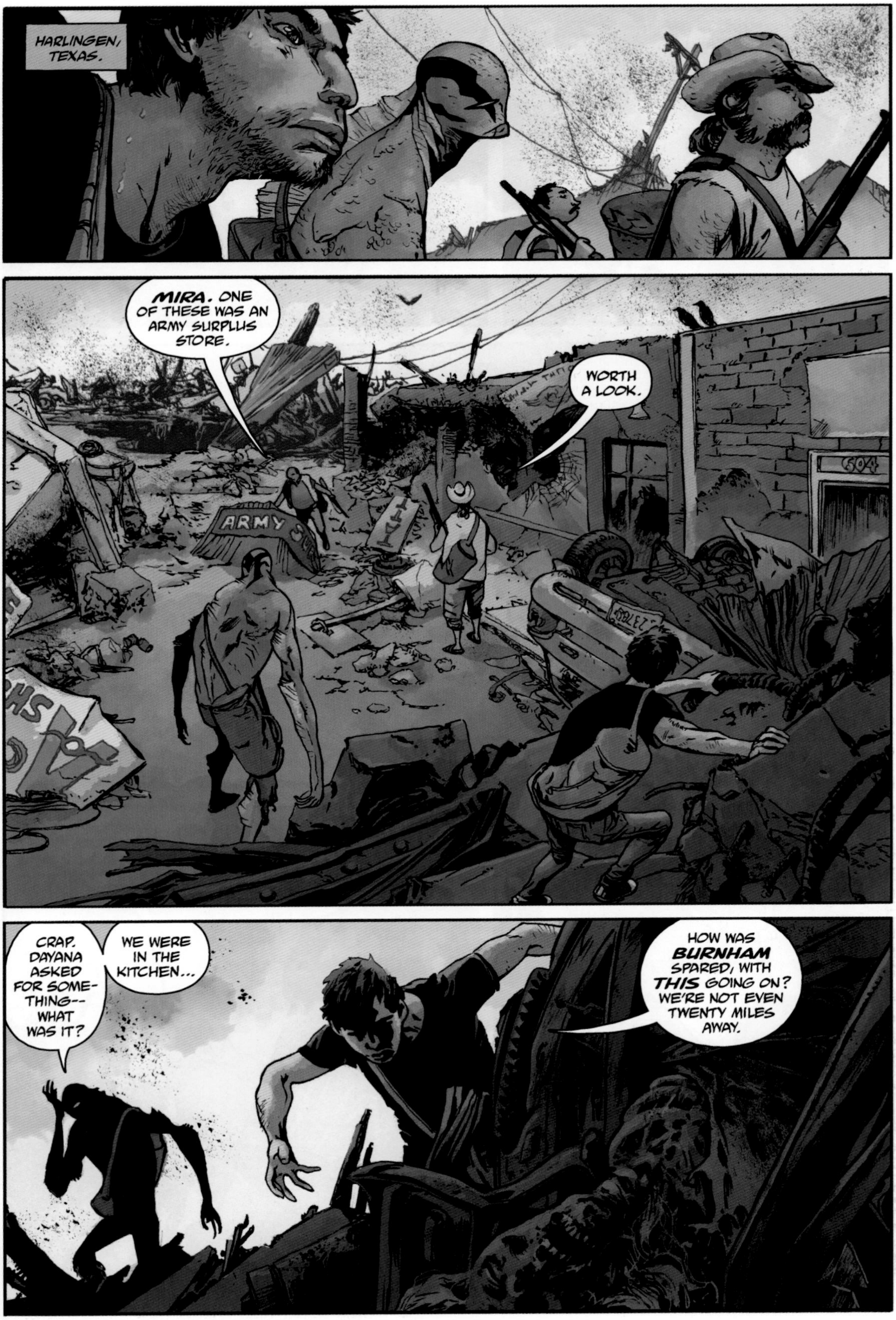
HARLINGEN, TEXAS.
MIRA. ONE OF THESE WAS AN ARMY SURPLUS STORE.
WORTH A LOOK.
ARMY
CRAP. DAYANA ASKED FOR SOMETHING-- WHAT WAS IT?
WE WERE IN THE KITCHEN...
HOW WAS BURNHAM SPARED, WITH THIS GOING ON? WE'RE NOT EVEN TWENTY MILES AWAY.

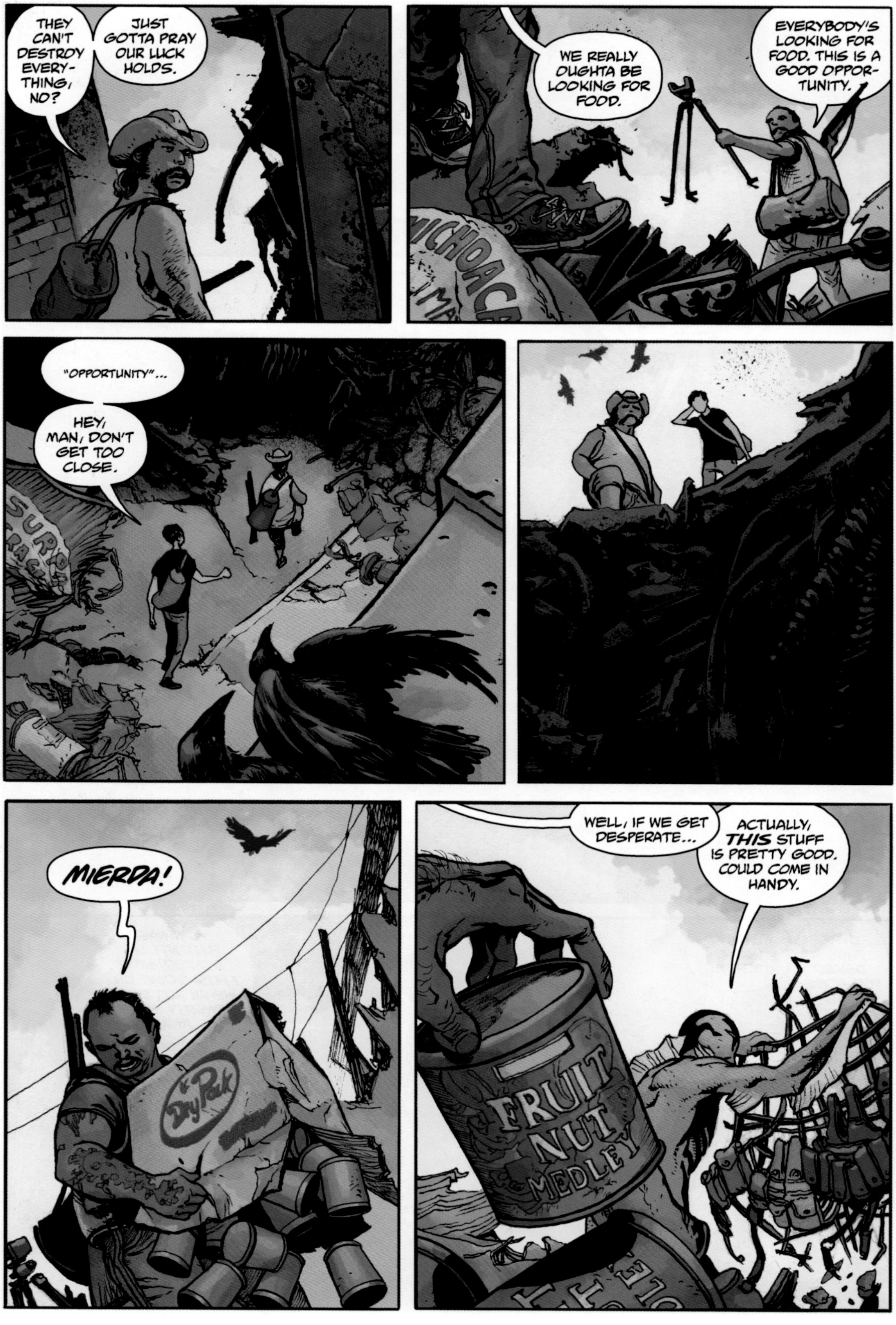
THEY CAN'T DESTROY EVERYTHING, NO?
JUST GOTTA PRAY OUR LUCK HOLDS.
WE REALLY OUGHTA BE LOOKING FOR FOOD.
EVERYBODY'S LOOKING FOR FOOD. THIS IS A GOOD OPPORTUNITY.
"OPPORTUNITY"...
HEY, MAN, DON'T GET TOO CLOSE.
MIERDA!
WELL, IF WE GET DESPERATE...
ACTUALLY, THIS STUFF IS PRETTY GOOD. COULD COME IN HANDY.
FRUIT NUT MEDLEY
Dry Pack

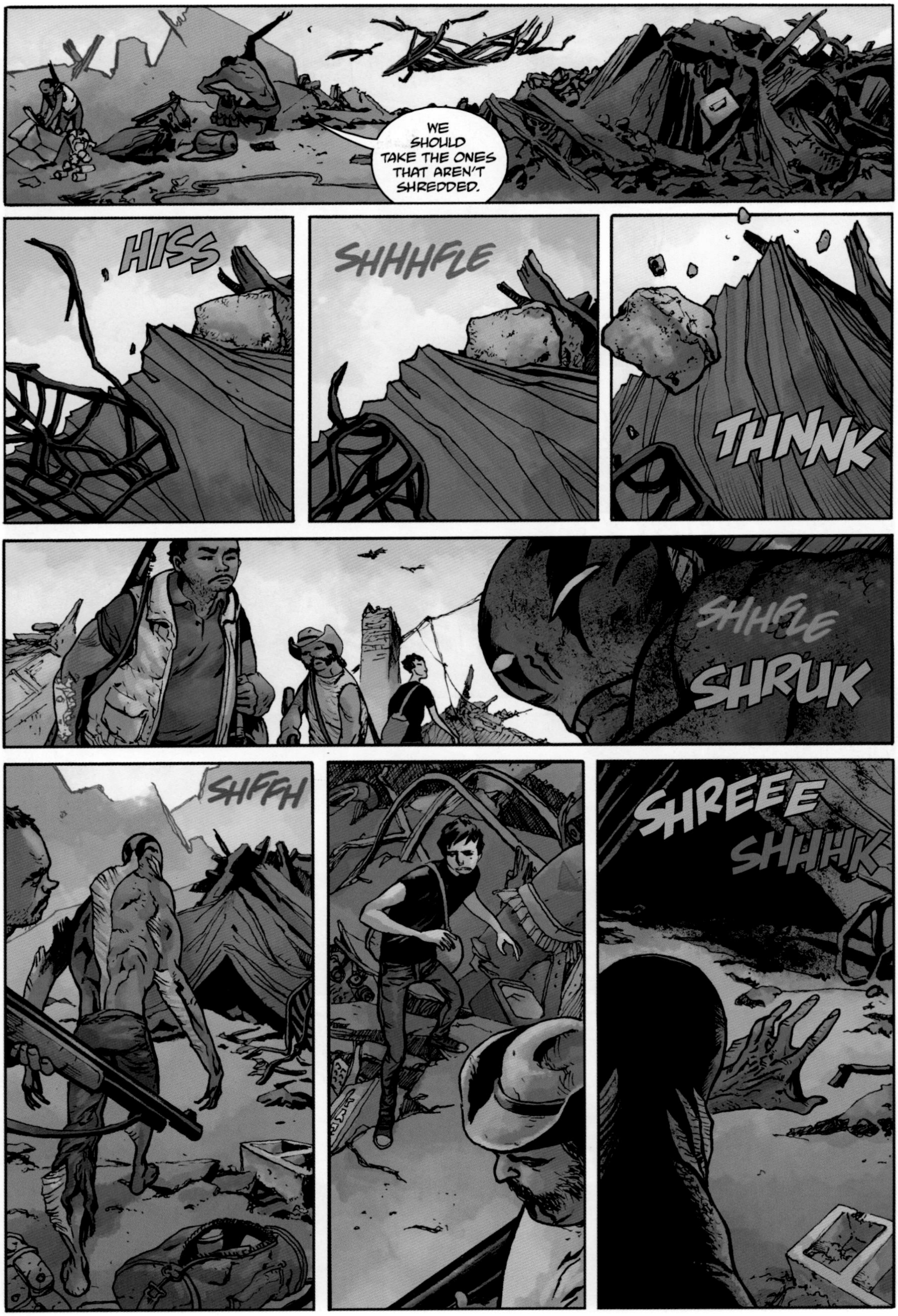
WE SHOULD TAKE THE ONES THAT AREN'T SHREDDED.
HISS
SHHHFLE
THNNK
SHHFLE
SHRUK
SHFFH
SHREEE
SHHHK

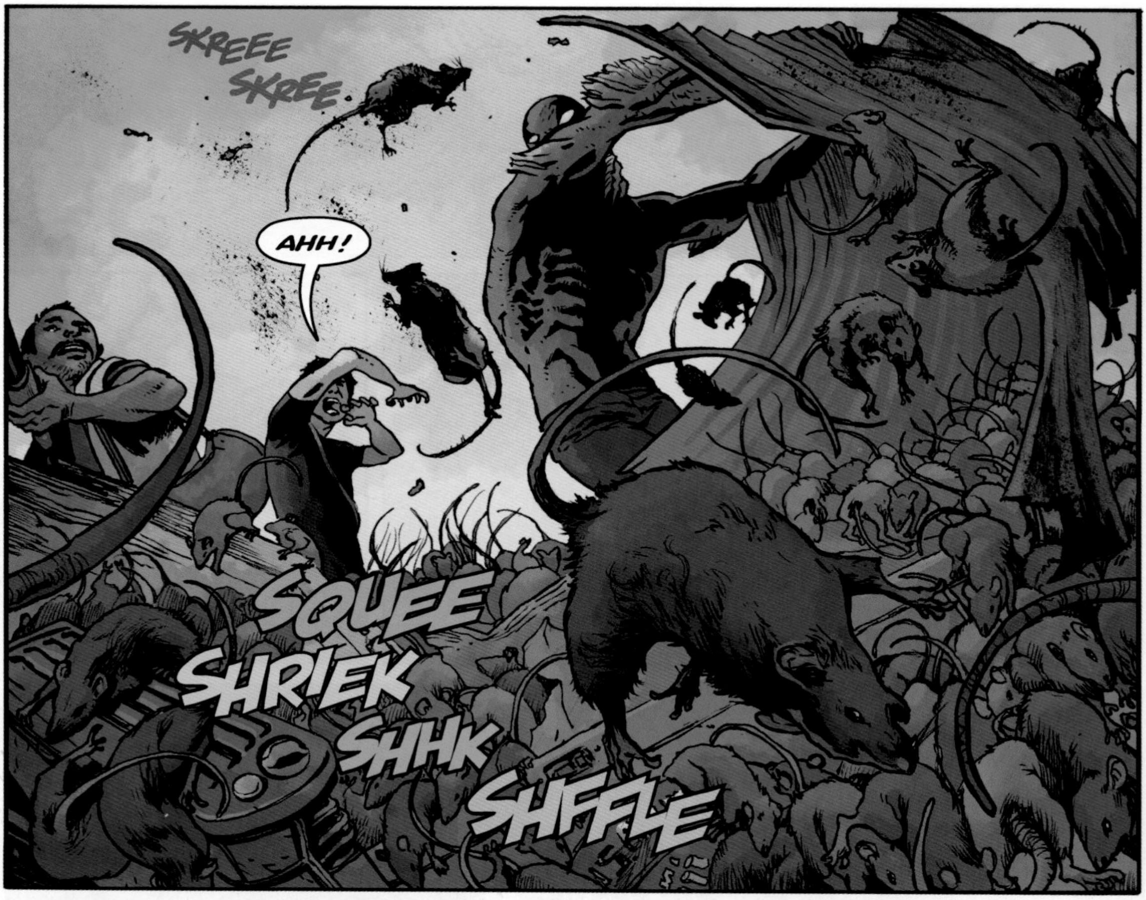
SKREEE
SKREE
AHH!
SQUEE
SHRIEK
SHHK
SHFFLE

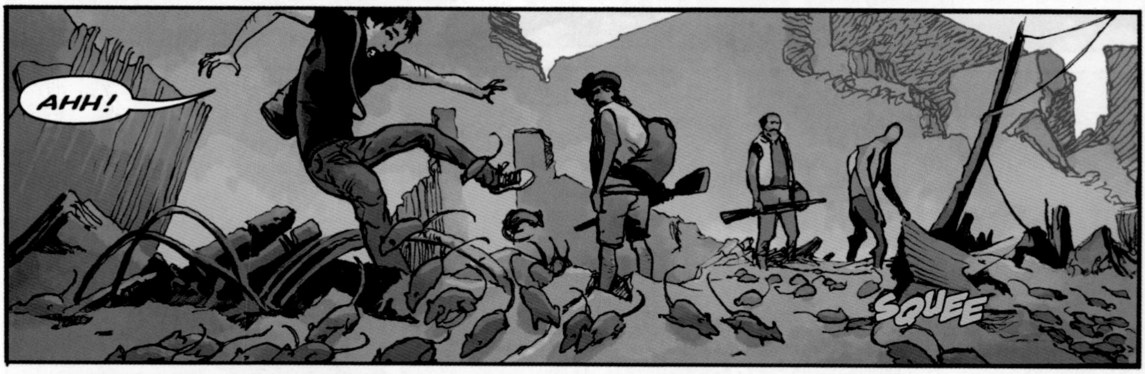
AHH!
SQUEE

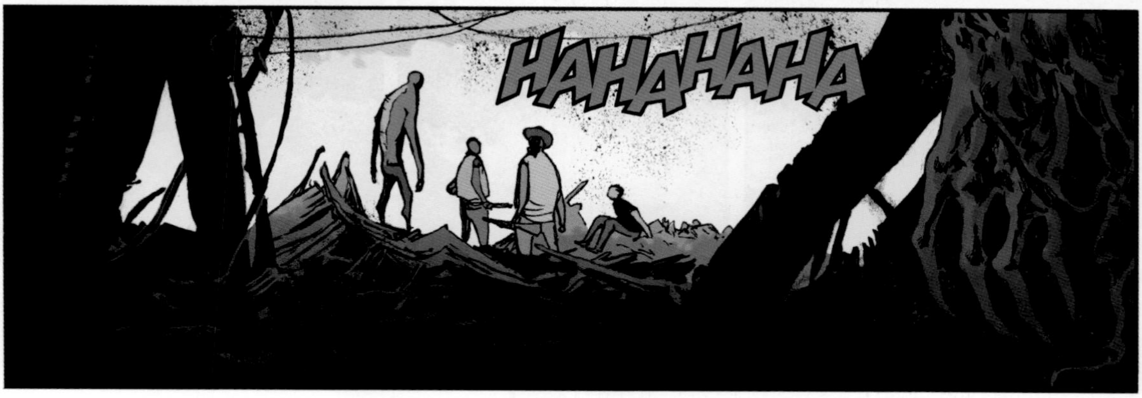
HAHAHAHA

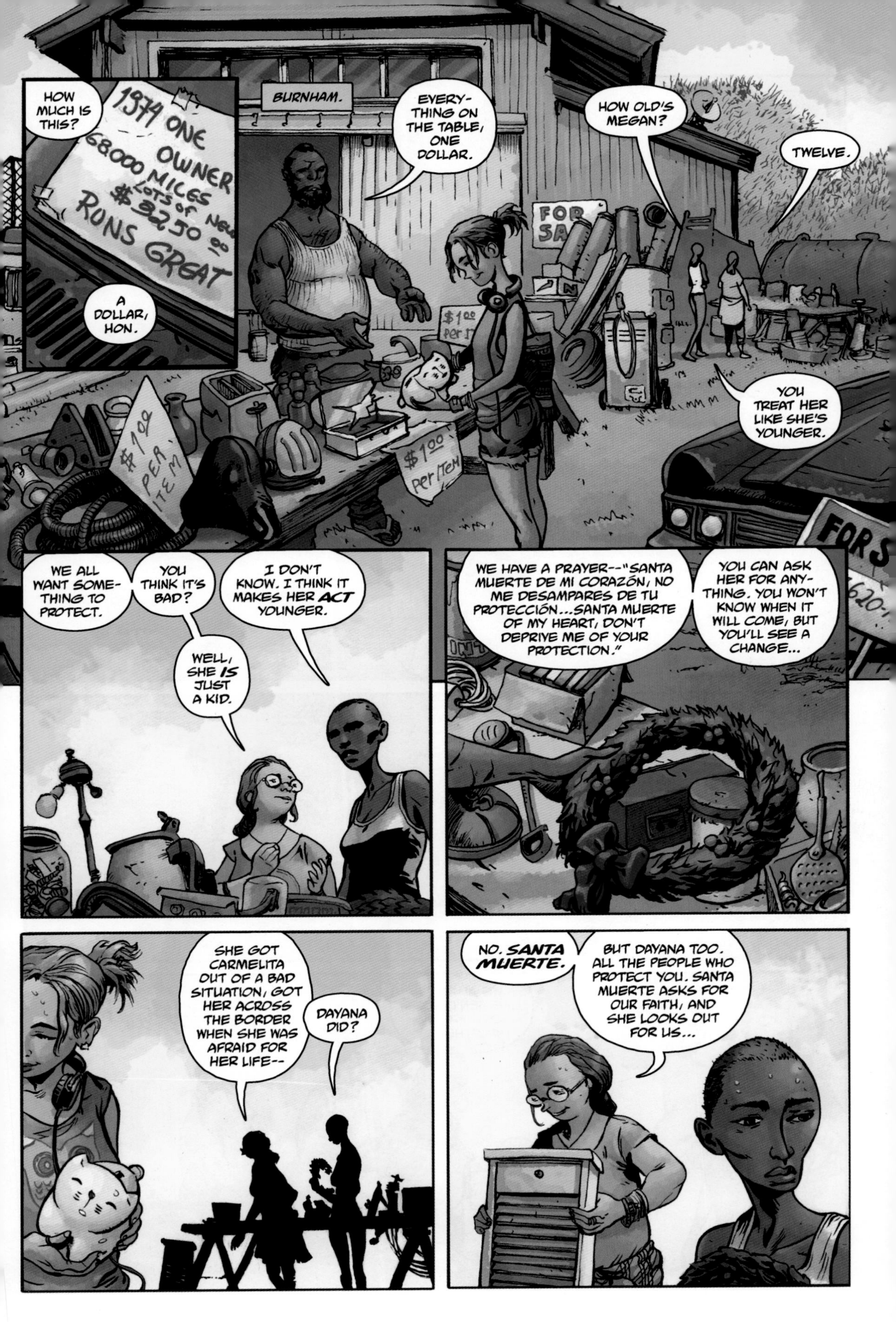
HOW MUCH IS THIS?
1974 ONE OWNER 68,000 MILES LOTS OF NEW $3250.00 RUNS GREAT
A DOLLAR, HON.
BURNHAM.
EVERY-THING ON THE TABLE, ONE DOLLAR.
$1.00 PER ITEM
$1.00 per ITEM
$1.00 per I
FOR SA
HOW OLD'S MEGAN?
TWELVE.
YOU TREAT HER LIKE SHE'S YOUNGER.
FOR S
WE ALL WANT SOME-THING TO PROTECT.
YOU THINK IT'S BAD?
I DON'T KNOW. I THINK IT MAKES HER ACT YOUNGER.
WELL, SHE IS JUST A KID.
WE HAVE A PRAYER--"SANTA MUERTE DE MI CORAZÓN, NO ME DESAMPARES DE TU PROTECCIÓN...SANTA MUERTE OF MY HEART, DON'T DEPRIVE ME OF YOUR PROTECTION."
YOU CAN ASK HER FOR ANY-THING. YOU WON'T KNOW WHEN IT WILL COME, BUT YOU'LL SEE A CHANGE...
SHE GOT CARMELITA OUT OF A BAD SITUATION, GOT HER ACROSS THE BORDER WHEN SHE WAS AFRAID FOR HER LIFE--
DAYANA DID?
NO. SANTA MUERTE.
BUT DAYANA TOO. ALL THE PEOPLE WHO PROTECT YOU. SANTA MUERTE ASKS FOR OUR FAITH, AND SHE LOOKS OUT FOR US...

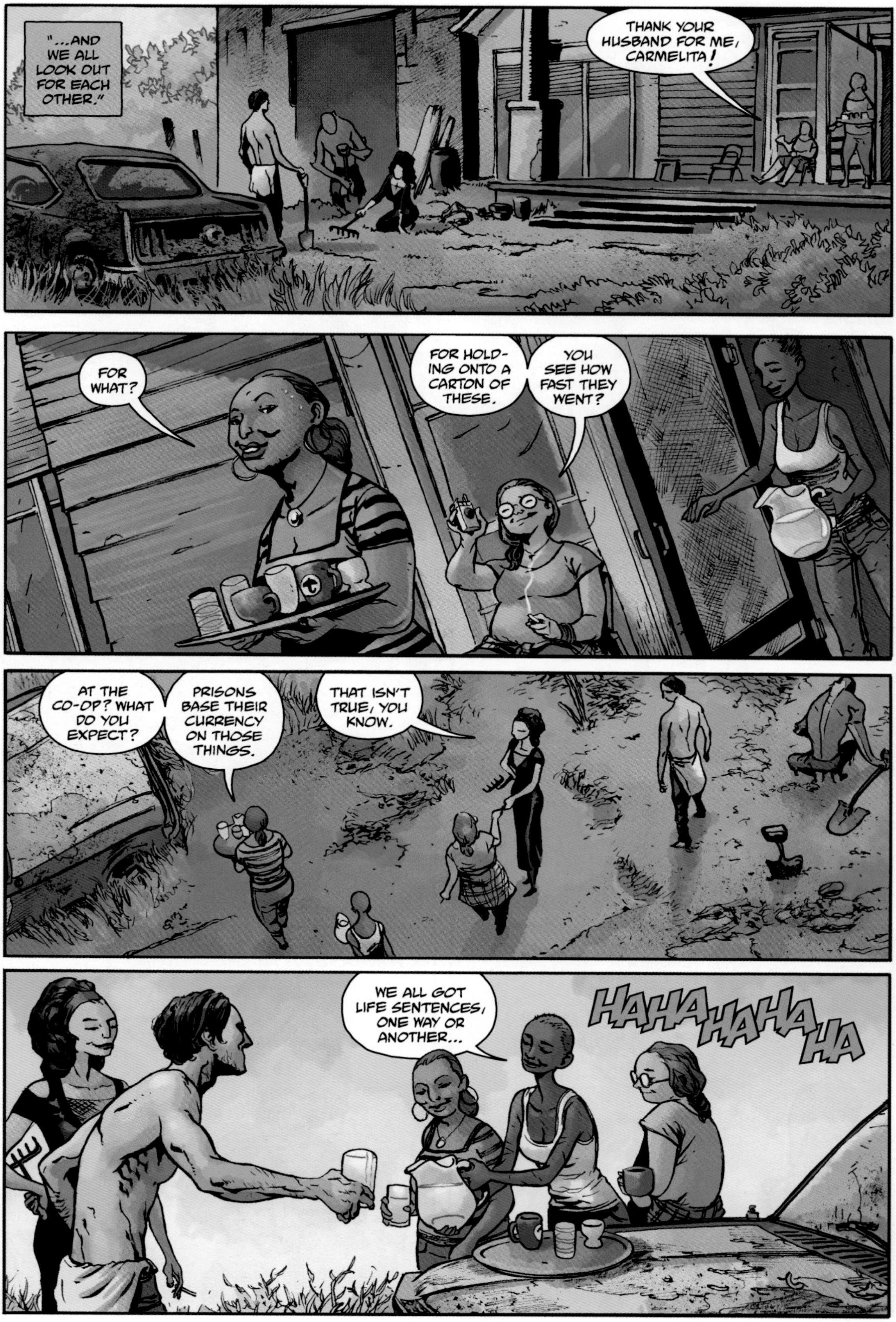
"...AND WE ALL LOOK OUT FOR EACH OTHER."
THANK YOUR HUSBAND FOR ME, CARMELITA!
FOR WHAT?
FOR HOLD-ING ONTO A CARTON OF THESE.
YOU SEE HOW FAST THEY WENT?
AT THE CO-OP? WHAT DO YOU EXPECT?
PRISONS BASE THEIR CURRENCY ON THOSE THINGS.
THAT ISN'T TRUE, YOU KNOW.
WE ALL GOT LIFE SENTENCES, ONE WAY OR ANOTHER...
HAHAHAHAHA

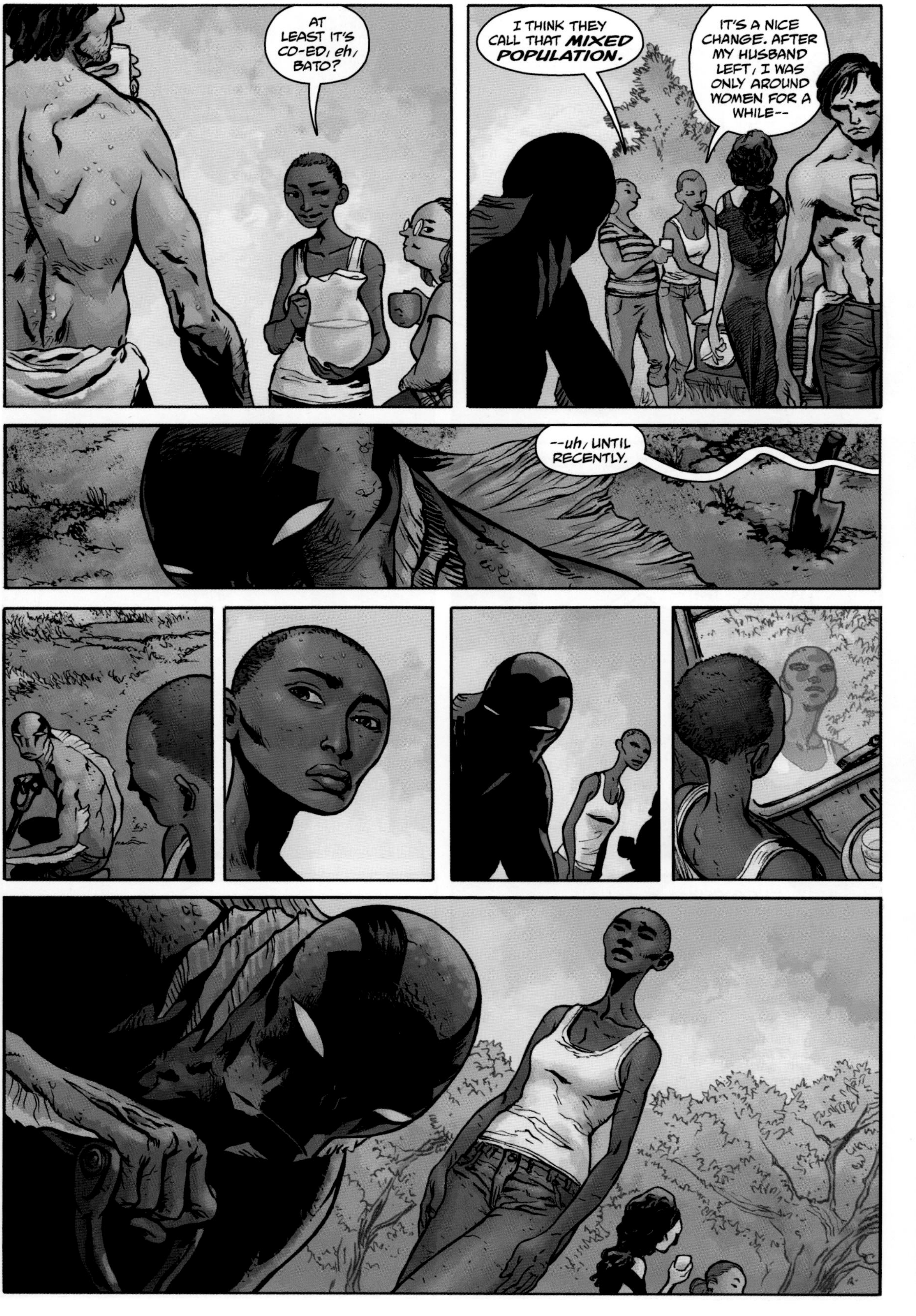
AT LEAST IT'S CO-ED, eh, BATO?
I THINK THEY CALL THAT MIXED POPULATION.
IT'S A NICE CHANGE. AFTER MY HUSBAND LEFT, I WAS ONLY AROUND WOMEN FOR A WHILE--
--uh, UNTIL RECENTLY.

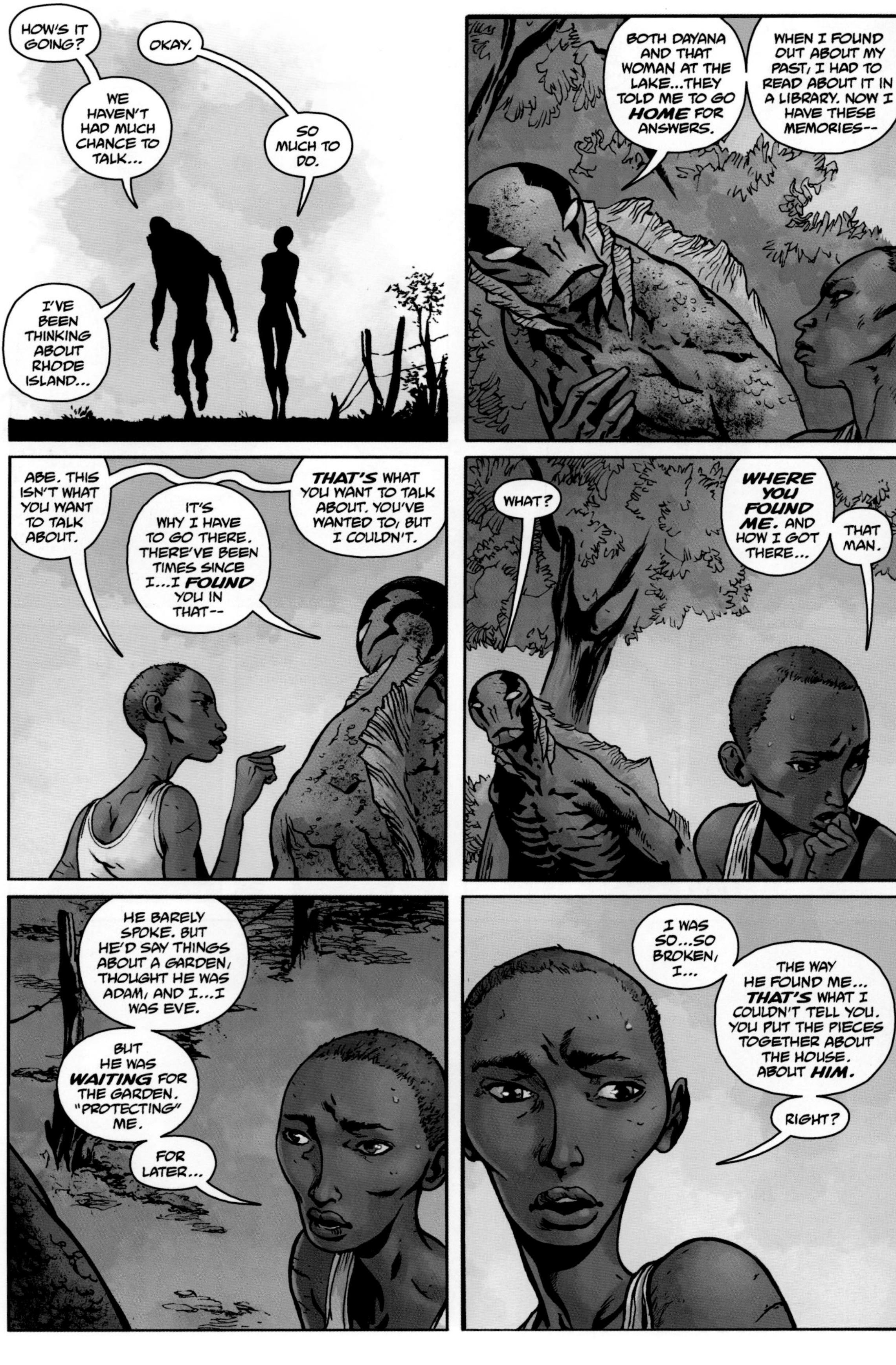
HOW'S IT GOING?
OKAY.
WE HAVEN'T HAD MUCH CHANCE TO TALK...
SO MUCH TO DO.
I'VE BEEN THINKING ABOUT RHODE ISLAND...
BOTH DAYANA AND THAT WOMAN AT THE LAKE...THEY TOLD ME TO GO HOME FOR ANSWERS.
WHEN I FOUND OUT ABOUT MY PAST, I HAD TO READ ABOUT IT IN A LIBRARY. NOW I HAVE THESE MEMORIES--
ABE. THIS ISN'T WHAT YOU WANT TO TALK ABOUT.
IT'S WHY I HAVE TO GO THERE. THERE'VE BEEN TIMES SINCE I...I FOUND YOU IN THAT--
THAT'S WHAT YOU WANT TO TALK ABOUT. YOU'VE WANTED TO, BUT I COULDN'T.
WHAT?
WHERE YOU FOUND ME. AND HOW I GOT THERE...
THAT MAN.
HE BARELY SPOKE. BUT HE'D SAY THINGS ABOUT A GARDEN, THOUGHT HE WAS ADAM, AND I...I WAS EVE.
BUT HE WAS WAITING FOR THE GARDEN. "PROTECTING" ME.
FOR LATER...
I WAS SO...SO BROKEN, I...
THE WAY HE FOUND ME... THAT'S WHAT I COULDN'T TELL YOU. YOU PUT THE PIECES TOGETHER ABOUT THE HOUSE. ABOUT HIM.
RIGHT?

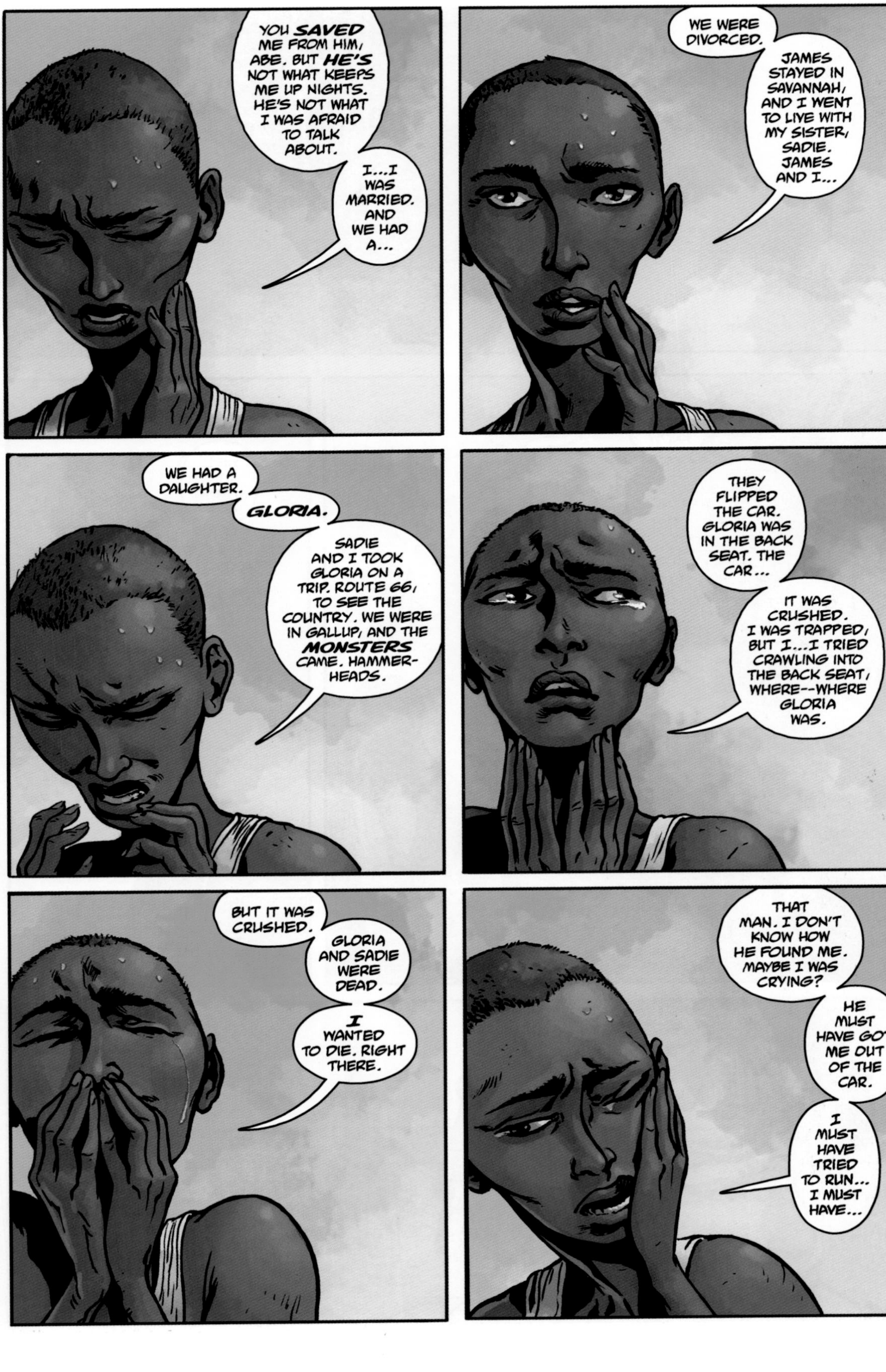
YOU SAVED ME FROM HIM, ABE. BUT HE'S NOT WHAT KEEPS ME UP NIGHTS. HE'S NOT WHAT I WAS AFRAID TO TALK ABOUT.
I...I WAS MARRIED. AND WE HAD A...
WE WERE DIVORCED.
JAMES STAYED IN SAVANNAH, AND I WENT TO LIVE WITH MY SISTER, SADIE. JAMES AND I...
WE HAD A DAUGHTER.
GLORIA.
SADIE AND I TOOK GLORIA ON A TRIP. ROUTE 66, TO SEE THE COUNTRY. WE WERE IN GALLUP, AND THE MONSTERS CAME. HAMMER-HEADS.
THEY FLIPPED THE CAR. GLORIA WAS IN THE BACK SEAT. THE CAR...
IT WAS CRUSHED. I WAS TRAPPED, BUT I...I TRIED CRAWLING INTO THE BACK SEAT, WHERE--WHERE GLORIA WAS.
BUT IT WAS CRUSHED.
GLORIA AND SADIE WERE DEAD.
I WANTED TO DIE. RIGHT THERE.
THAT MAN. I DON'T KNOW HOW HE FOUND ME. MAYBE I WAS CRYING?
HE MUST HAVE GOT ME OUT OF THE CAR.
I MUST HAVE TRIED TO RUN... I MUST HAVE...

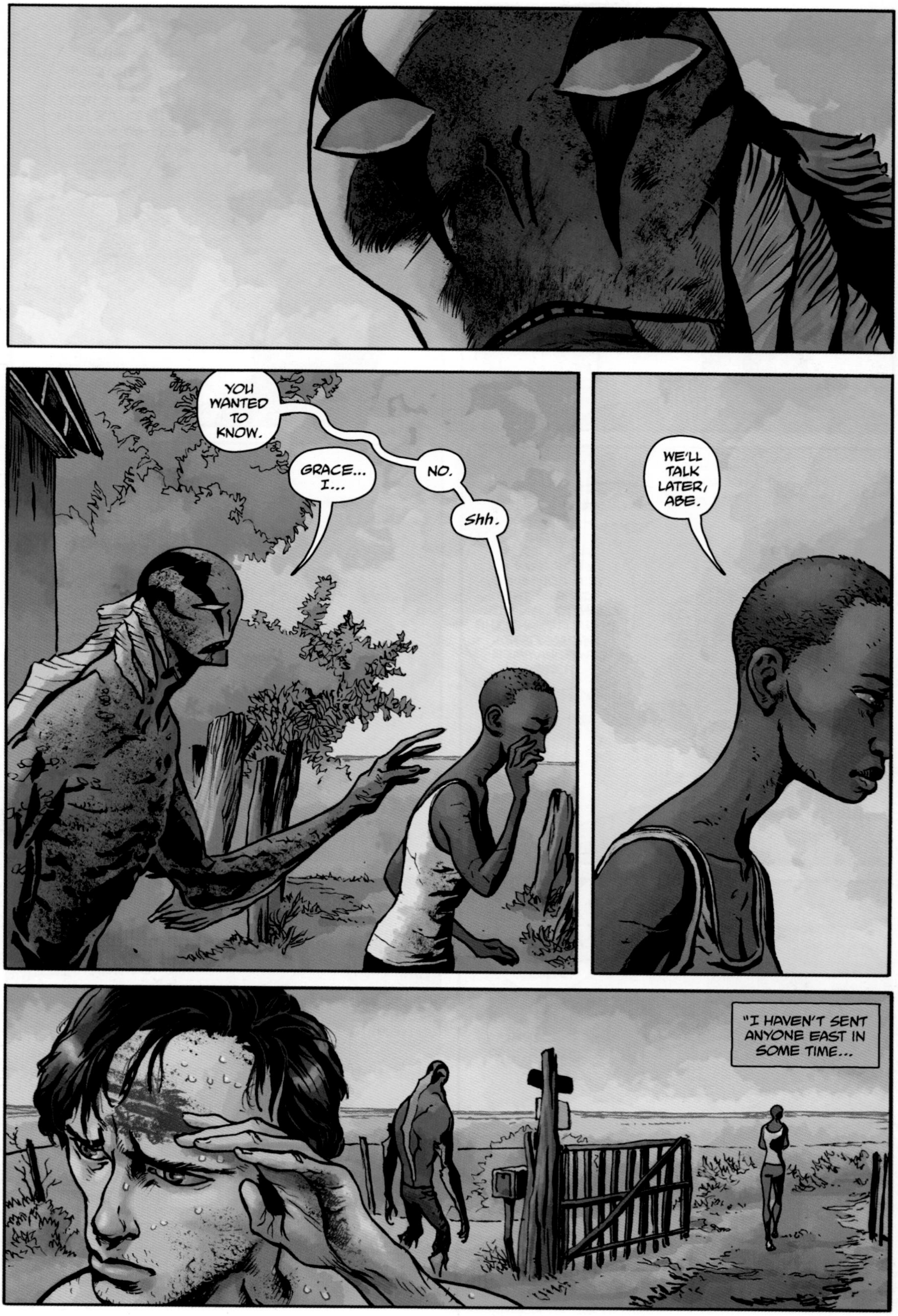
YOU WANTED TO KNOW.
GRACE... I...
NO.
Shh.
WE'LL TALK LATER, ABE.
"I HAVEN'T SENT ANYONE EAST IN SOME TIME...

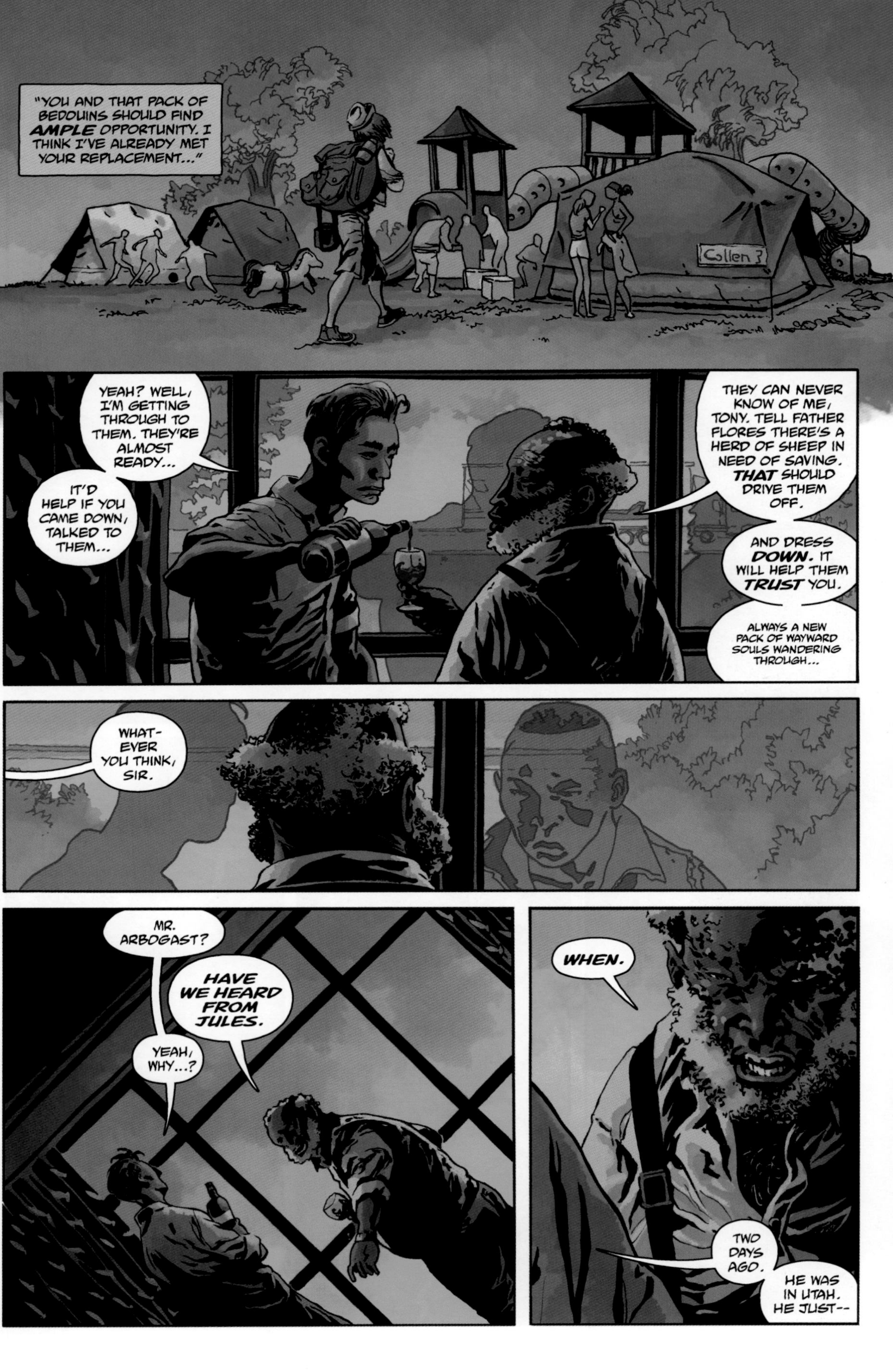
"YOU AND THAT PACK OF BEDOUINS SHOULD FIND AMPLE OPPORTUNITY. I THINK I'VE ALREADY MET YOUR REPLACEMENT..."
Collen 3
YEAH? WELL, I'M GETTING THROUGH TO THEM. THEY'RE ALMOST READY...
IT'D HELP IF YOU CAME DOWN, TALKED TO THEM...
THEY CAN NEVER KNOW OF ME, TONY. TELL FATHER FLORES THERE'S A HERD OF SHEEP IN NEED OF SAVING. THAT SHOULD DRIVE THEM OFF.
AND DRESS DOWN. IT WILL HELP THEM TRUST YOU.
ALWAYS A NEW PACK OF WAYWARD SOULS WANDERING THROUGH...
WHAT-EVER YOU THINK, SIR.
MR. ARBOGAST?
HAVE WE HEARD FROM JULES.
YEAH, WHY...?
WHEN.
TWO DAYS AGO.
HE WAS IN UTAH. HE JUST--

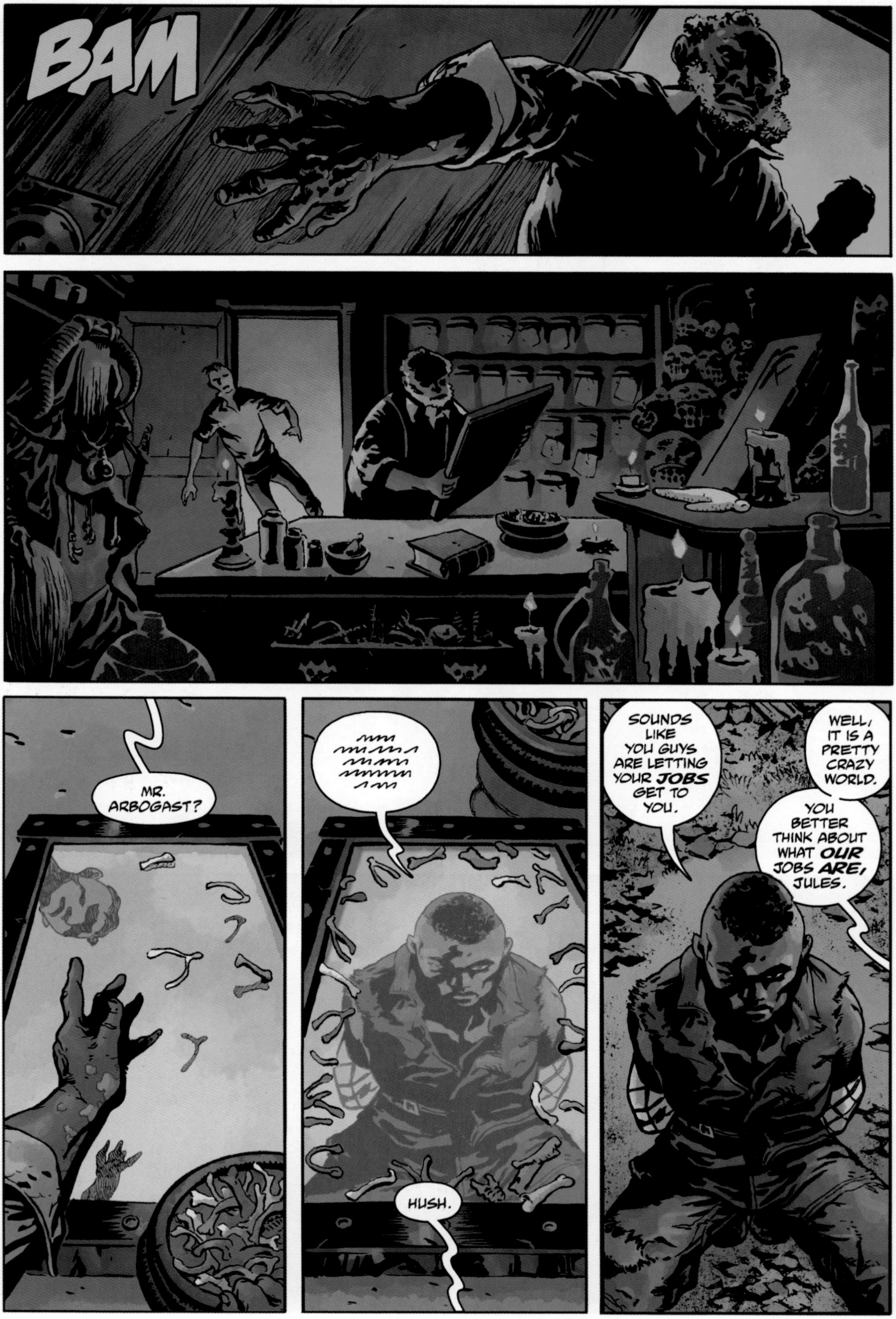
BAM
MR. ARBOGAST?
HUSH.
SOUNDS LIKE YOU GUYS ARE LETTING YOUR JOBS GET TO YOU.
WELL, IT IS A PRETTY CRAZY WORLD.
YOU BETTER THINK ABOUT WHAT OUR JOBS ARE, JULES.

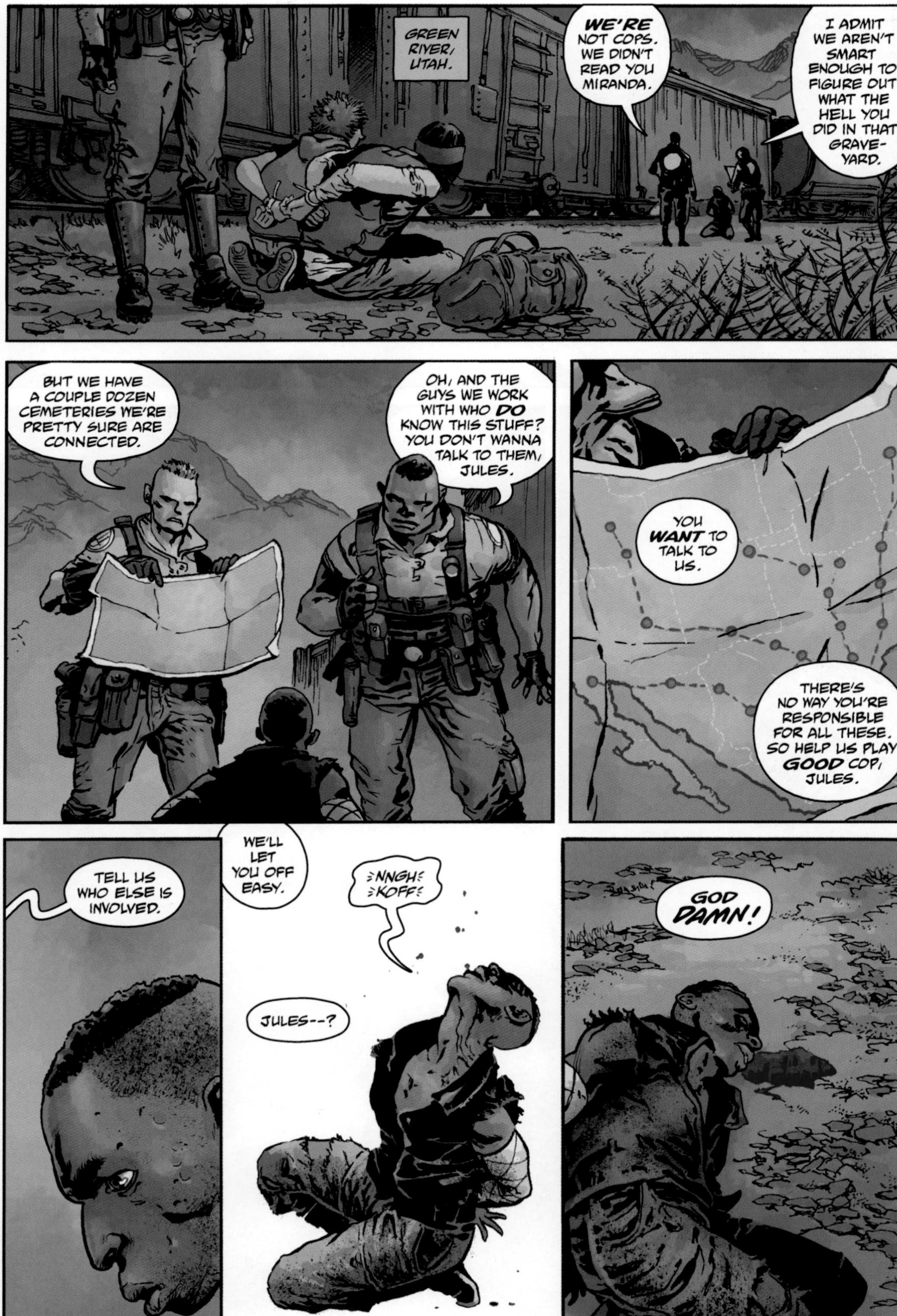
GREEN RIVER, UTAH.
WE'RE NOT COPS. WE DIDN'T READ YOU MIRANDA.
I ADMIT WE AREN'T SMART ENOUGH TO FIGURE OUT WHAT THE HELL YOU DID IN THAT GRAVE-YARD.
BUT WE HAVE A COUPLE DOZEN CEMETERIES WE'RE PRETTY SURE ARE CONNECTED.
OH, AND THE GUYS WE WORK WITH WHO DO KNOW THIS STUFF? YOU DON'T WANNA TALK TO THEM, JULES.
YOU WANT TO TALK TO US.
THERE'S NO WAY YOU'RE RESPONSIBLE FOR ALL THESE. SO HELP US PLAY GOOD COP, JULES.
TELL US WHO ELSE IS INVOLVED.
WE'LL LET YOU OFF EASY.
NNGH KOFF
JULES--?
GOD DAMN!

HE... HE DIDN'T SEEM LIKE HE WAS GONNA SAY ANY-THING...

HE DID NOT SEEM...?

DO YOU THINK I DID THAT *LIGHTLY?* YOU HAVE SOME *HUNCH* THAT JULES *MAY* NOT HAVE CONDEMNED ALL OF OUR WORK...?

TOK

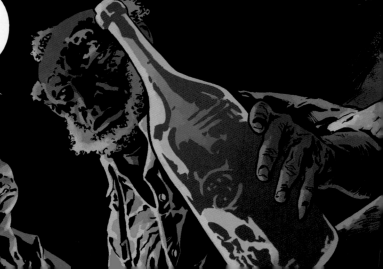

BE GLAD YOUR LIVES ARE IN *MY* HANDS, RATHER THAN YOUR OWN.

HAVE FAITH IN THIS POWER, TONY, AS *YOU* BRING THOSE LOST SOULS TO SPREAD THE WORD EAST...AND BRING THE *RAPTURE* TO MAN, BEFORE IT'S TOO LATE...

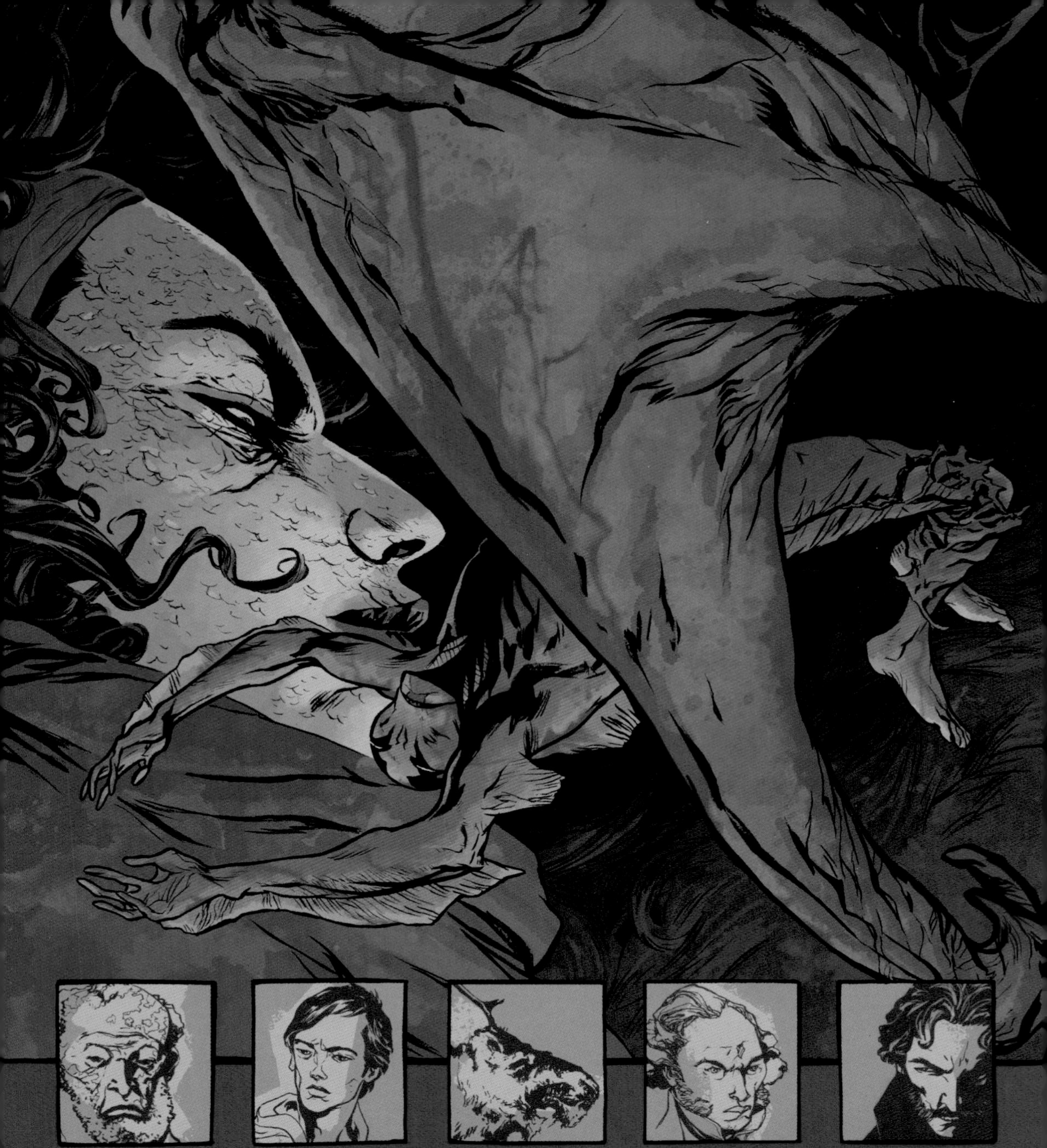

DAYANA

With the guidance and protection of la Santa Muerte, Dayana has kept her extended family together in the face of the worldwide crisis. But her adopted hometown on the Texas-Mexico border finally grew too dangerous. Now, with Abe Sapien, she's brought her small group to a stable town on the otherwise-devastated Texas Gulf Coast.

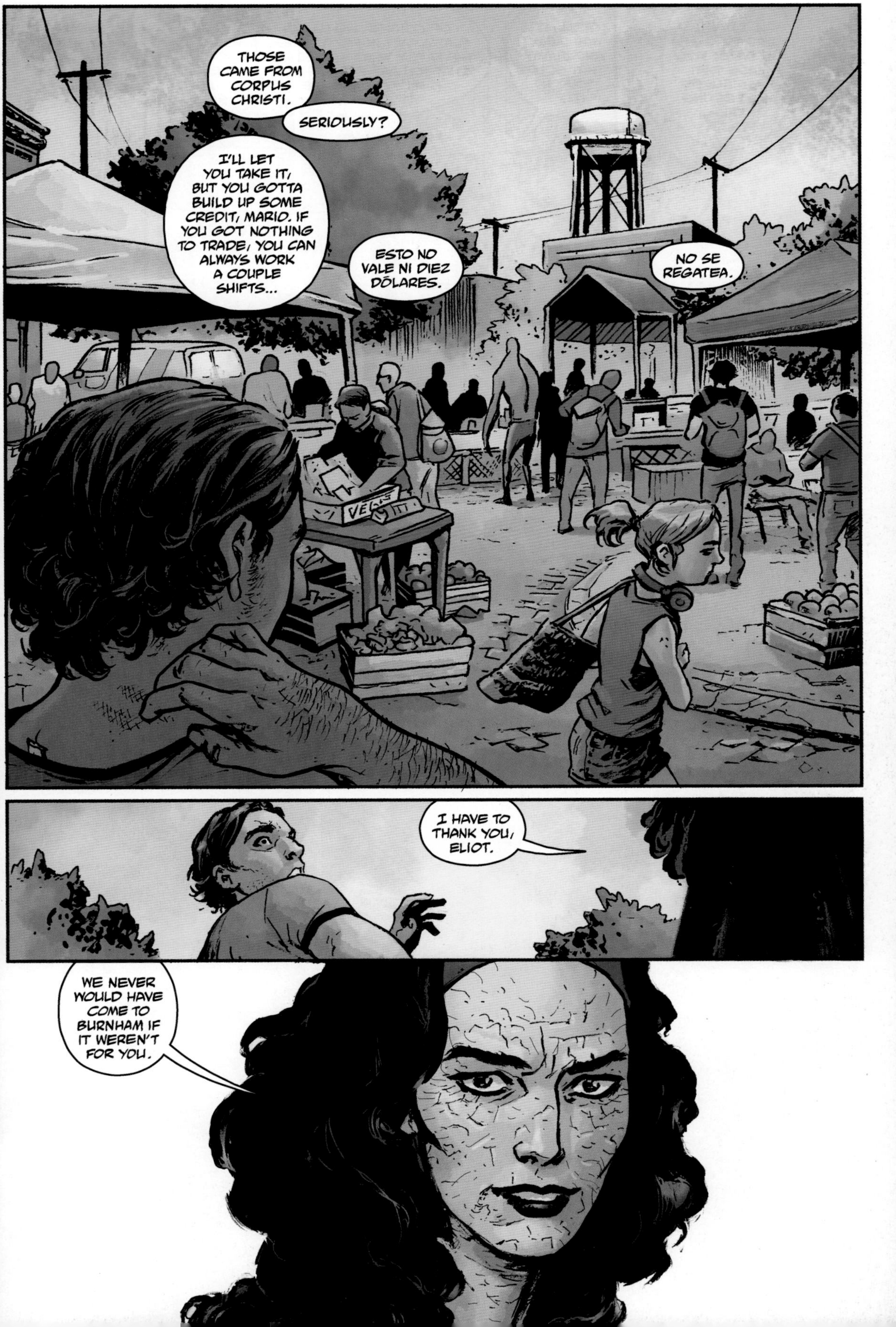
THOSE CAME FROM CORPUS CHRISTI.
SERIOUSLY?
I'LL LET YOU TAKE IT, BUT YOU GOTTA BUILD UP SOME CREDIT, MARIO. IF YOU GOT NOTHING TO TRADE, YOU CAN ALWAYS WORK A COUPLE SHIFTS...
ESTO NO VALE NI DIEZ DÓLARES.
NO SE REGATEA.
I HAVE TO THANK YOU, ELIOT.
WE NEVER WOULD HAVE COME TO BURNHAM IF IT WEREN'T FOR YOU.

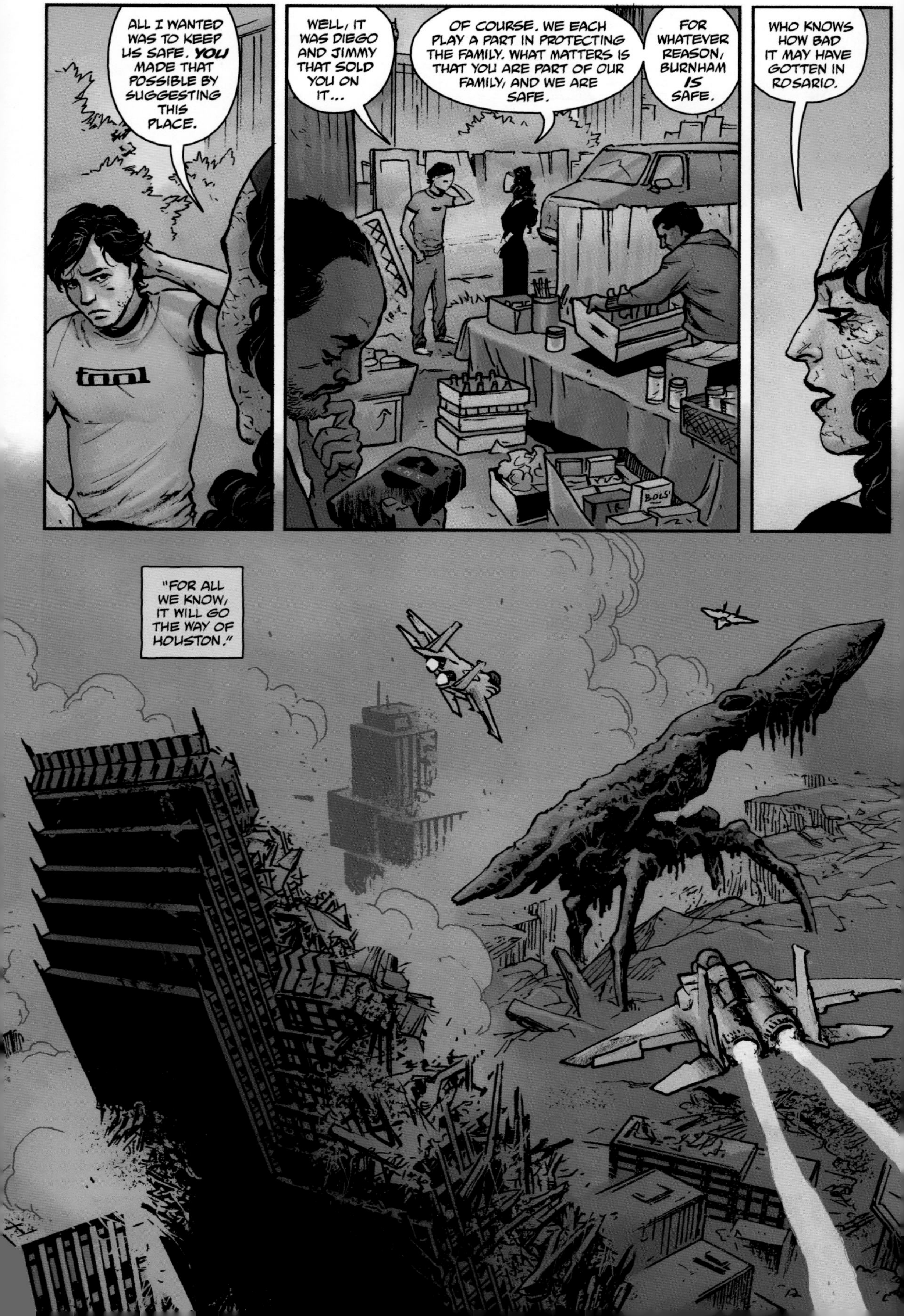
ALL I WANTED WAS TO KEEP US SAFE. YOU MADE THAT POSSIBLE BY SUGGESTING THIS PLACE.
WELL, IT WAS DIEGO AND JIMMY THAT SOLD YOU ON IT...
OF COURSE. WE EACH PLAY A PART IN PROTECTING THE FAMILY. WHAT MATTERS IS THAT YOU ARE PART OF OUR FAMILY, AND WE ARE SAFE.
FOR WHATEVER REASON, BURNHAM IS SAFE.
WHO KNOWS HOW BAD IT MAY HAVE GOTTEN IN ROSARIO.
"FOR ALL WE KNOW, IT WILL GO THE WAY OF HOUSTON."
tool

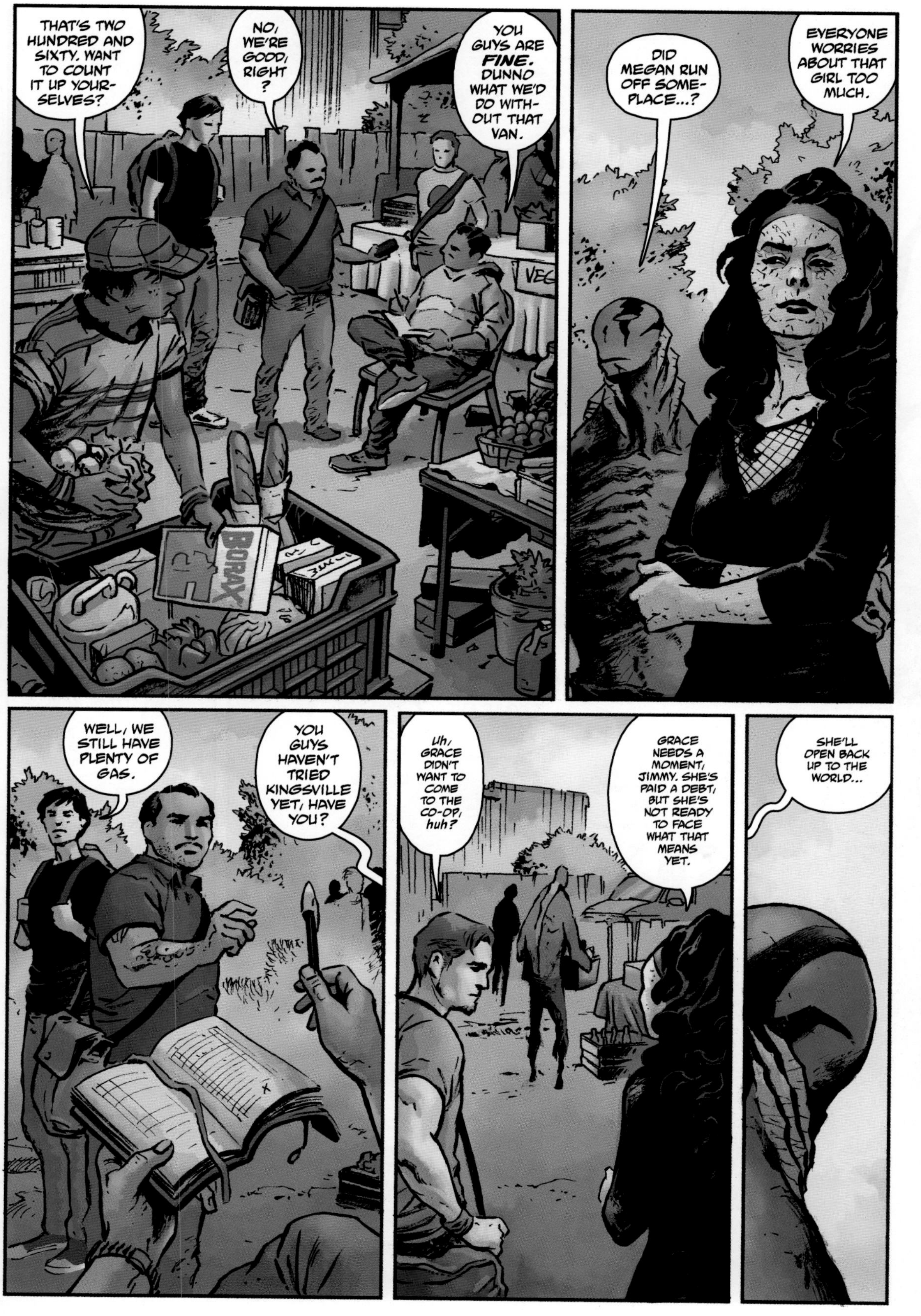
THAT'S TWO HUNDRED AND SIXTY. WANT TO COUNT IT UP YOURSELVES?
NO, WE'RE GOOD, RIGHT?
YOU GUYS ARE FINE. DUNNO WHAT WE'D DO WITHOUT THAT VAN.
BORAX
DID MEGAN RUN OFF SOMEPLACE...?
EVERYONE WORRIES ABOUT THAT GIRL TOO MUCH.
WELL, WE STILL HAVE PLENTY OF GAS.
YOU GUYS HAVEN'T TRIED KINGSVILLE YET, HAVE YOU?
Uh, GRACE DIDN'T WANT TO COME TO THE CO-OP, huh?
GRACE NEEDS A MOMENT, JIMMY. SHE'S PAID A DEBT, BUT SHE'S NOT READY TO FACE WHAT THAT MEANS YET.
SHE'LL OPEN BACK UP TO THE WORLD...

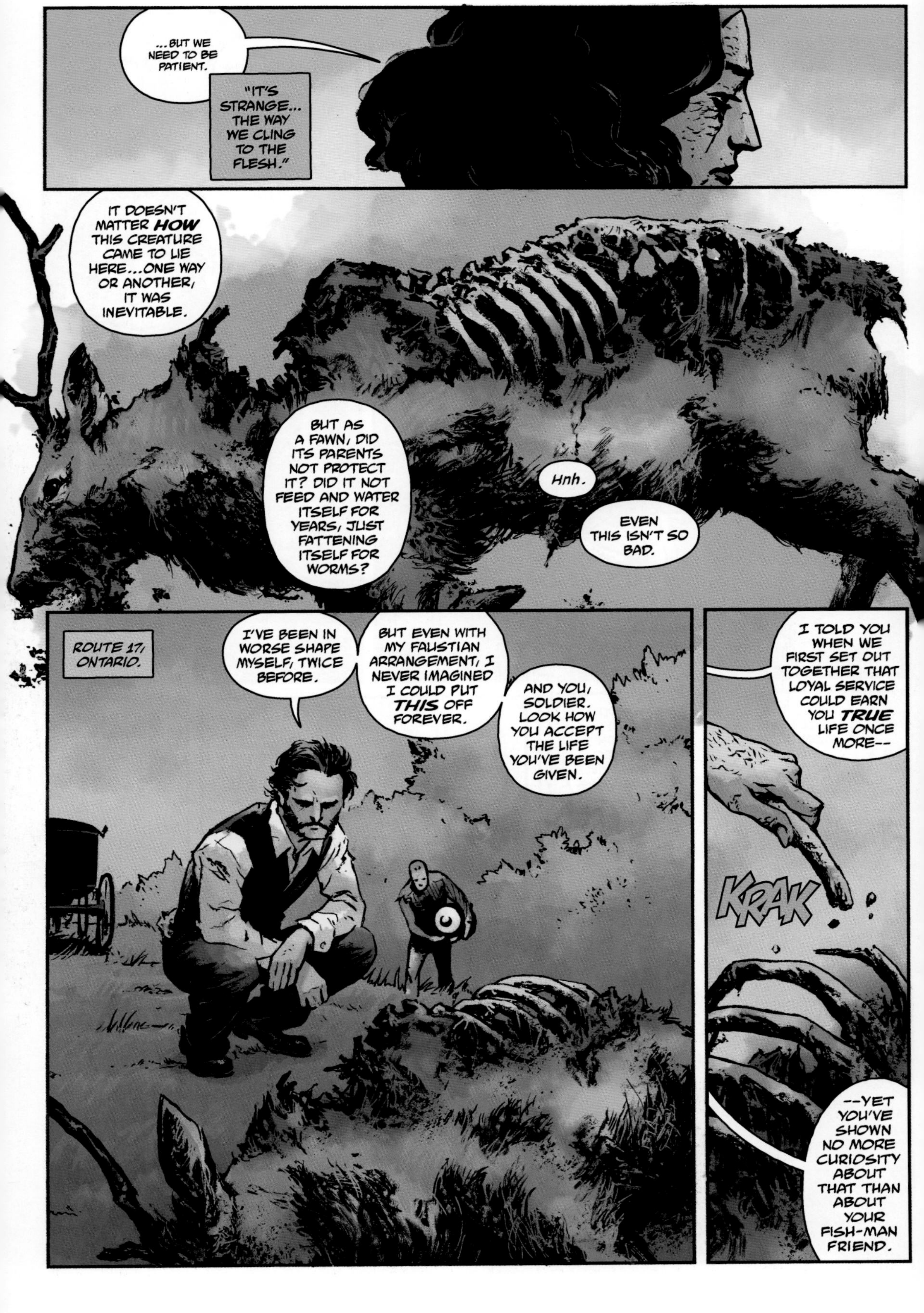
...BUT WE NEED TO BE PATIENT.
"IT'S STRANGE... THE WAY WE CLING TO THE FLESH."
IT DOESN'T MATTER HOW THIS CREATURE CAME TO LIE HERE...ONE WAY OR ANOTHER, IT WAS INEVITABLE.
BUT AS A FAWN, DID ITS PARENTS NOT PROTECT IT? DID IT NOT FEED AND WATER ITSELF FOR YEARS, JUST FATTENING ITSELF FOR WORMS?
Hnh.
EVEN THIS ISN'T SO BAD.
ROUTE 17, ONTARIO.
I'VE BEEN IN WORSE SHAPE MYSELF, TWICE BEFORE.
BUT EVEN WITH MY FAUSTIAN ARRANGEMENT, I NEVER IMAGINED I COULD PUT THIS OFF FOREVER.
AND YOU, SOLDIER. LOOK HOW YOU ACCEPT THE LIFE YOU'VE BEEN GIVEN.
I TOLD YOU WHEN WE FIRST SET OUT TOGETHER THAT LOYAL SERVICE COULD EARN YOU TRUE LIFE ONCE MORE--
KRAK
--YET YOU'VE SHOWN NO MORE CURIOSITY ABOUT THAT THAN ABOUT YOUR FISH-MAN FRIEND.

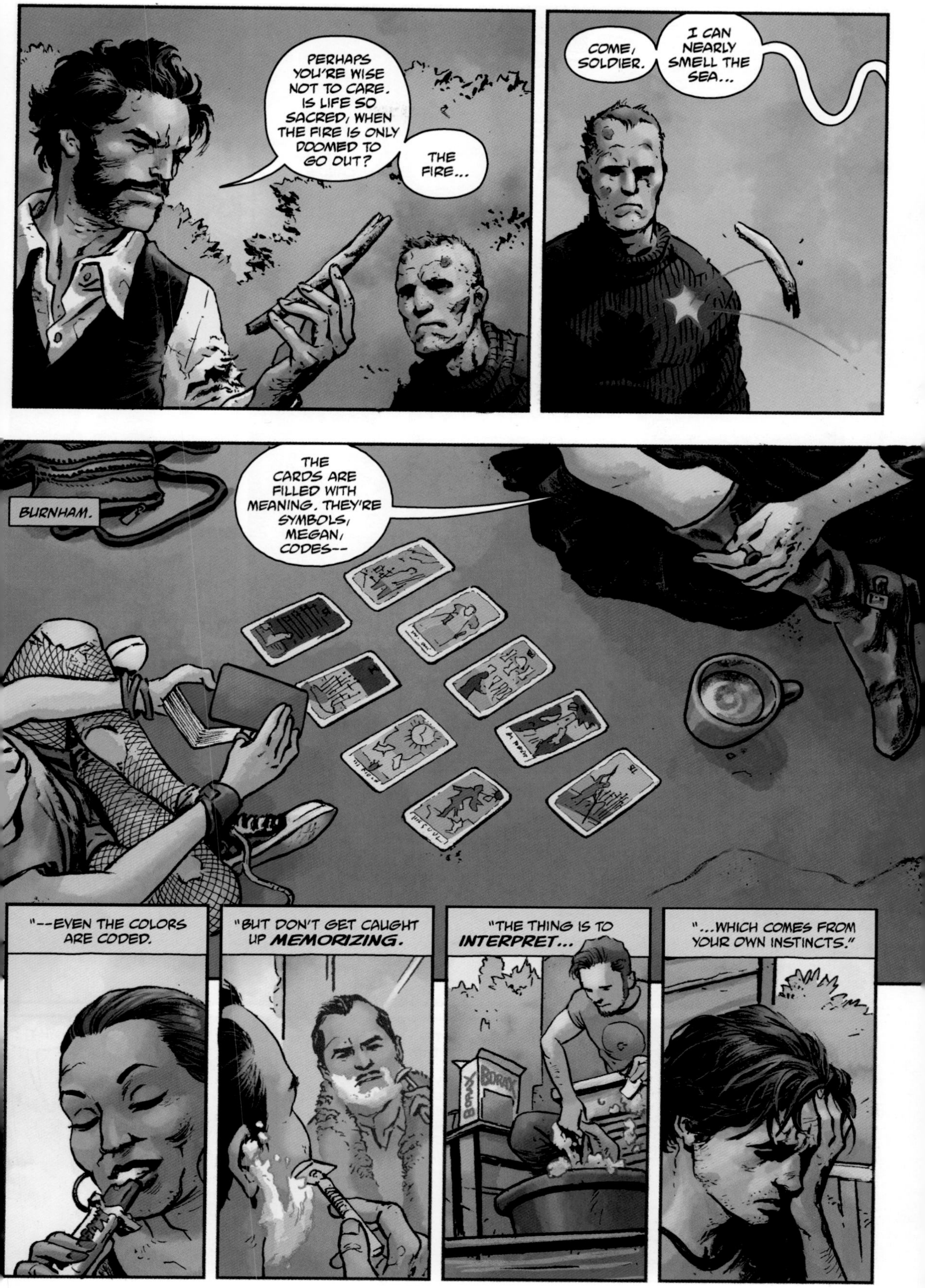
PERHAPS YOU'RE WISE NOT TO CARE. IS LIFE SO SACRED, WHEN THE FIRE IS ONLY DOOMED TO GO OUT?
THE FIRE...
COME, SOLDIER.
I CAN NEARLY SMELL THE SEA...
BURNHAM.
THE CARDS ARE FILLED WITH MEANING. THEY'RE SYMBOLS, MEGAN, CODES--
"--EVEN THE COLORS ARE CODED.
"BUT DON'T GET CAUGHT UP MEMORIZING.
"THE THING IS TO INTERPRET...
"...WHICH COMES FROM YOUR OWN INSTINCTS."
BORAX

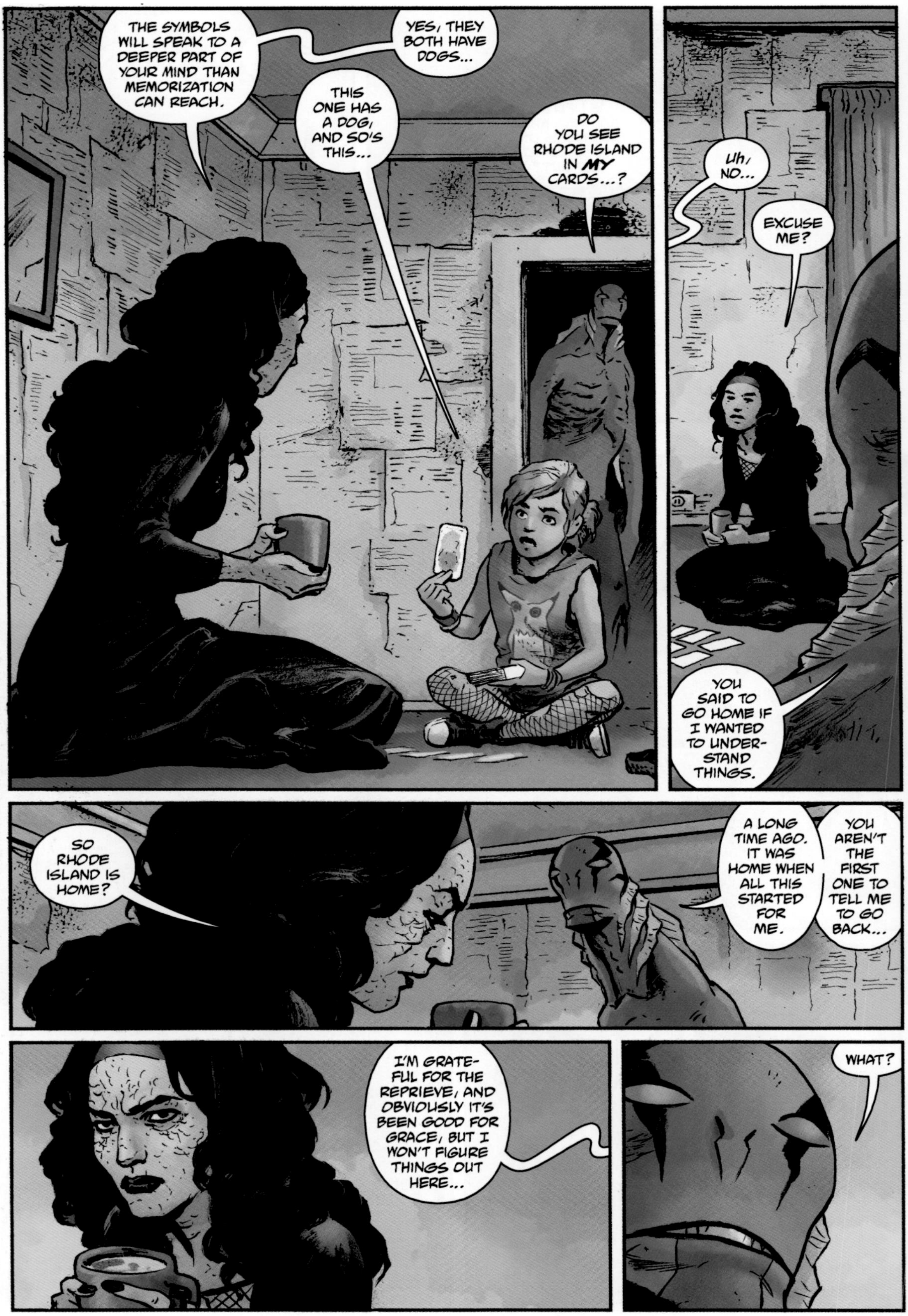
THE SYMBOLS WILL SPEAK TO A DEEPER PART OF YOUR MIND THAN MEMORIZATION CAN REACH.
YES, THEY BOTH HAVE DOGS...
THIS ONE HAS A DOG, AND SO'S THIS...
DO YOU SEE RHODE ISLAND IN *MY* CARDS...?
UH, NO...
EXCUSE ME?
YOU SAID TO GO HOME IF I WANTED TO UNDER-STAND THINGS.
SO RHODE ISLAND IS HOME?
A LONG TIME AGO. IT WAS HOME WHEN ALL THIS STARTED FOR ME.
YOU AREN'T THE FIRST ONE TO TELL ME TO GO BACK...
I'M GRATE-FUL FOR THE REPRIEVE, AND OBVIOUSLY IT'S BEEN GOOD FOR GRACE, BUT I WON'T FIGURE THINGS OUT HERE...
WHAT?

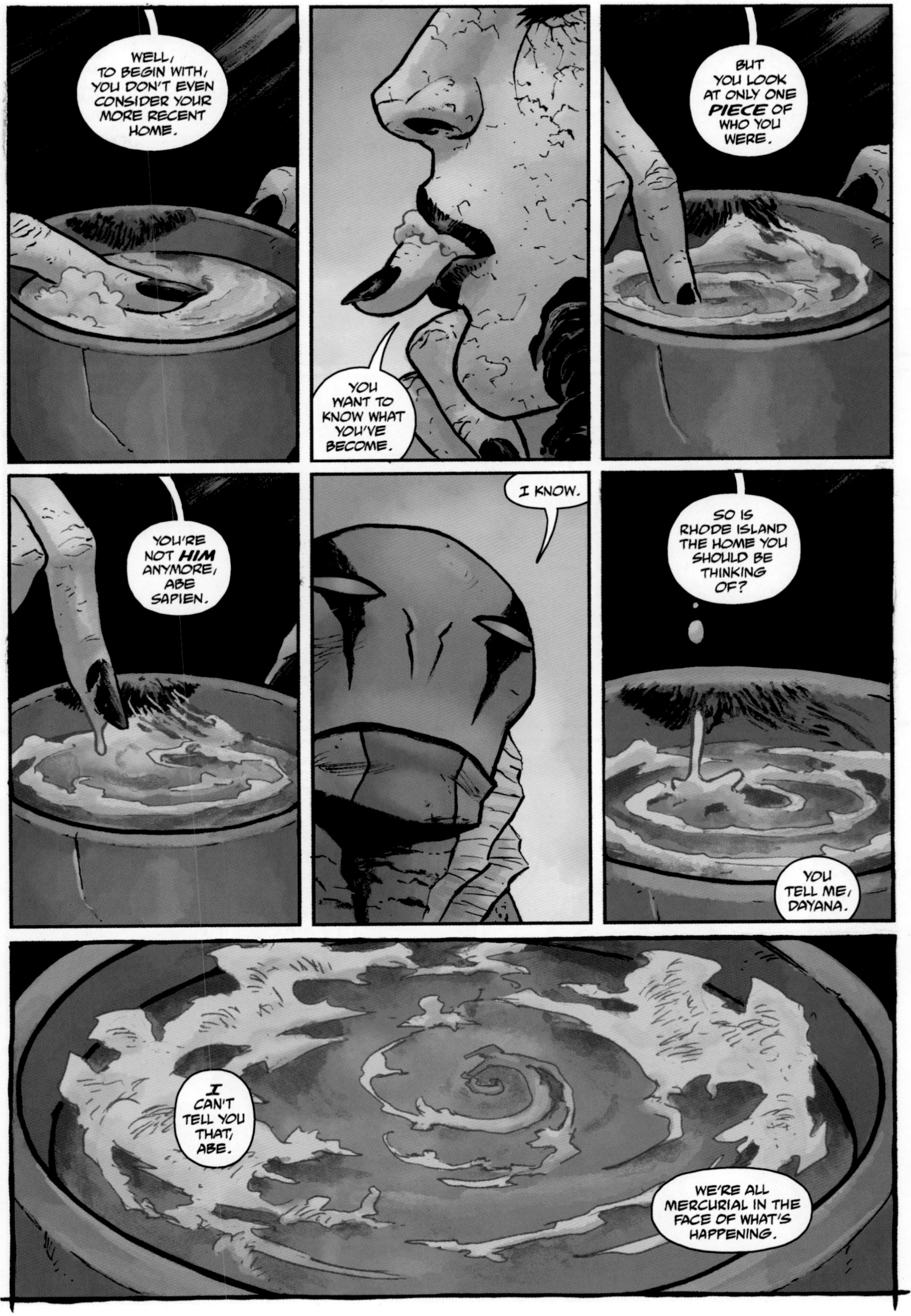
WELL, TO BEGIN WITH, YOU DON'T EVEN CONSIDER YOUR MORE RECENT HOME.
YOU WANT TO KNOW WHAT YOU'VE BECOME.
BUT YOU LOOK AT ONLY ONE PIECE OF WHO YOU WERE.
YOU'RE NOT HIM ANYMORE, ABE SAPIEN.
I KNOW.
SO IS RHODE ISLAND THE HOME YOU SHOULD BE THINKING OF?
YOU TELL ME, DAYANA.
I CAN'T TELL YOU THAT, ABE.
WE'RE ALL MERCURIAL IN THE FACE OF WHAT'S HAPPENING.

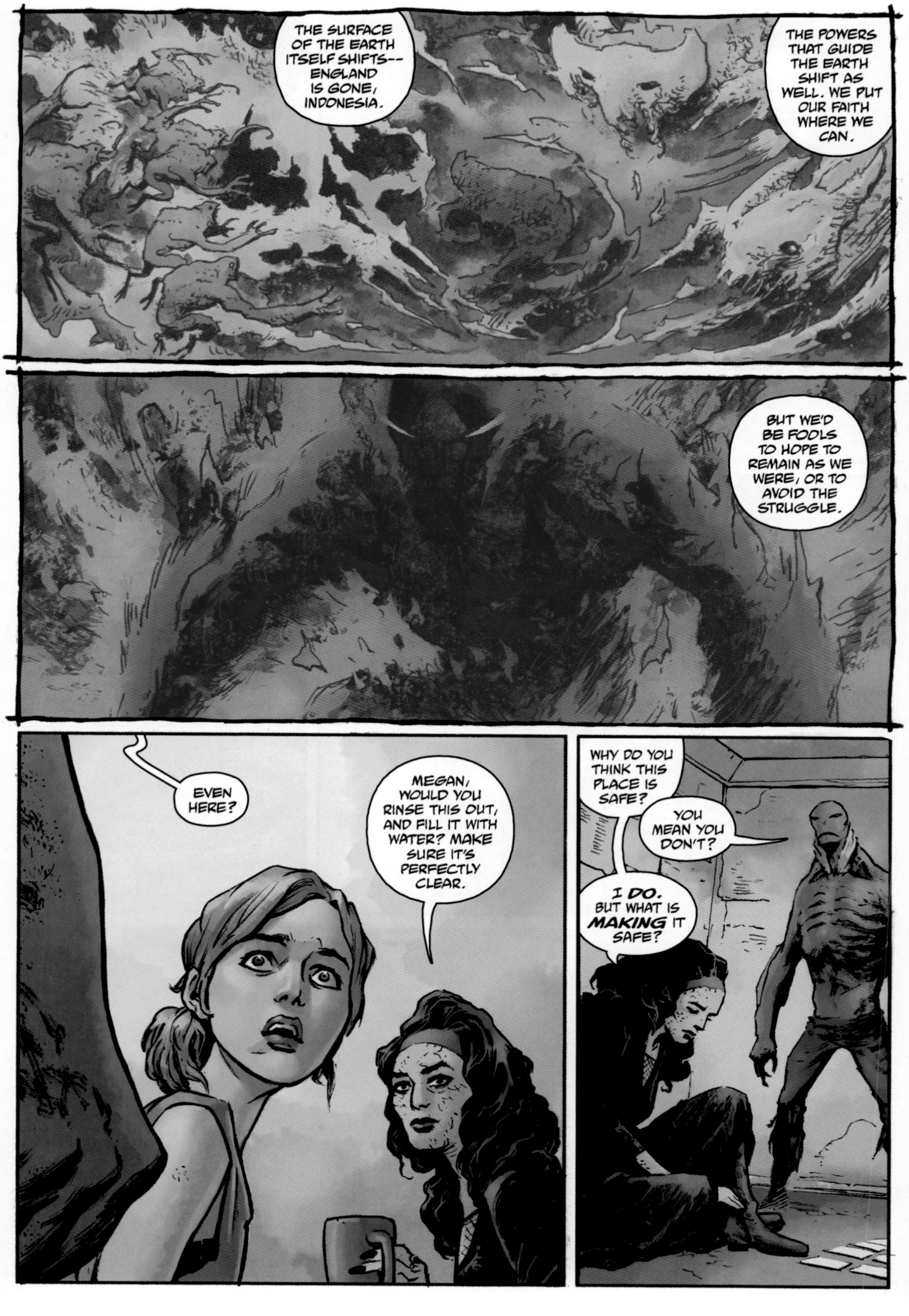
THE SURFACE OF THE EARTH ITSELF SHIFTS-- ENGLAND IS GONE, INDONESIA.
THE POWERS THAT GUIDE THE EARTH SHIFT AS WELL. WE PUT OUR FAITH WHERE WE CAN.
BUT WE'D BE FOOLS TO HOPE TO REMAIN AS WE WERE, OR TO AVOID THE STRUGGLE.
EVEN HERE?
MEGAN, WOULD YOU RINSE THIS OUT, AND FILL IT WITH WATER? MAKE SURE IT'S PERFECTLY CLEAR.
WHY DO YOU THINK THIS PLACE IS SAFE?
YOU MEAN YOU DON'T?
I DO. BUT WHAT IS MAKING IT SAFE?

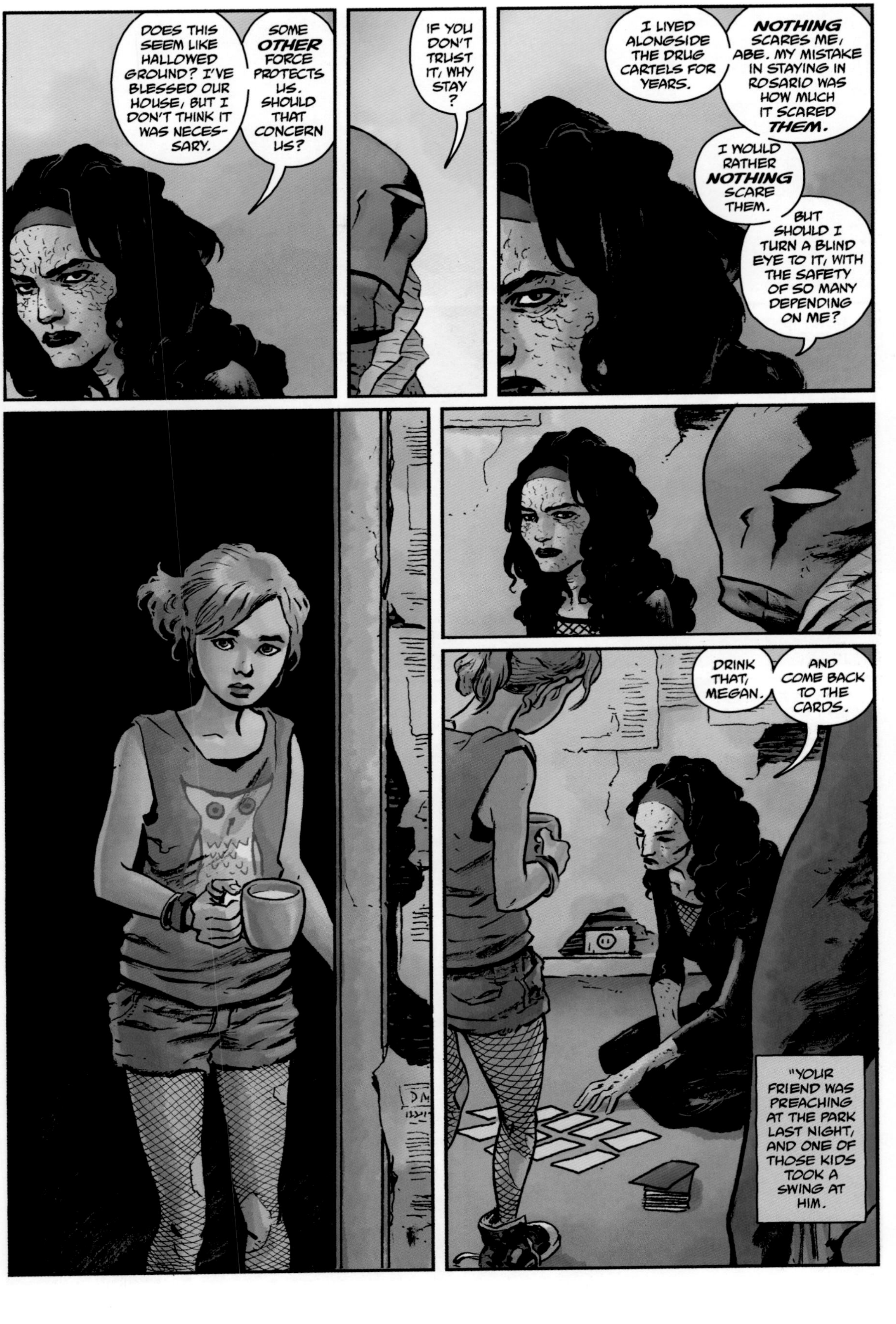
DOES THIS SEEM LIKE HALLOWED GROUND? I'VE BLESSED OUR HOUSE, BUT I DON'T THINK IT WAS NECES-SARY.
SOME **OTHER** FORCE PROTECTS US. SHOULD THAT CONCERN US?
IF YOU DON'T TRUST IT, WHY STAY?
I LIVED ALONGSIDE THE DRUG CARTELS FOR YEARS.
NOTHING SCARES ME, ABE. MY MISTAKE IN STAYING IN ROSARIO WAS HOW MUCH IT SCARED **THEM.**
I WOULD RATHER **NOTHING** SCARE THEM.
BUT SHOULD I TURN A BLIND EYE TO IT, WITH THE SAFETY OF SO MANY DEPENDING ON ME?
DRINK THAT, MEGAN.
AND COME BACK TO THE CARDS.
"YOUR FRIEND WAS PREACHING AT THE PARK LAST NIGHT, AND ONE OF THOSE KIDS TOOK A SWING AT HIM.

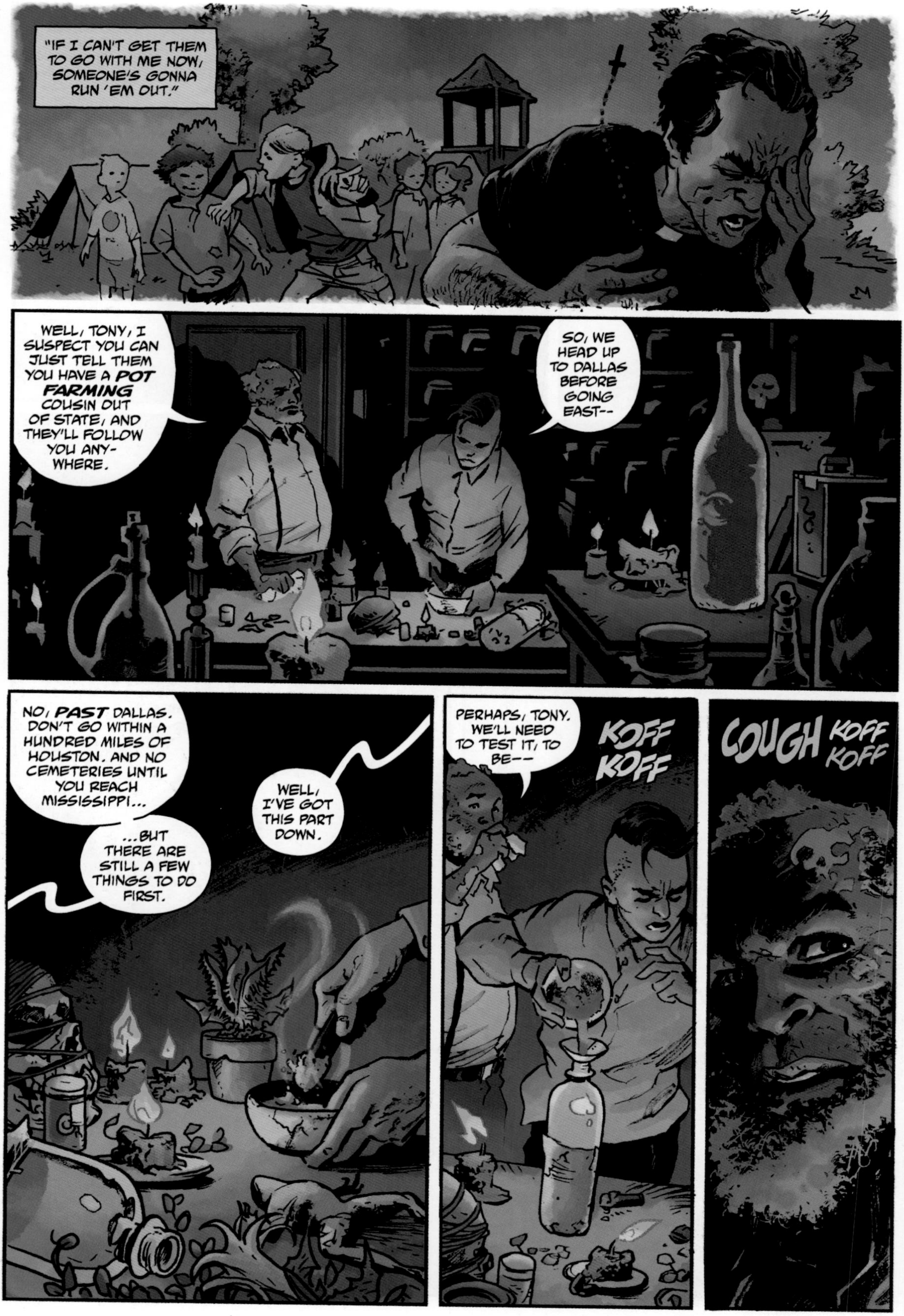
"IF I CAN'T GET THEM TO GO WITH ME NOW, SOMEONE'S GONNA RUN 'EM OUT."
WELL, TONY, I SUSPECT YOU CAN JUST TELL THEM YOU HAVE A POT FARMING COUSIN OUT OF STATE, AND THEY'LL FOLLOW YOU ANYWHERE.
SO, WE HEAD UP TO DALLAS BEFORE GOING EAST--
NO, PAST DALLAS. DON'T GO WITHIN A HUNDRED MILES OF HOUSTON. AND NO CEMETERIES UNTIL YOU REACH MISSISSIPPI...
...BUT THERE ARE STILL A FEW THINGS TO DO FIRST.
WELL, I'VE GOT THIS PART DOWN.
PERHAPS, TONY. WE'LL NEED TO TEST IT, TO BE--
KOFF KOFF
COUGH KOFF KOFF

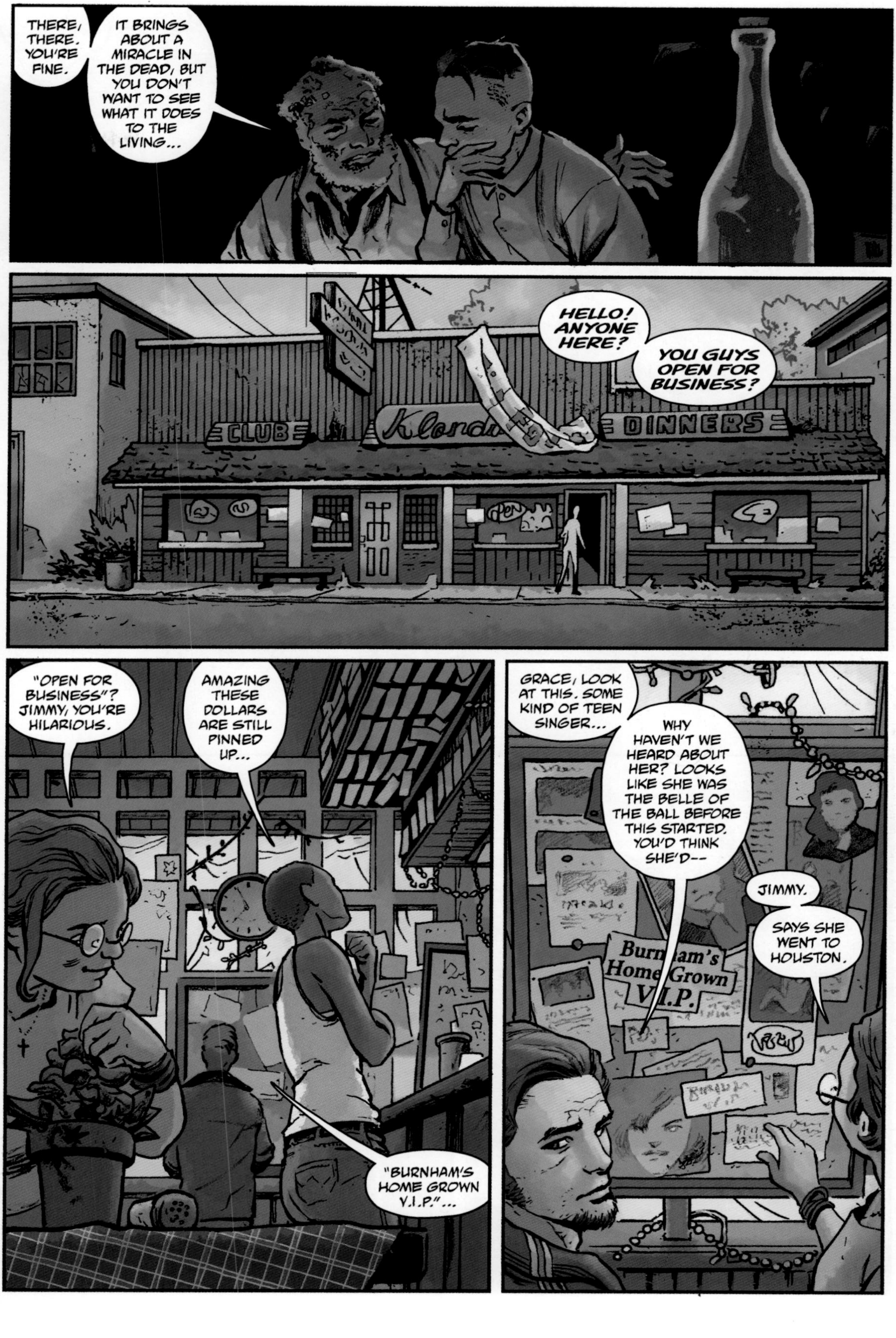
THERE, THERE. YOU'RE FINE.
IT BRINGS ABOUT A MIRACLE IN THE DEAD, BUT YOU DON'T WANT TO SEE WHAT IT DOES TO THE LIVING...
CLUB
DINNERS
HELLO! ANYONE HERE?
YOU GUYS OPEN FOR BUSINESS?
"OPEN FOR BUSINESS"? JIMMY, YOU'RE HILARIOUS.
AMAZING THESE DOLLARS ARE STILL PINNED UP...
"BURNHAM'S HOME GROWN V.I.P."...
GRACE, LOOK AT THIS. SOME KIND OF TEEN SINGER...
WHY HAVEN'T WE HEARD ABOUT HER? LOOKS LIKE SHE WAS THE BELLE OF THE BALL BEFORE THIS STARTED. YOU'D THINK SHE'D--
Burnham's Home Grown V.I.P.
JIMMY.
SAYS SHE WENT TO HOUSTON.

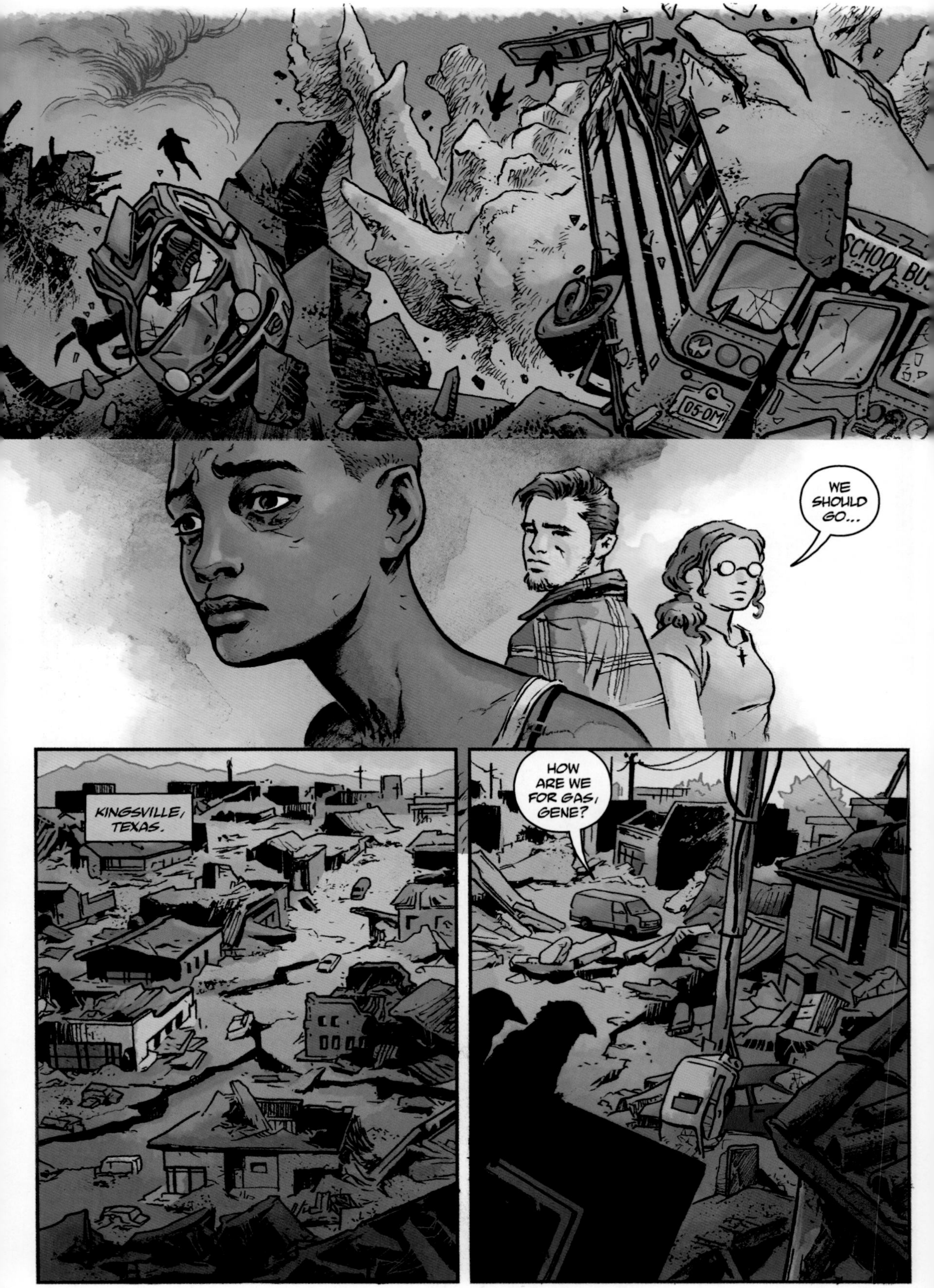

SCHOOL BUS
05-DM
WE SHOULD GO...
KINGSVILLE, TEXAS.
HOW ARE WE FOR GAS, GENE?

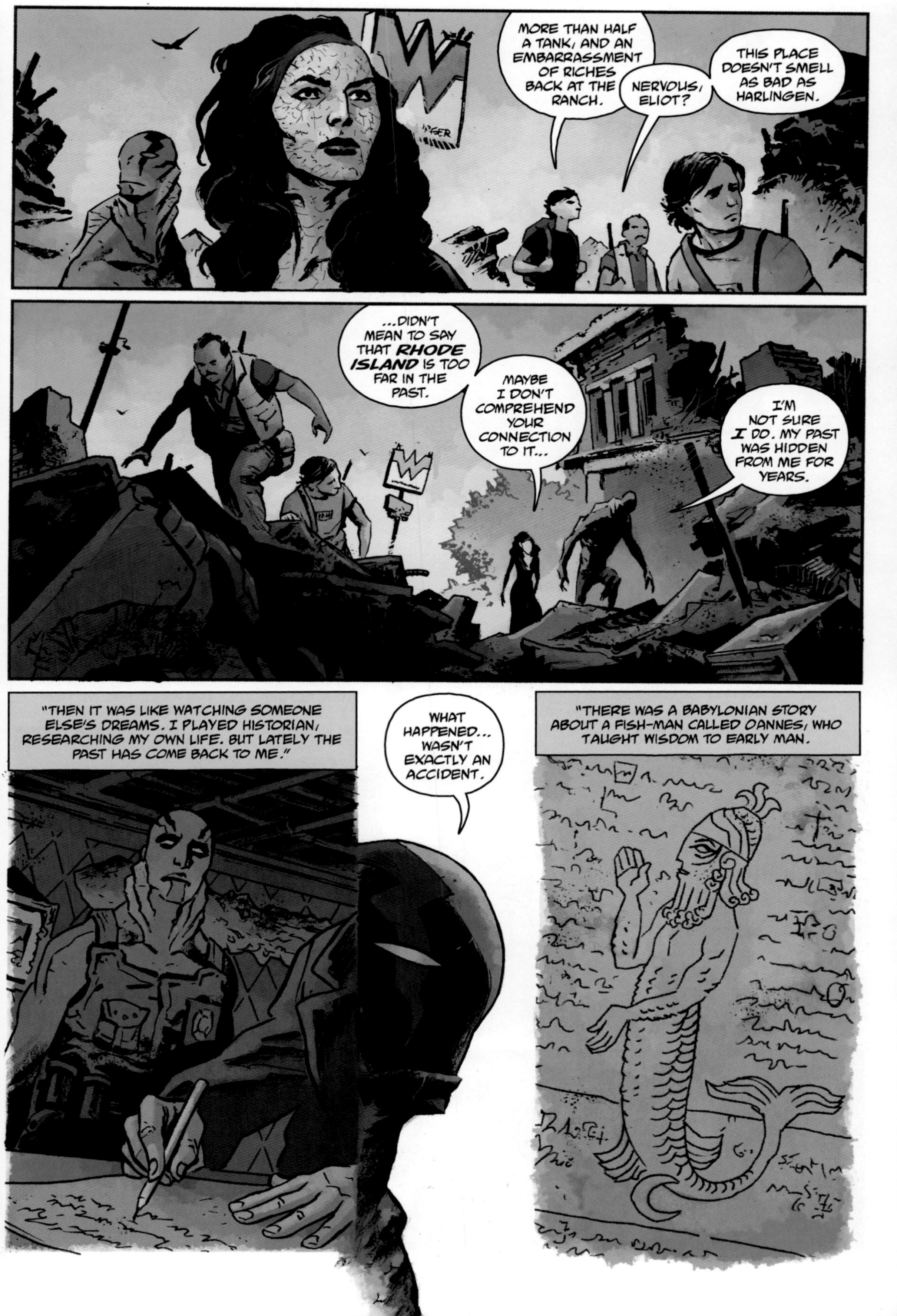
MORE THAN HALF A TANK, AND AN EMBARRASSMENT OF RICHES BACK AT THE RANCH.
NERVOUS, ELIOT?
THIS PLACE DOESN'T SMELL AS BAD AS HARLINGEN.
...DIDN'T MEAN TO SAY THAT RHODE ISLAND IS TOO FAR IN THE PAST.
MAYBE I DON'T COMPREHEND YOUR CONNECTION TO IT...
I'M NOT SURE I DO. MY PAST WAS HIDDEN FROM ME FOR YEARS.
"THEN IT WAS LIKE WATCHING SOMEONE ELSE'S DREAMS. I PLAYED HISTORIAN, RESEARCHING MY OWN LIFE. BUT LATELY THE PAST HAS COME BACK TO ME."
WHAT HAPPENED... WASN'T EXACTLY AN ACCIDENT.
"THERE WAS A BABYLONIAN STORY ABOUT A FISH-MAN CALLED OANNES, WHO TAUGHT WISDOM TO EARLY MAN.

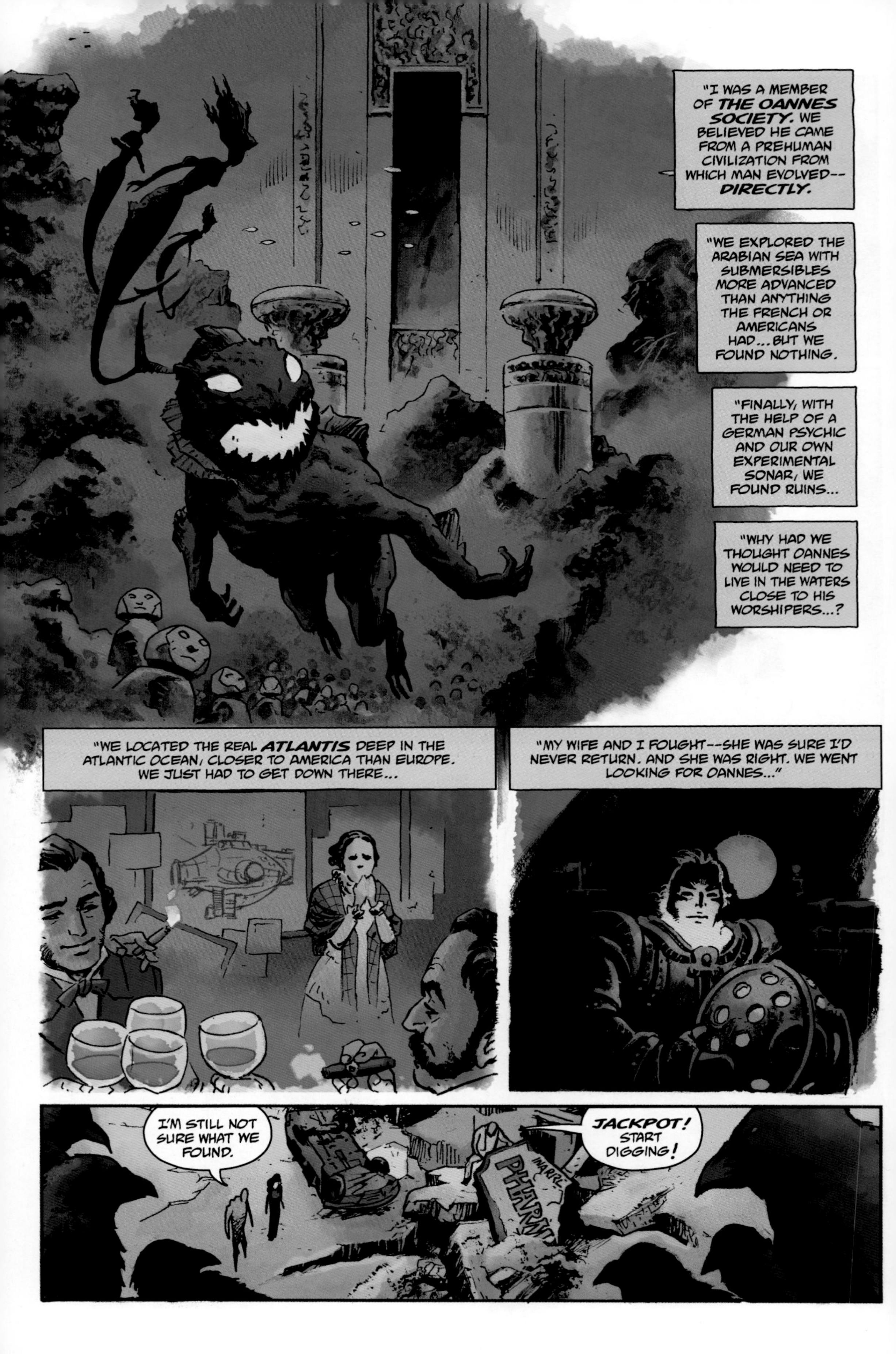
"I WAS A MEMBER OF THE OANNES SOCIETY. WE BELIEVED HE CAME FROM A PREHUMAN CIVILIZATION FROM WHICH MAN EVOLVED--DIRECTLY.
"WE EXPLORED THE ARABIAN SEA WITH SUBMERSIBLES MORE ADVANCED THAN ANYTHING THE FRENCH OR AMERICANS HAD... BUT WE FOUND NOTHING.
"FINALLY, WITH THE HELP OF A GERMAN PSYCHIC AND OUR OWN EXPERIMENTAL SONAR, WE FOUND RUINS...
"WHY HAD WE THOUGHT OANNES WOULD NEED TO LIVE IN THE WATERS CLOSE TO HIS WORSHIPERS...?
"WE LOCATED THE REAL ATLANTIS DEEP IN THE ATLANTIC OCEAN, CLOSER TO AMERICA THAN EUROPE. WE JUST HAD TO GET DOWN THERE...
"MY WIFE AND I FOUGHT--SHE WAS SURE I'D NEVER RETURN. AND SHE WAS RIGHT. WE WENT LOOKING FOR OANNES..."
I'M STILL NOT SURE WHAT WE FOUND.
JACKPOT! START DIGGING!

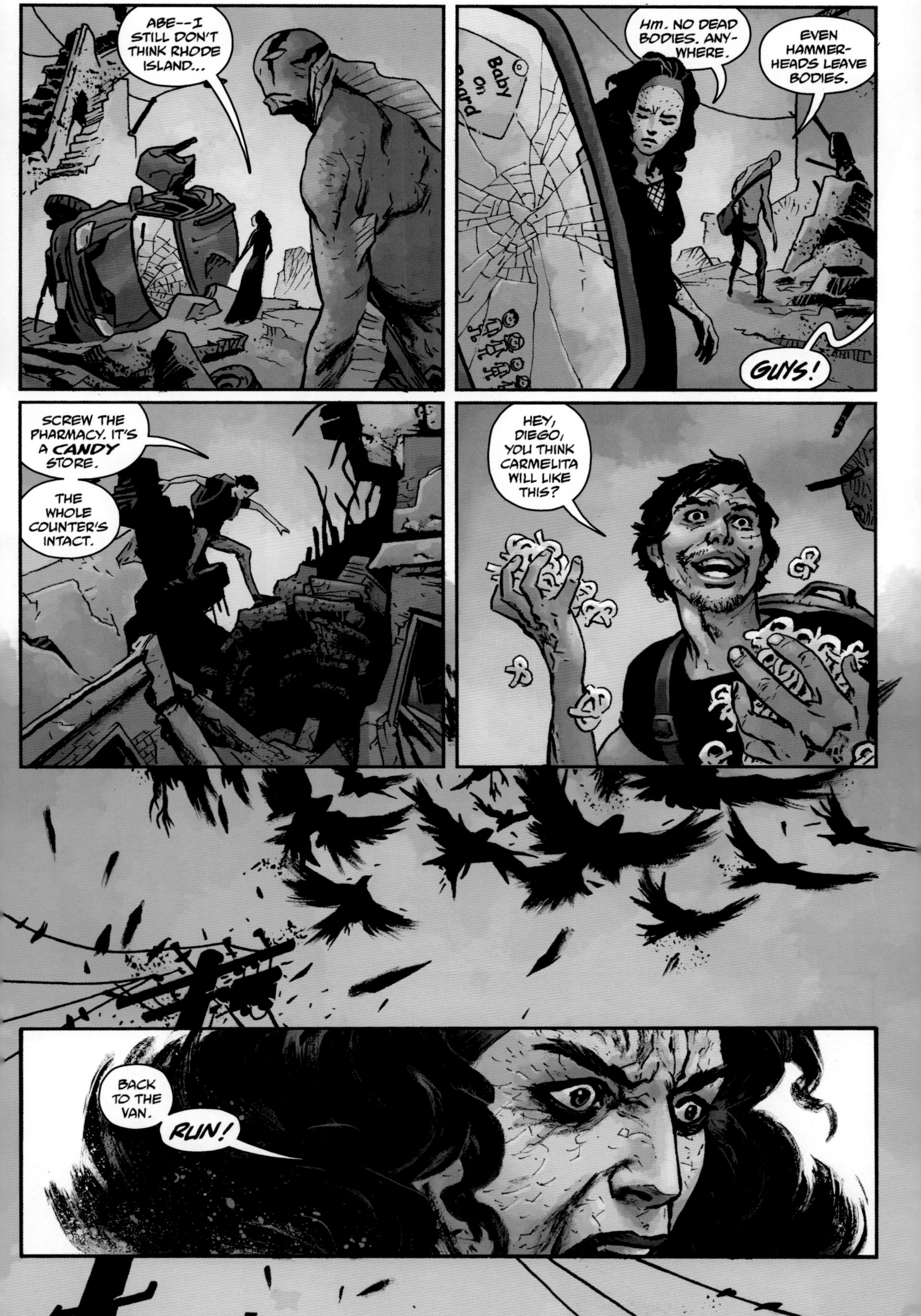
ABE--I STILL DON'T THINK RHODE ISLAND...
Baby On Board
Hm. NO DEAD BODIES. ANYWHERE.
EVEN HAMMERHEADS LEAVE BODIES.
GUYS!
SCREW THE PHARMACY. IT'S A CANDY STORE.
THE WHOLE COUNTER'S INTACT.
HEY, DIEGO, YOU THINK CARMELITA WILL LIKE THIS?
BACK TO THE VAN.
RUN!

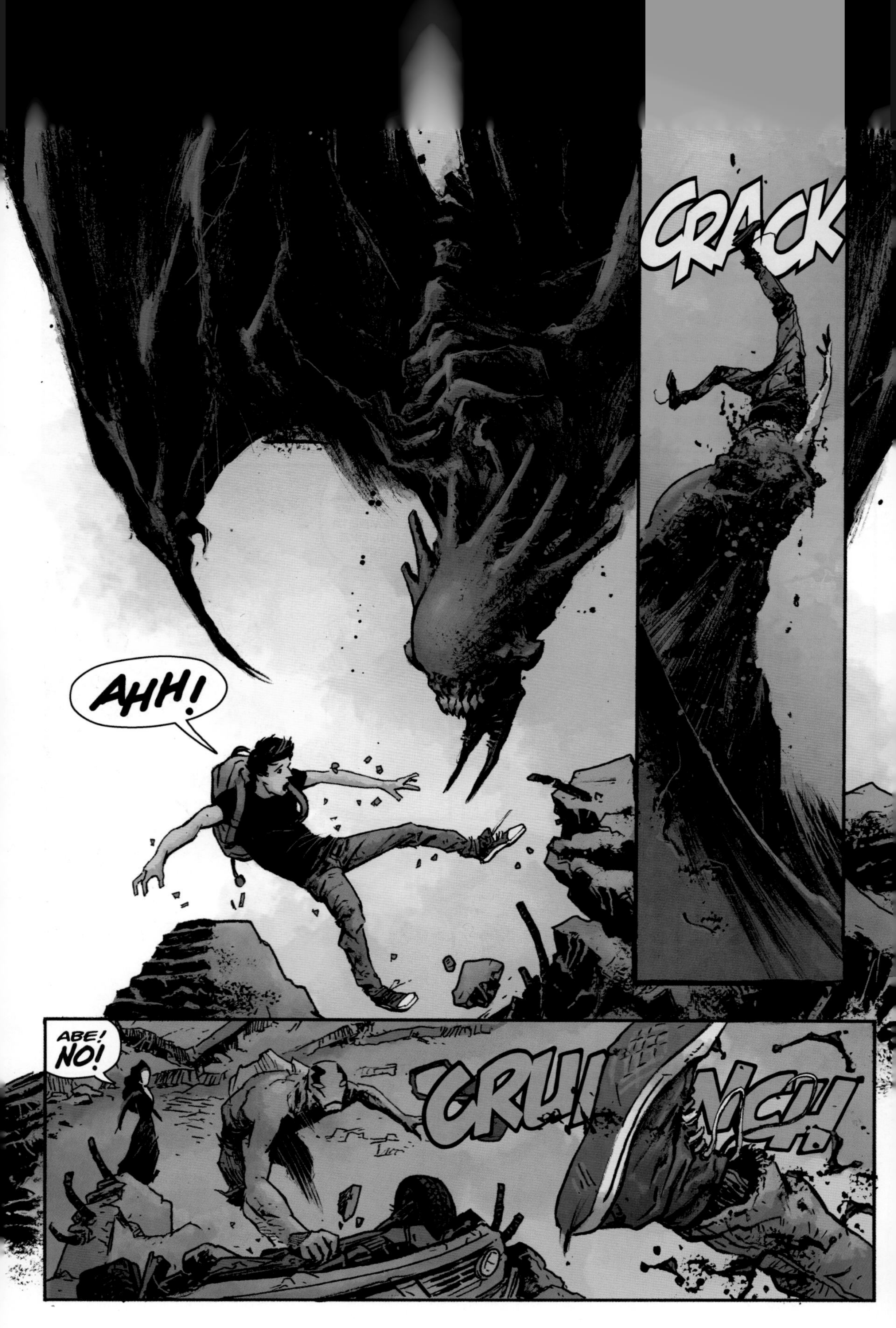

CRACK
AHH!
ABE! NO!
CRUNCH

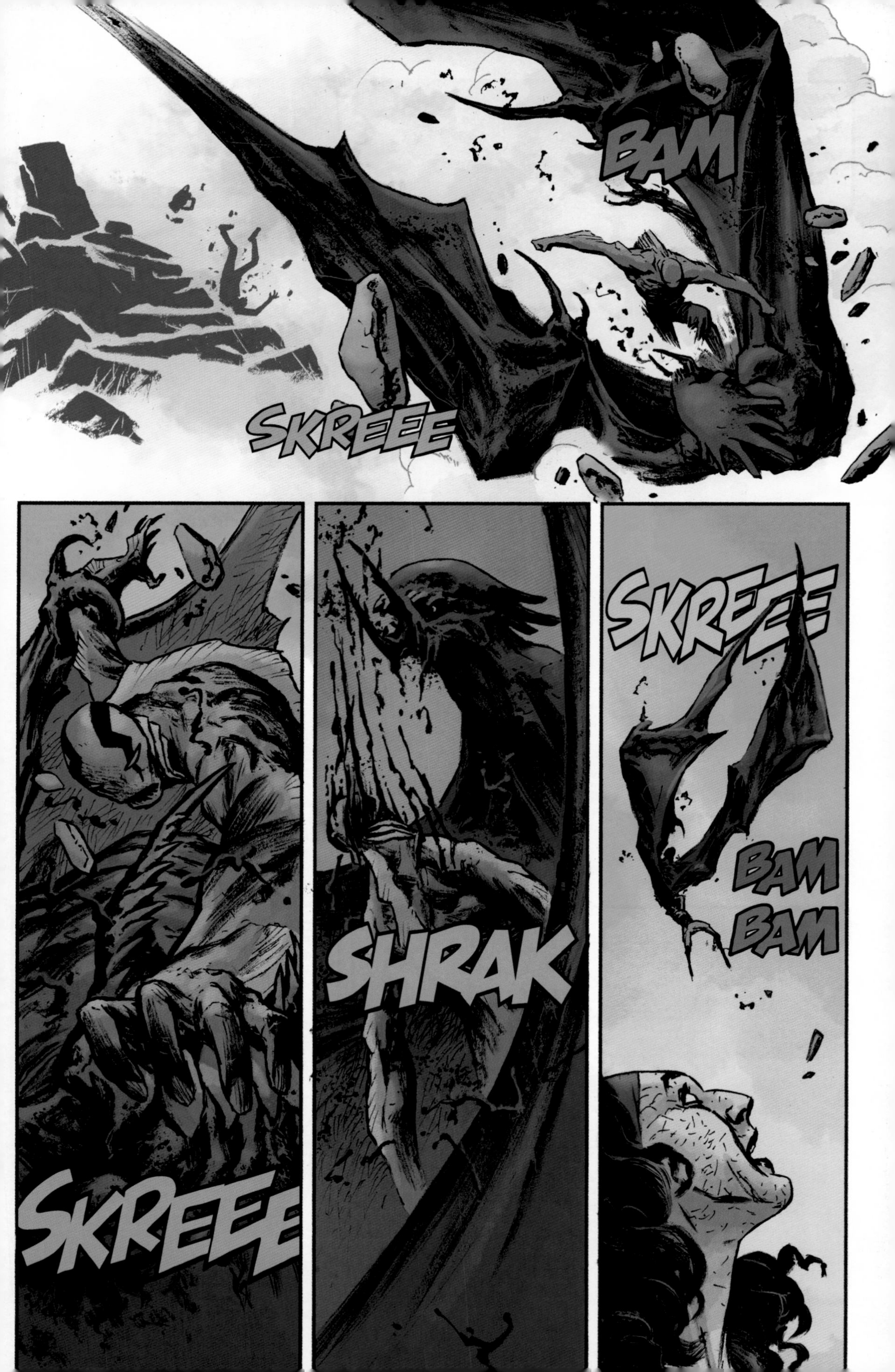
BAM
SKREEE
SKREEE
SHRAK
SKREEE
BAM
BAM
!

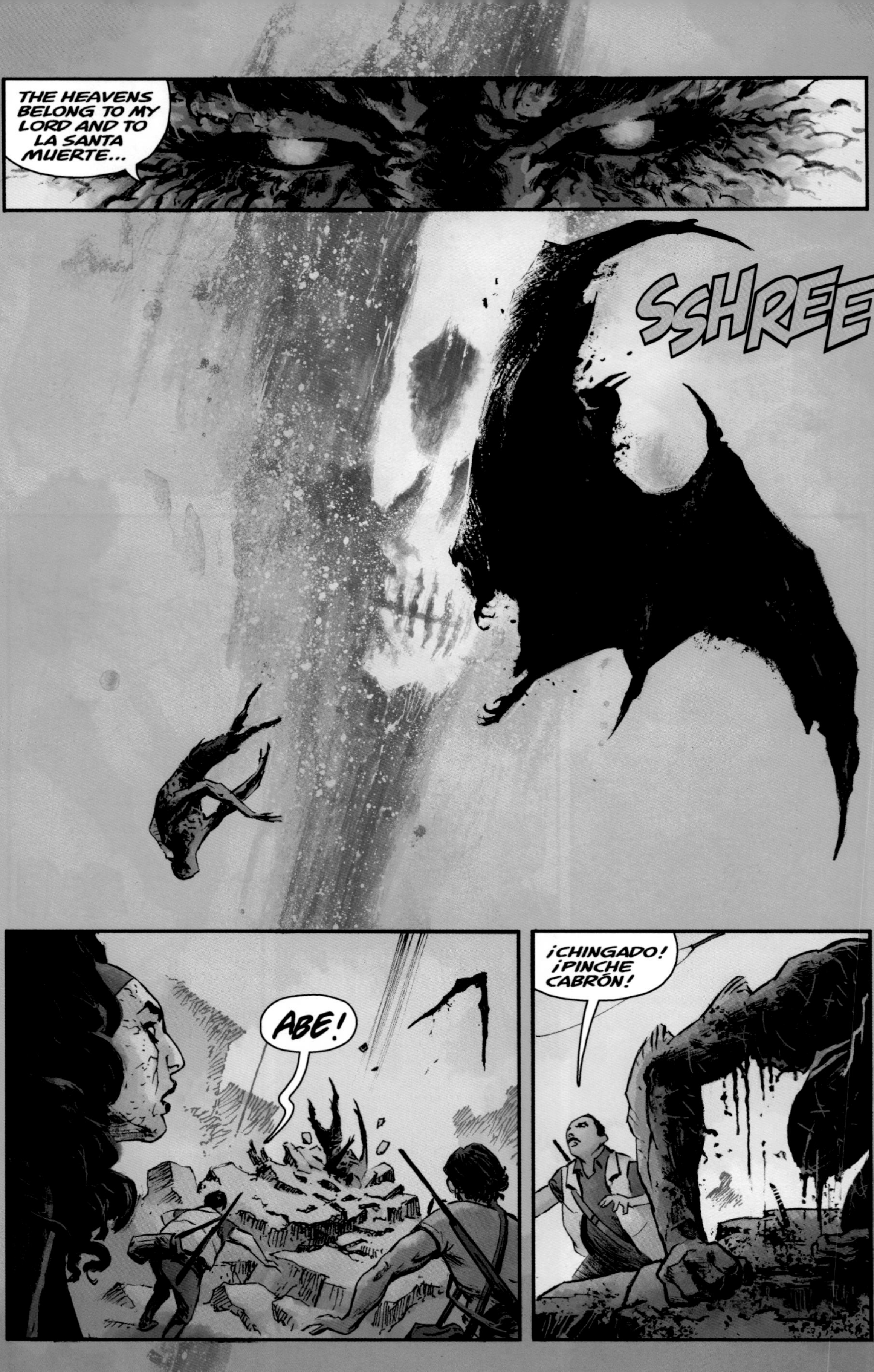
THE HEAVENS BELONG TO MY LORD AND TO LA SANTA MUERTE...
SSHREE
ABE!
¡CHINGADO! ¡PINCHE CABRÓN!

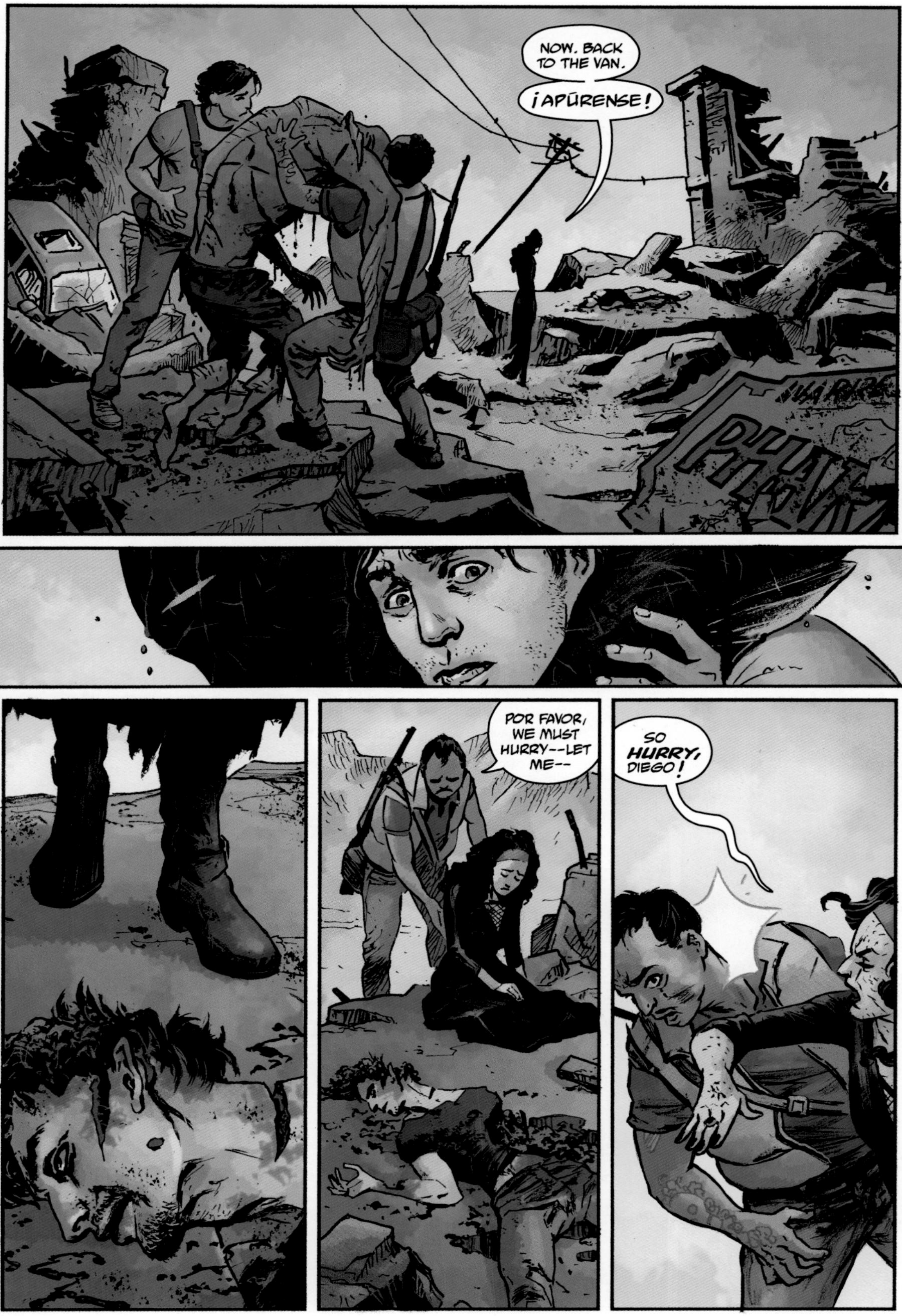
NOW. BACK TO THE VAN.
¡APÚRENSE!
POR FAVOR, WE MUST HURRY--LET ME--
SO HURRY, DIEGO!

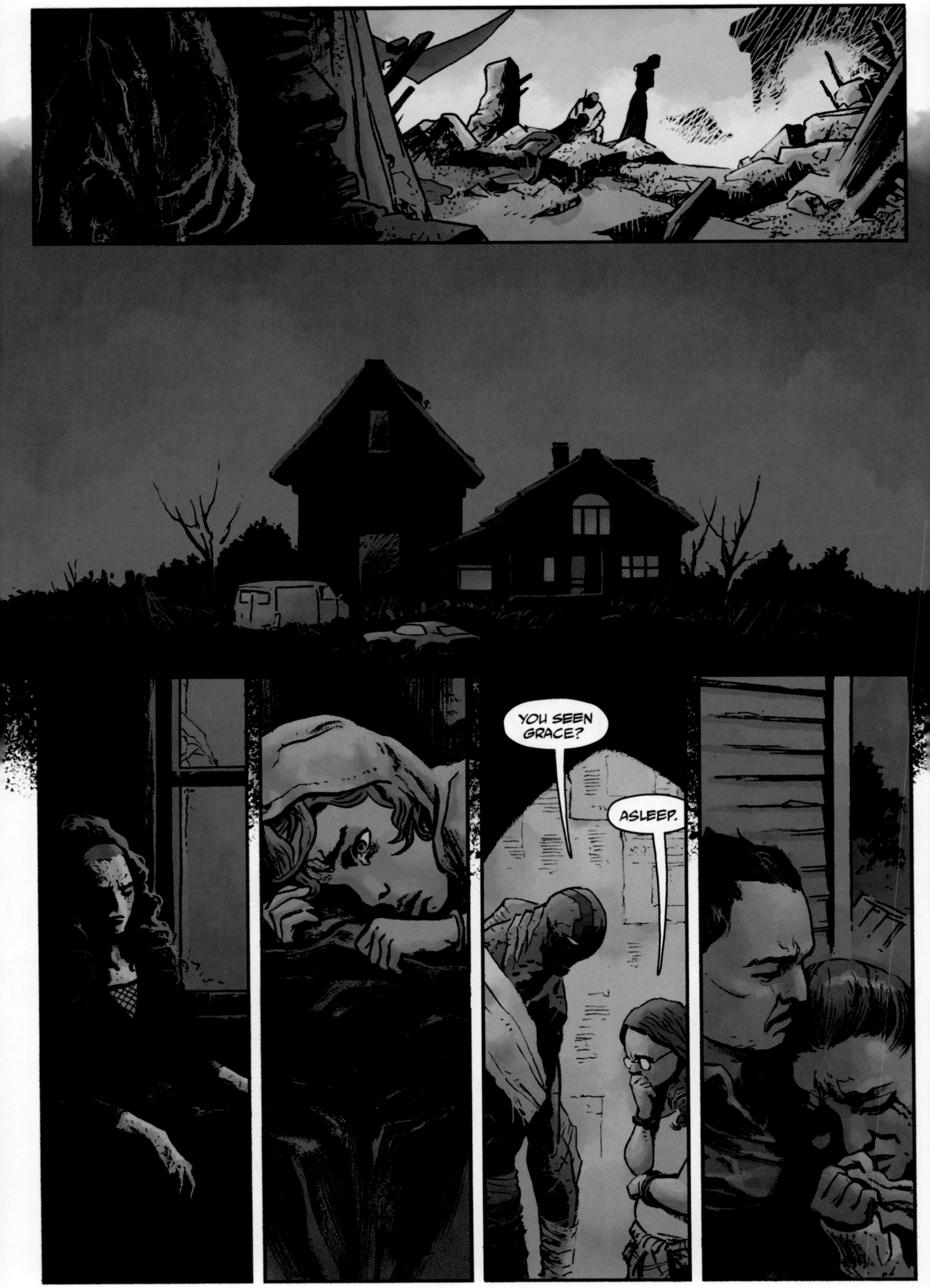
YOU SEEN GRACE?
ASLEEP.

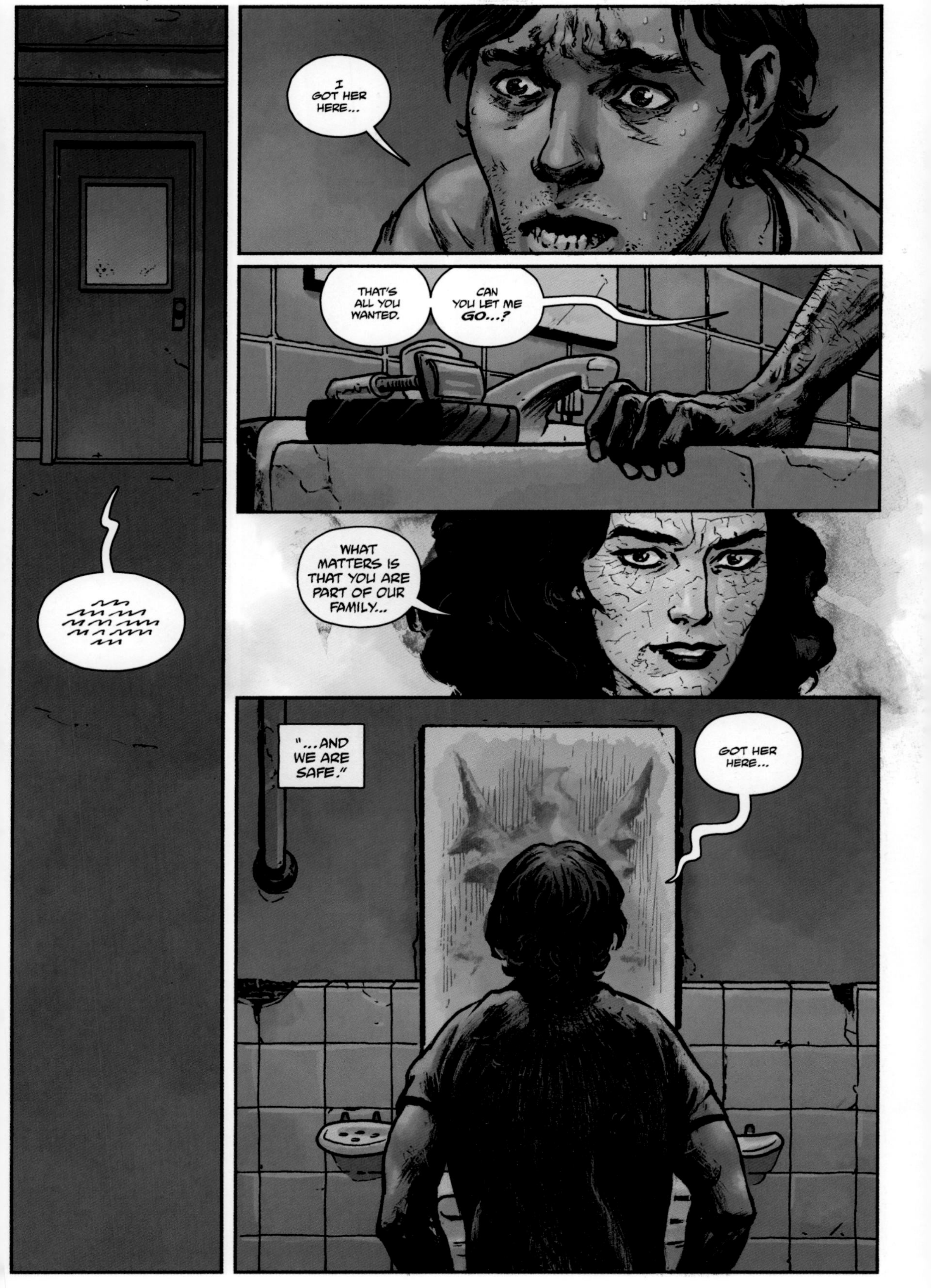
I GOT HER HERE...
THAT'S ALL YOU WANTED.
CAN YOU LET ME GO...?
WHAT MATTERS IS THAT YOU ARE PART OF OUR FAMILY...
"...AND WE ARE SAFE."
GOT HER HERE...

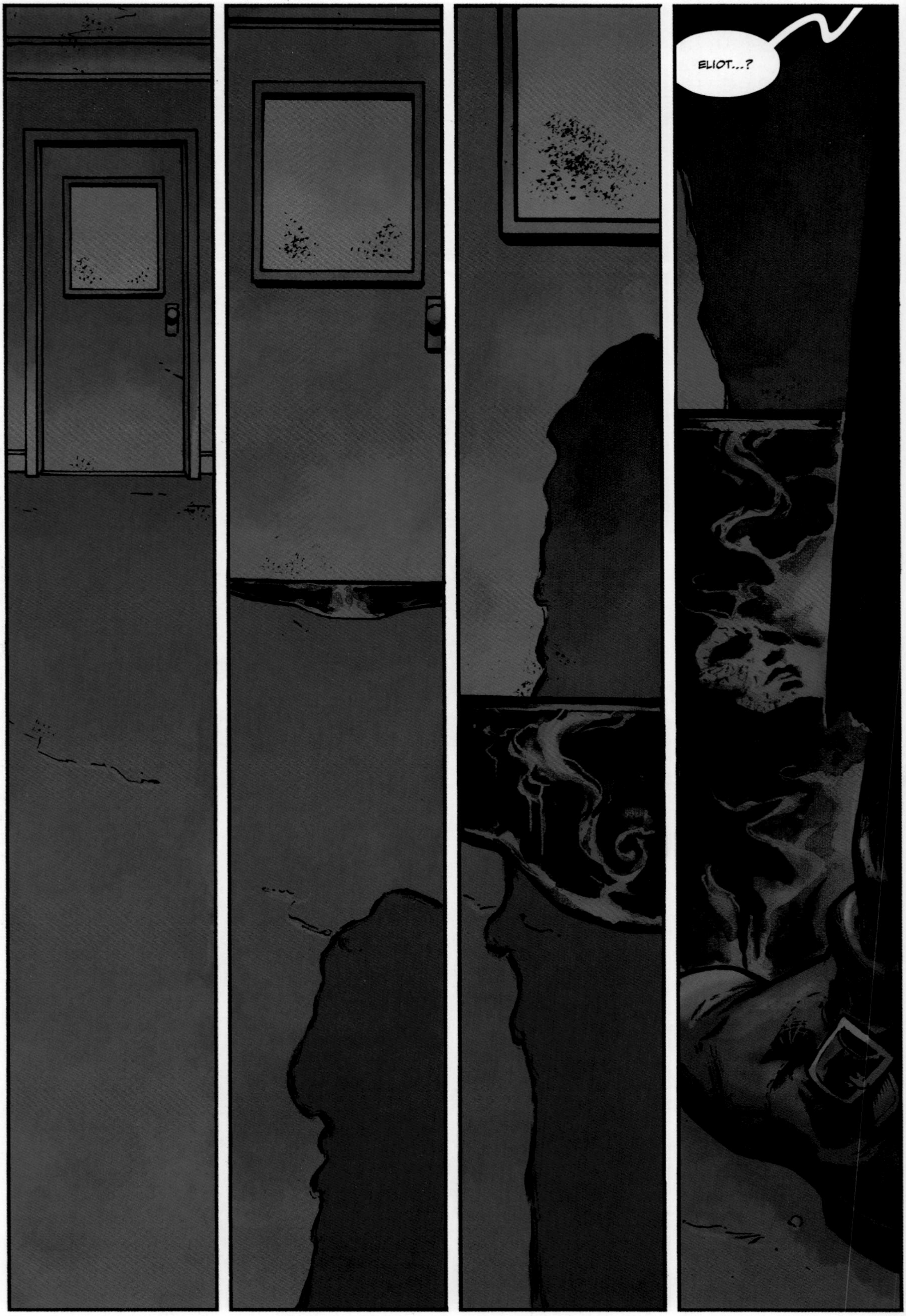
ELIOT...?

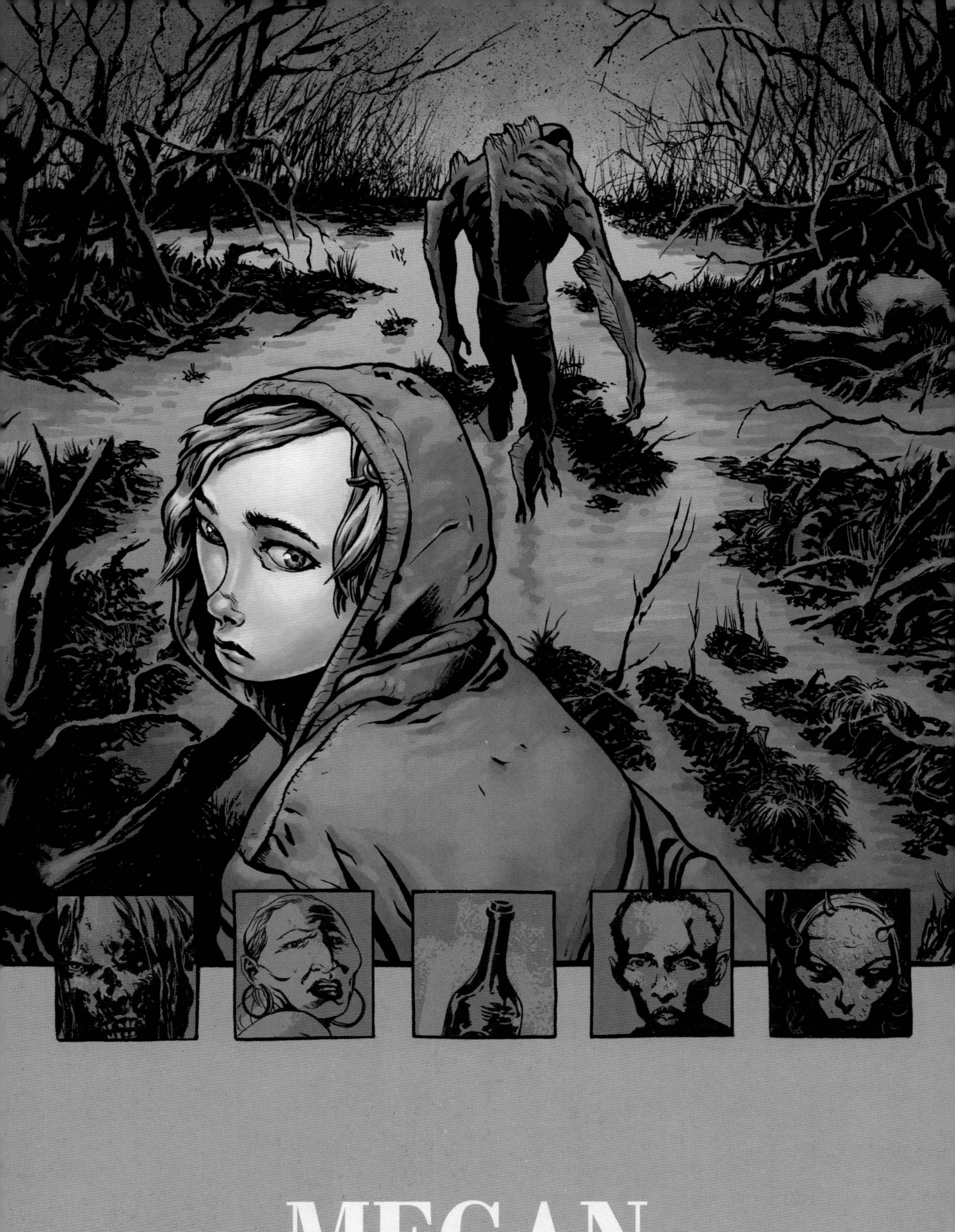

MEGAN

Megan grew up in Rosario, Texas, a middle-class kid in an impoverished border town with few friends and a world defined by her parents and her mother's brother. She can barely remember that normal life now, after her parents were killed by hammerheads and her uncle has exposed her to one end-of-the-world cult after another.

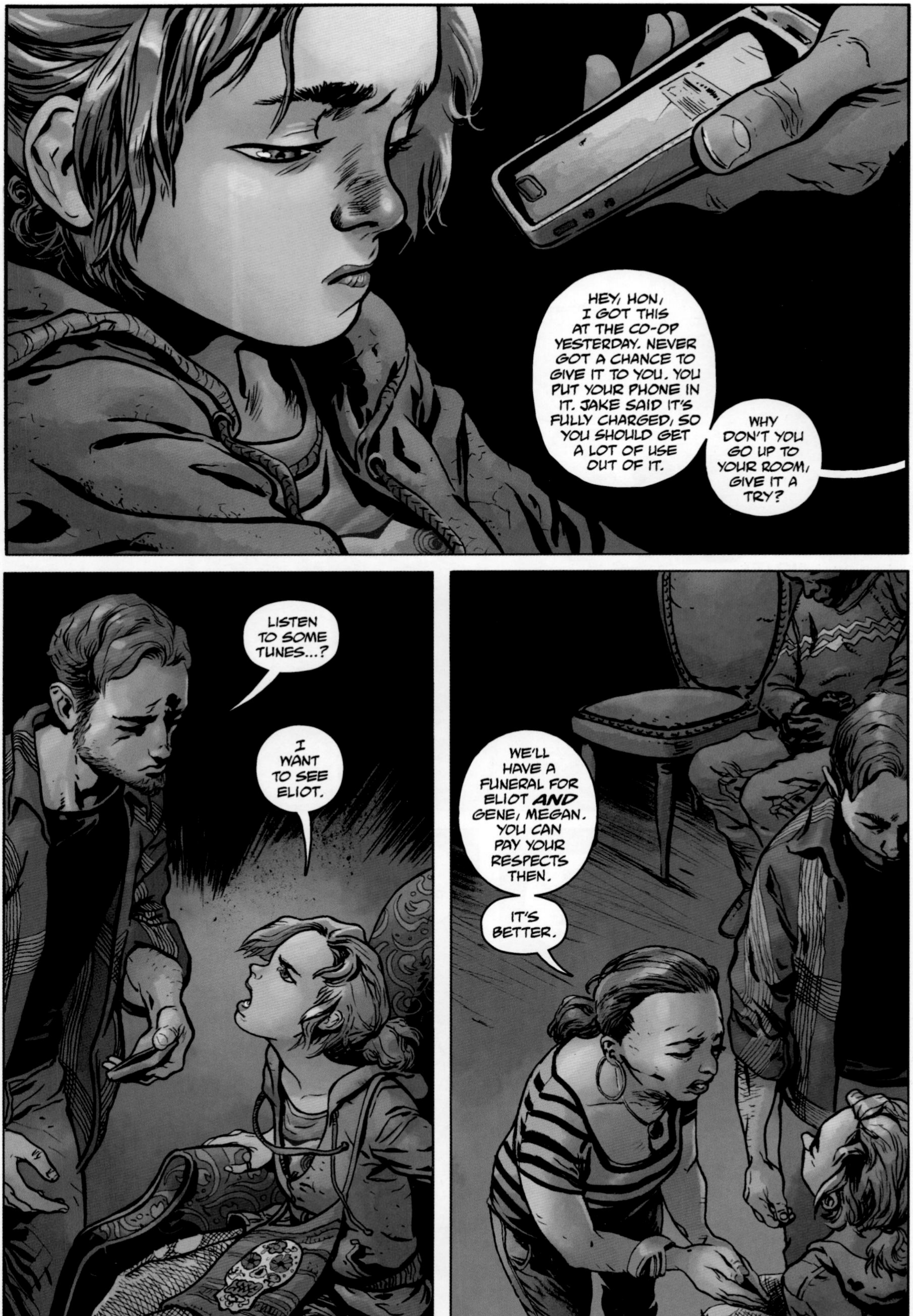
HEY, HON, I GOT THIS AT THE CO-OP YESTERDAY. NEVER GOT A CHANCE TO GIVE IT TO YOU. YOU PUT YOUR PHONE IN IT. JAKE SAID IT'S FULLY CHARGED, SO YOU SHOULD GET A LOT OF USE OUT OF IT.
WHY DON'T YOU GO UP TO YOUR ROOM, GIVE IT A TRY?
LISTEN TO SOME TUNES...?
I WANT TO SEE ELIOT.
WE'LL HAVE A FUNERAL FOR ELIOT AND GENE, MEGAN. YOU CAN PAY YOUR RESPECTS THEN.
IT'S BETTER.

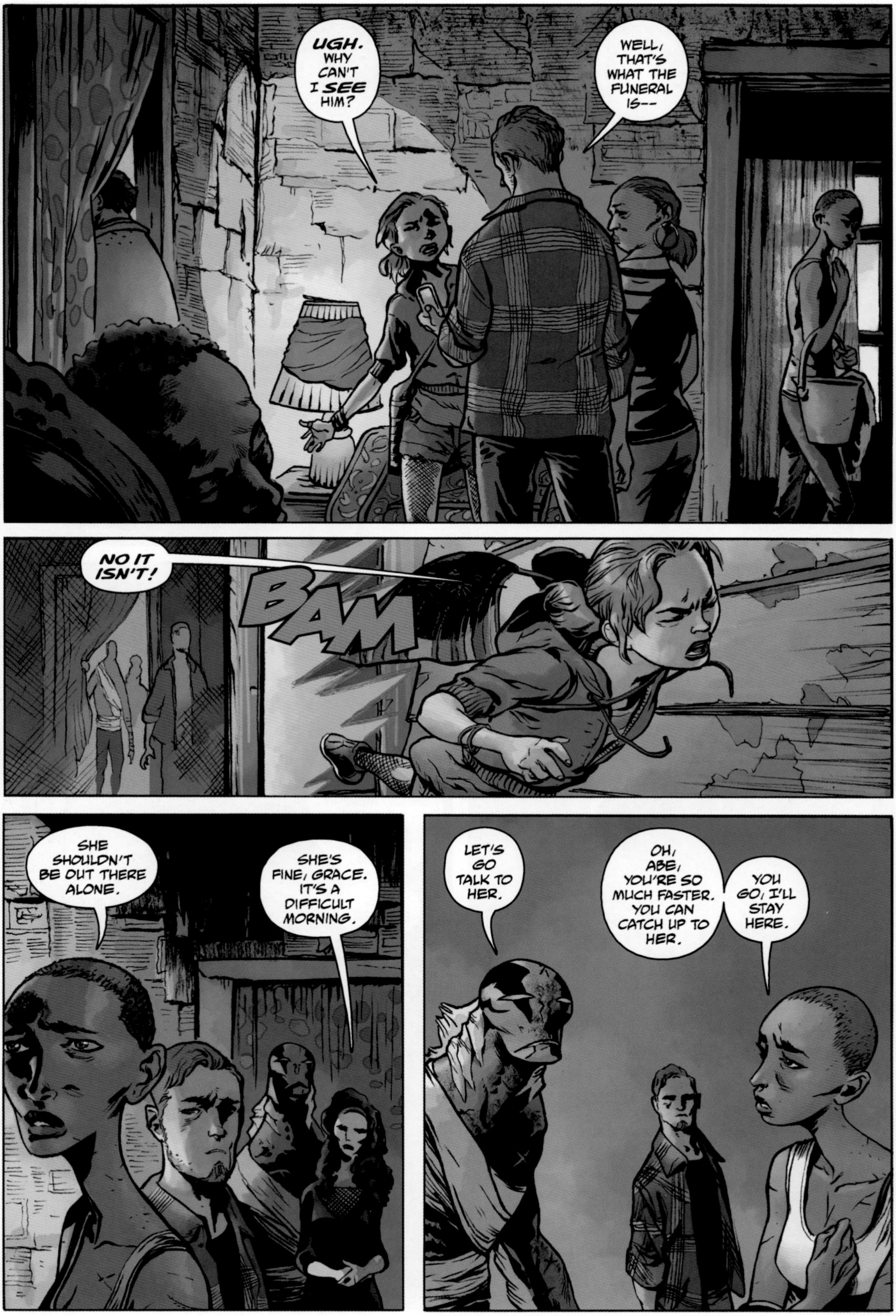
UGH. WHY CAN'T I SEE HIM?
WELL, THAT'S WHAT THE FUNERAL IS--
NO IT ISN'T!
BAM
SHE SHOULDN'T BE OUT THERE ALONE.
SHE'S FINE, GRACE. IT'S A DIFFICULT MORNING.
LET'S GO TALK TO HER.
OH, ABE, YOU'RE SO MUCH FASTER. YOU CAN CATCH UP TO HER.
YOU GO, I'LL STAY HERE.

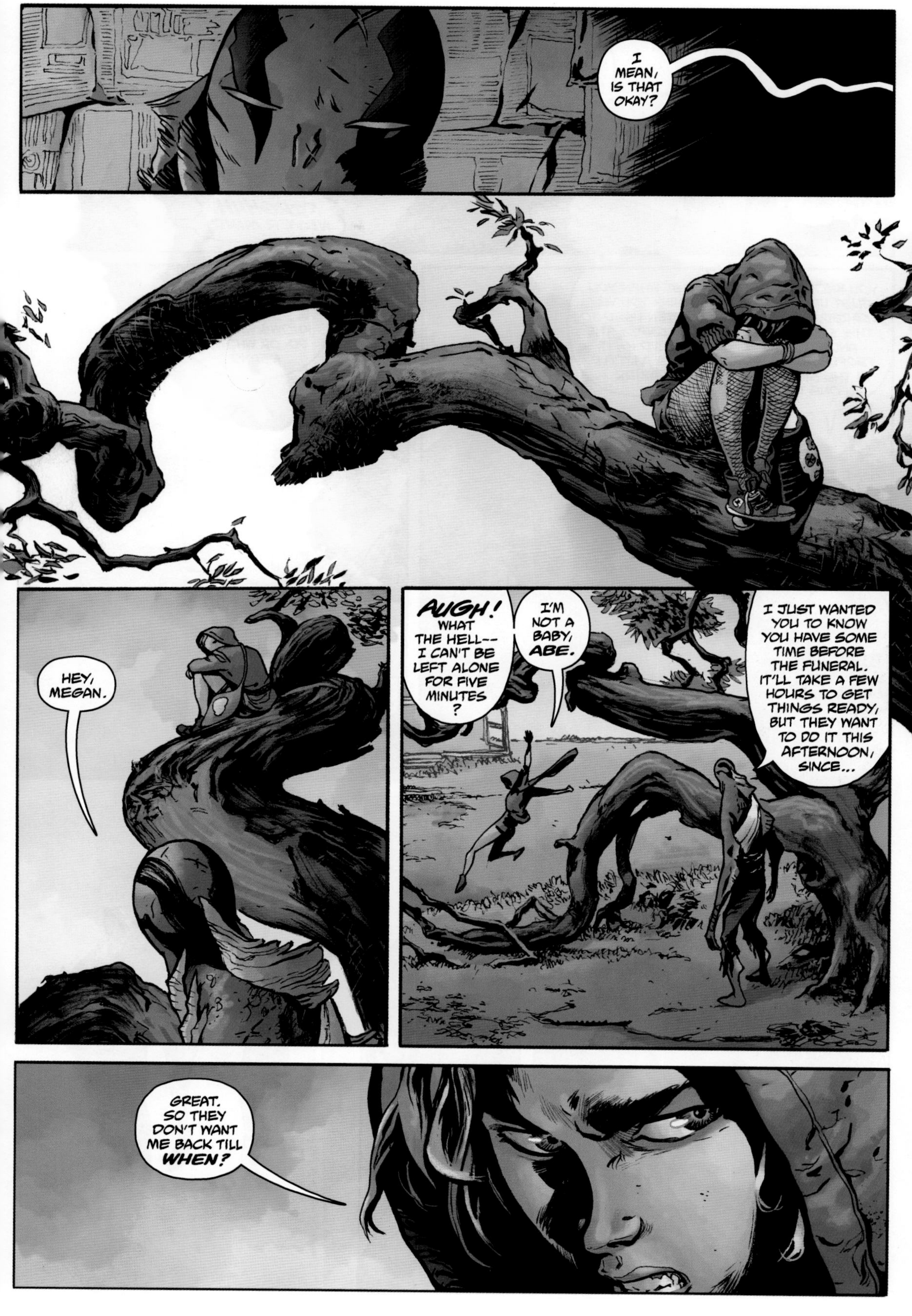
I MEAN, IS THAT OKAY?
HEY, MEGAN.
AUGH! WHAT THE HELL-- I CAN'T BE LEFT ALONE FOR FIVE MINUTES?
I'M NOT A BABY, ABE.
I JUST WANTED YOU TO KNOW YOU HAVE SOME TIME BEFORE THE FUNERAL. IT'LL TAKE A FEW HOURS TO GET THINGS READY, BUT THEY WANT TO DO IT THIS AFTERNOON, SINCE...
GREAT. SO THEY DON'T WANT ME BACK TILL WHEN?

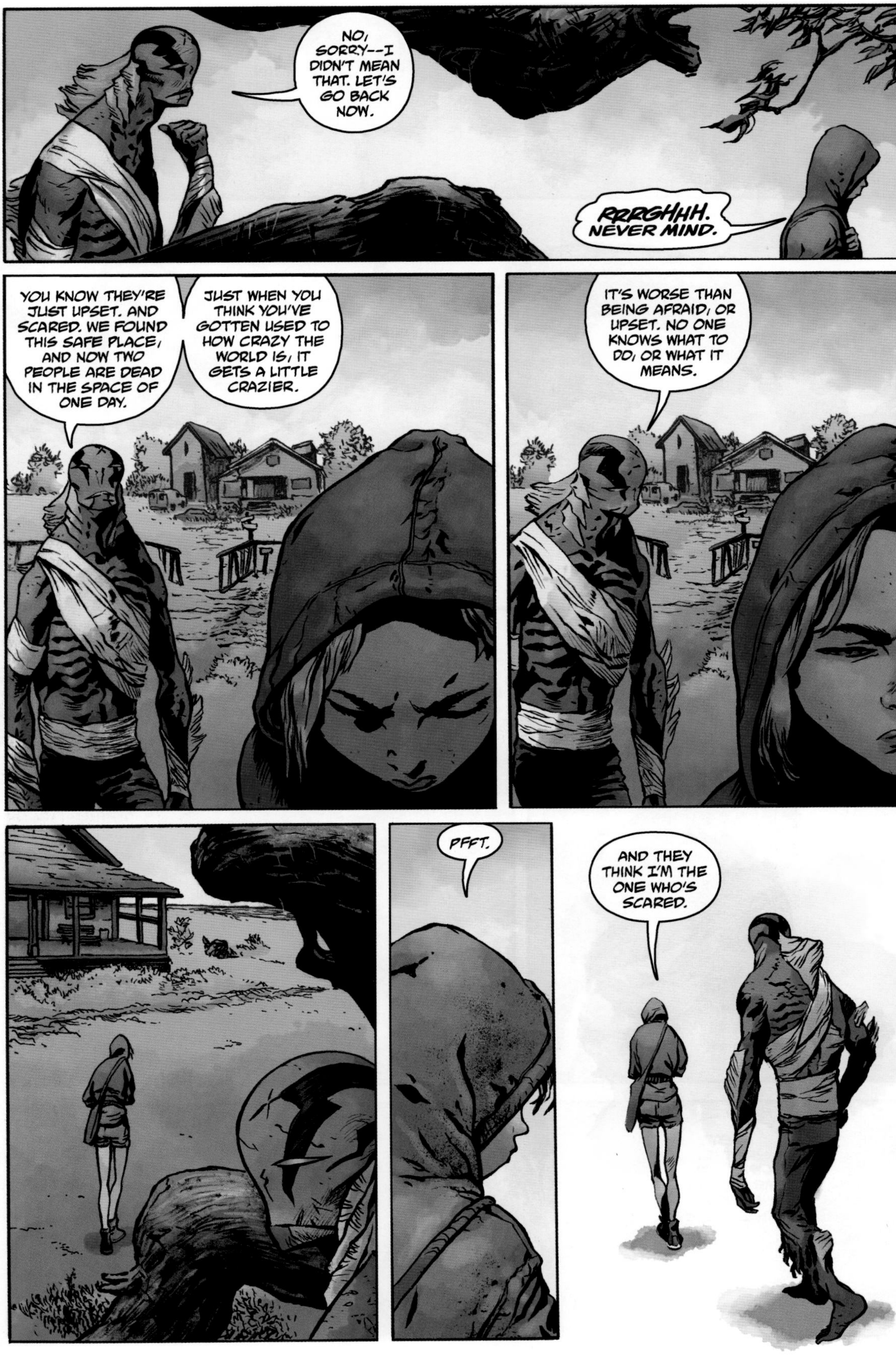
NO, SORRY--I DIDN'T MEAN THAT. LET'S GO BACK NOW.
RRRGHHH. NEVER MIND.
YOU KNOW THEY'RE JUST UPSET. AND SCARED. WE FOUND THIS SAFE PLACE, AND NOW TWO PEOPLE ARE DEAD IN THE SPACE OF ONE DAY.
JUST WHEN YOU THINK YOU'VE GOTTEN USED TO HOW CRAZY THE WORLD IS, IT GETS A LITTLE CRAZIER.
IT'S WORSE THAN BEING AFRAID, OR UPSET. NO ONE KNOWS WHAT TO DO, OR WHAT IT MEANS.
PFFT.
AND THEY THINK I'M THE ONE WHO'S SCARED.

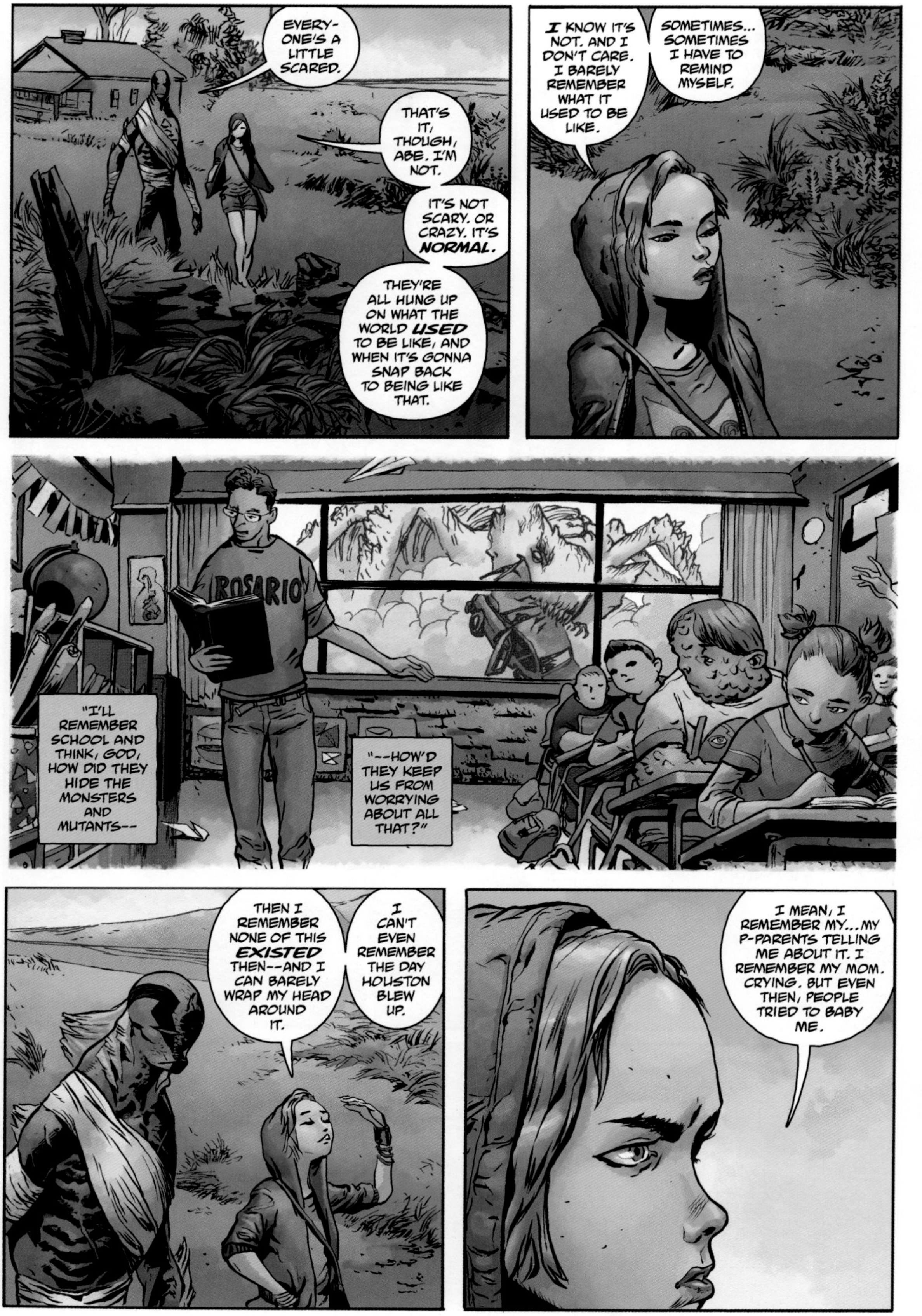
EVERY-ONE'S A LITTLE SCARED.
THAT'S IT, THOUGH, ABE. I'M NOT.
IT'S NOT SCARY. OR CRAZY. IT'S NORMAL.
THEY'RE ALL HUNG UP ON WHAT THE WORLD USED TO BE LIKE, AND WHEN IT'S GONNA SNAP BACK TO BEING LIKE THAT.
I KNOW IT'S NOT. AND I DON'T CARE. I BARELY REMEMBER WHAT IT USED TO BE LIKE.
SOMETIMES... SOMETIMES I HAVE TO REMIND MYSELF.
ROSARIO
"I'LL REMEMBER SCHOOL AND THINK, GOD, HOW DID THEY HIDE THE MONSTERS AND MUTANTS--
"--HOW'D THEY KEEP US FROM WORRYING ABOUT ALL THAT?"
THEN I REMEMBER NONE OF THIS EXISTED THEN--AND I CAN BARELY WRAP MY HEAD AROUND IT.
I CAN'T EVEN REMEMBER THE DAY HOUSTON BLEW UP.
I MEAN, I REMEMBER MY...MY P-PARENTS TELLING ME ABOUT IT. I REMEMBER MY MOM. CRYING. BUT EVEN THEN, PEOPLE TRIED TO BABY ME.

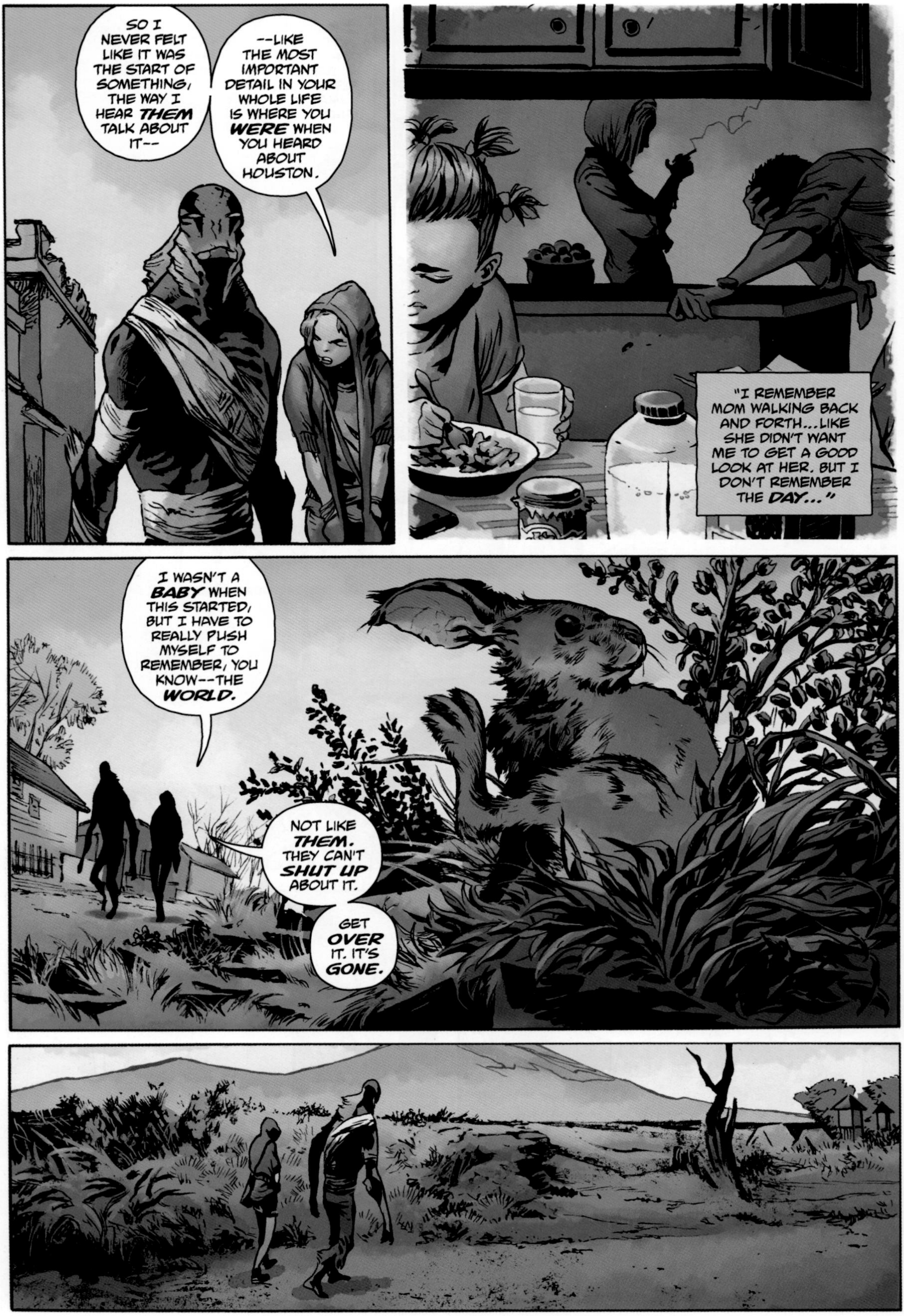
SO I NEVER FELT LIKE IT WAS THE START OF SOMETHING, THE WAY I HEAR THEM TALK ABOUT IT--
--LIKE THE MOST IMPORTANT DETAIL IN YOUR WHOLE LIFE IS WHERE YOU WERE WHEN YOU HEARD ABOUT HOUSTON.
"I REMEMBER MOM WALKING BACK AND FORTH... LIKE SHE DIDN'T WANT ME TO GET A GOOD LOOK AT HER. BUT I DON'T REMEMBER THE DAY..."
I WASN'T A BABY WHEN THIS STARTED, BUT I HAVE TO REALLY PUSH MYSELF TO REMEMBER, YOU KNOW--THE WORLD.
NOT LIKE THEM. THEY CAN'T SHUT UP ABOUT IT.
GET OVER IT. IT'S GONE.

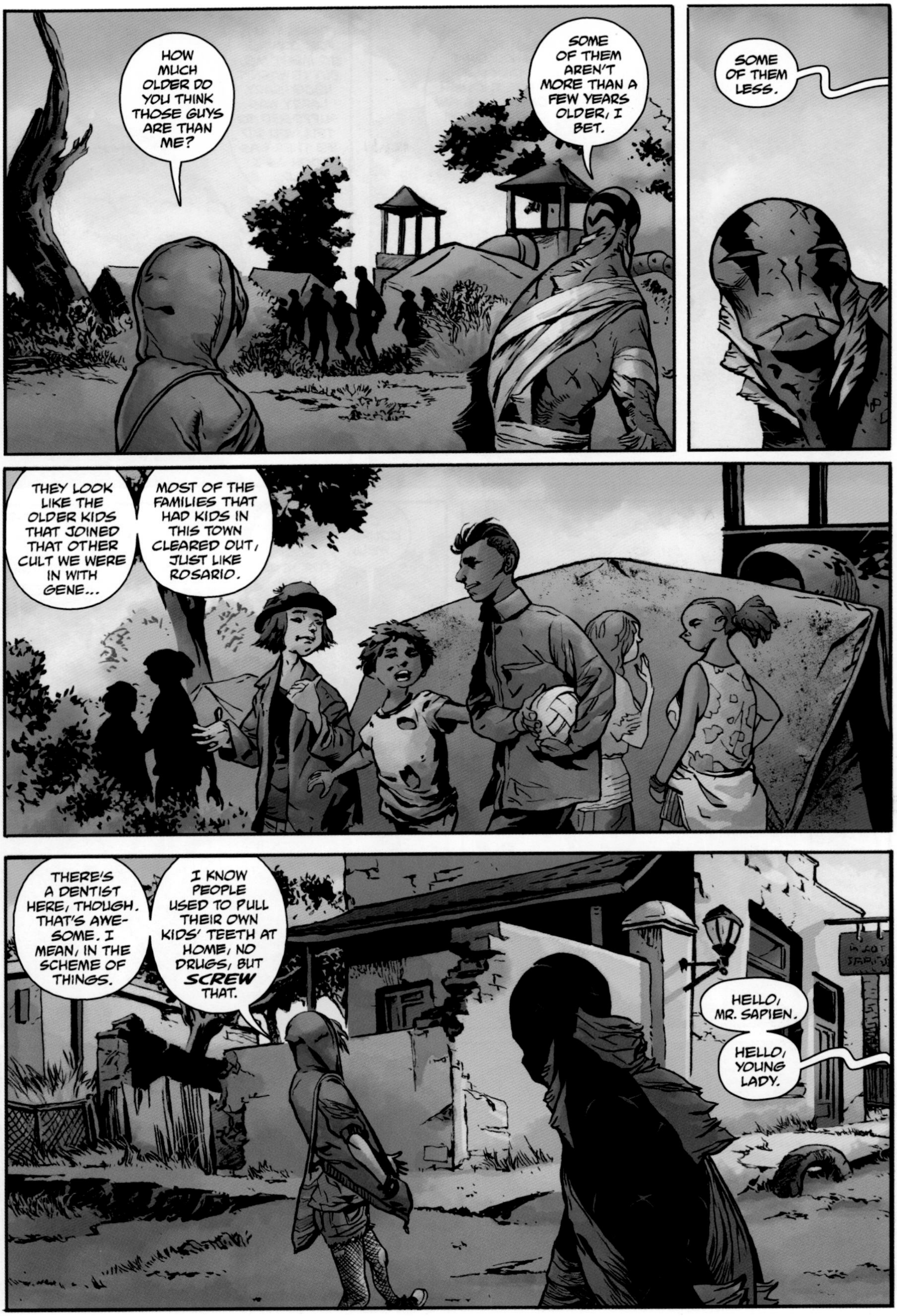
HOW MUCH OLDER DO YOU THINK THOSE GUYS ARE THAN ME?
SOME OF THEM AREN'T MORE THAN A FEW YEARS OLDER, I BET.
SOME OF THEM LESS.
THEY LOOK LIKE THE OLDER KIDS THAT JOINED THAT OTHER CULT WE WERE IN WITH GENE...
MOST OF THE FAMILIES THAT HAD KIDS IN THIS TOWN CLEARED OUT, JUST LIKE ROSARIO.
THERE'S A DENTIST HERE, THOUGH. THAT'S AWE-SOME. I MEAN, IN THE SCHEME OF THINGS.
I KNOW PEOPLE USED TO PULL THEIR OWN KIDS' TEETH AT HOME, NO DRUGS, BUT SCREW THAT.
HELLO, MR. SAPIEN.
HELLO, YOUNG LADY.

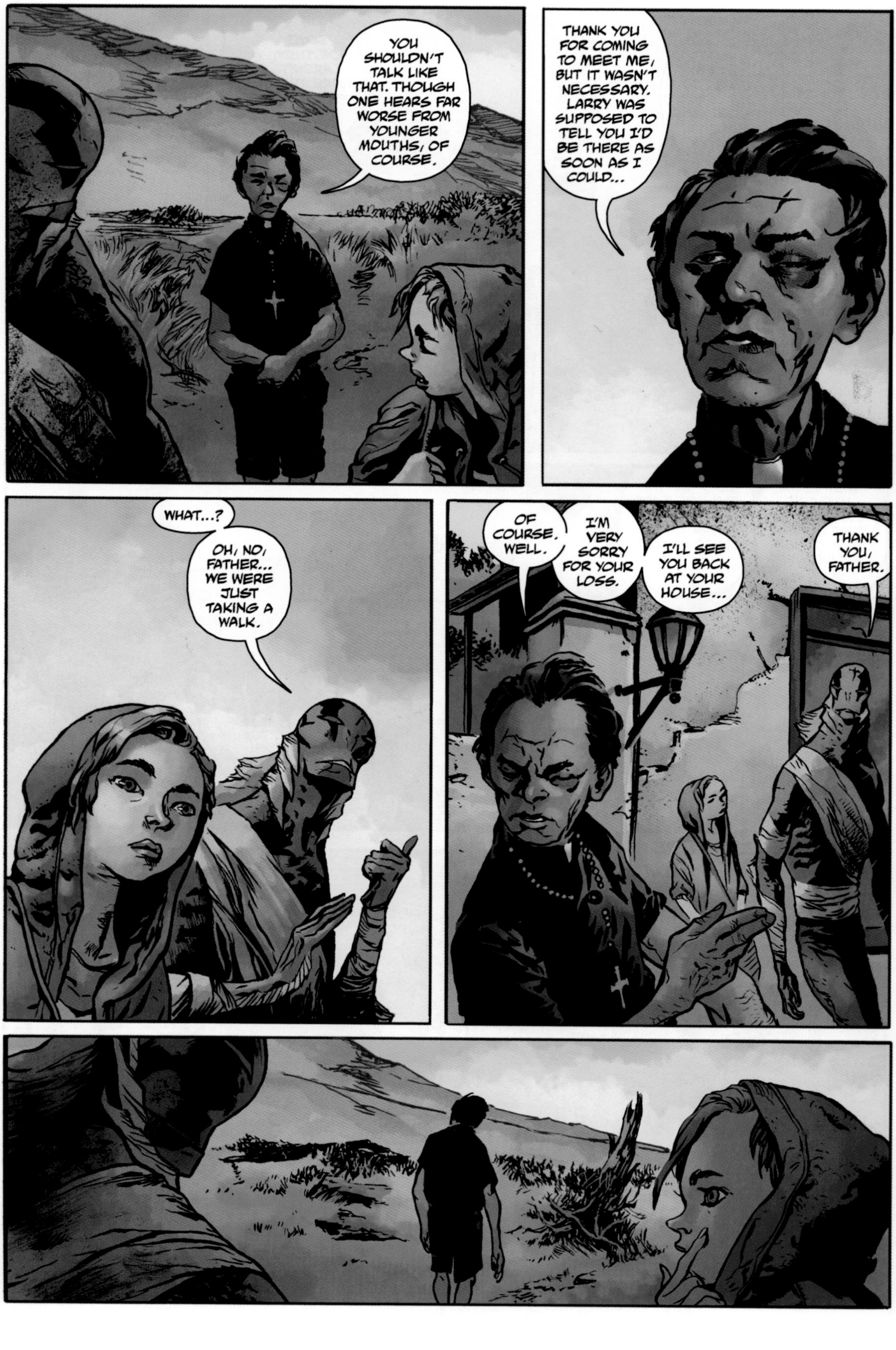
YOU SHOULDN'T TALK LIKE THAT. THOUGH ONE HEARS FAR WORSE FROM YOUNGER MOUTHS, OF COURSE.
THANK YOU FOR COMING TO MEET ME, BUT IT WASN'T NECESSARY. LARRY WAS SUPPOSED TO TELL YOU I'D BE THERE AS SOON AS I COULD...
WHAT...?
OH, NO, FATHER... WE WERE JUST TAKING A WALK.
OF COURSE. WELL.
I'M VERY SORRY FOR YOUR LOSS.
I'LL SEE YOU BACK AT YOUR HOUSE...
THANK YOU, FATHER.

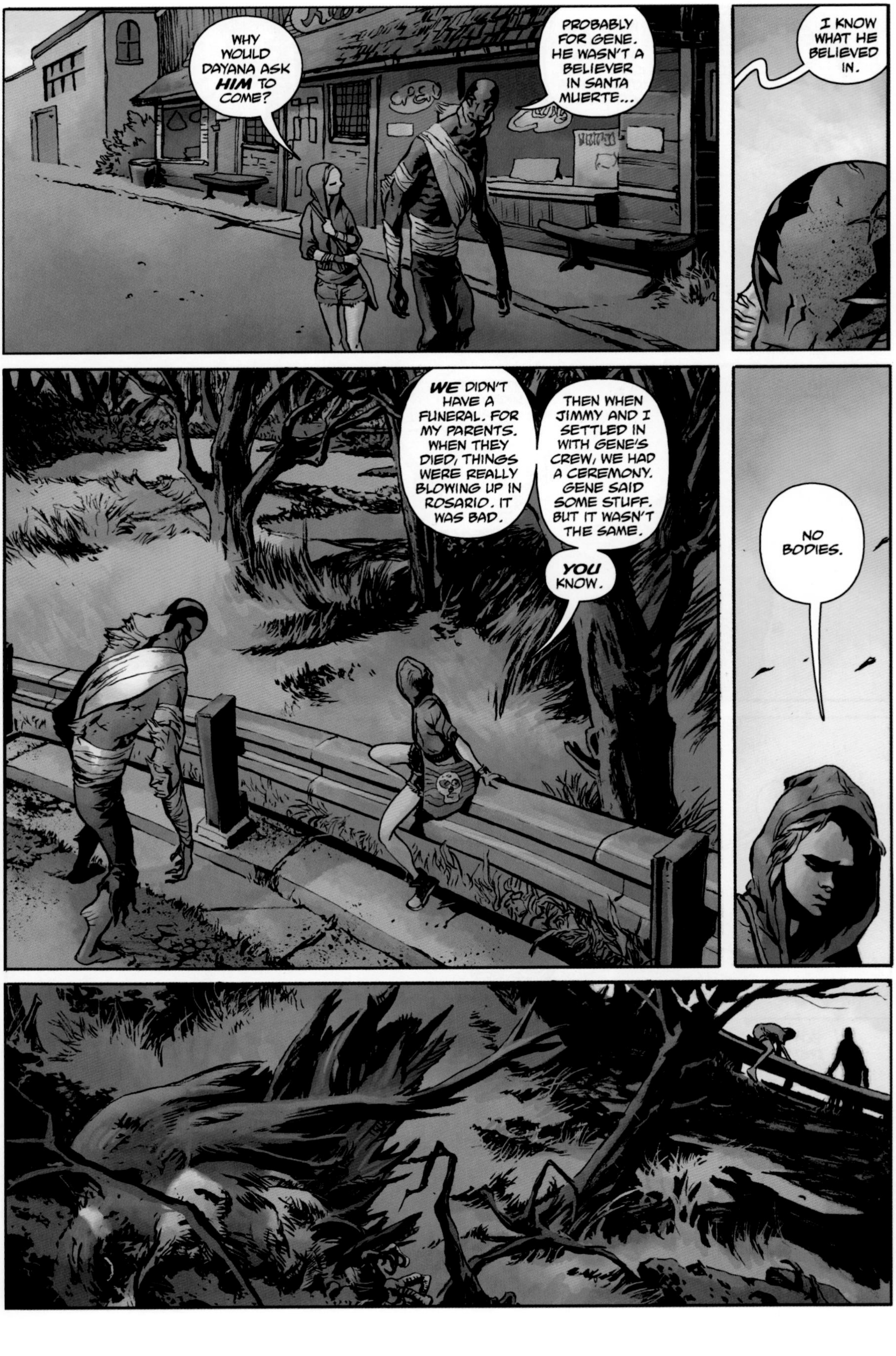
WHY WOULD DAYANA ASK HIM TO COME?
PROBABLY FOR GENE. HE WASN'T A BELIEVER IN SANTA MUERTE...
I KNOW WHAT HE BELIEVED IN.
WE DIDN'T HAVE A FUNERAL. FOR MY PARENTS. WHEN THEY DIED, THINGS WERE REALLY BLOWING UP IN ROSARIO. IT WAS BAD.
THEN WHEN JIMMY AND I SETTLED IN WITH GENE'S CREW, WE HAD A CEREMONY. GENE SAID SOME STUFF. BUT IT WASN'T THE SAME.
YOU KNOW.
NO BODIES.

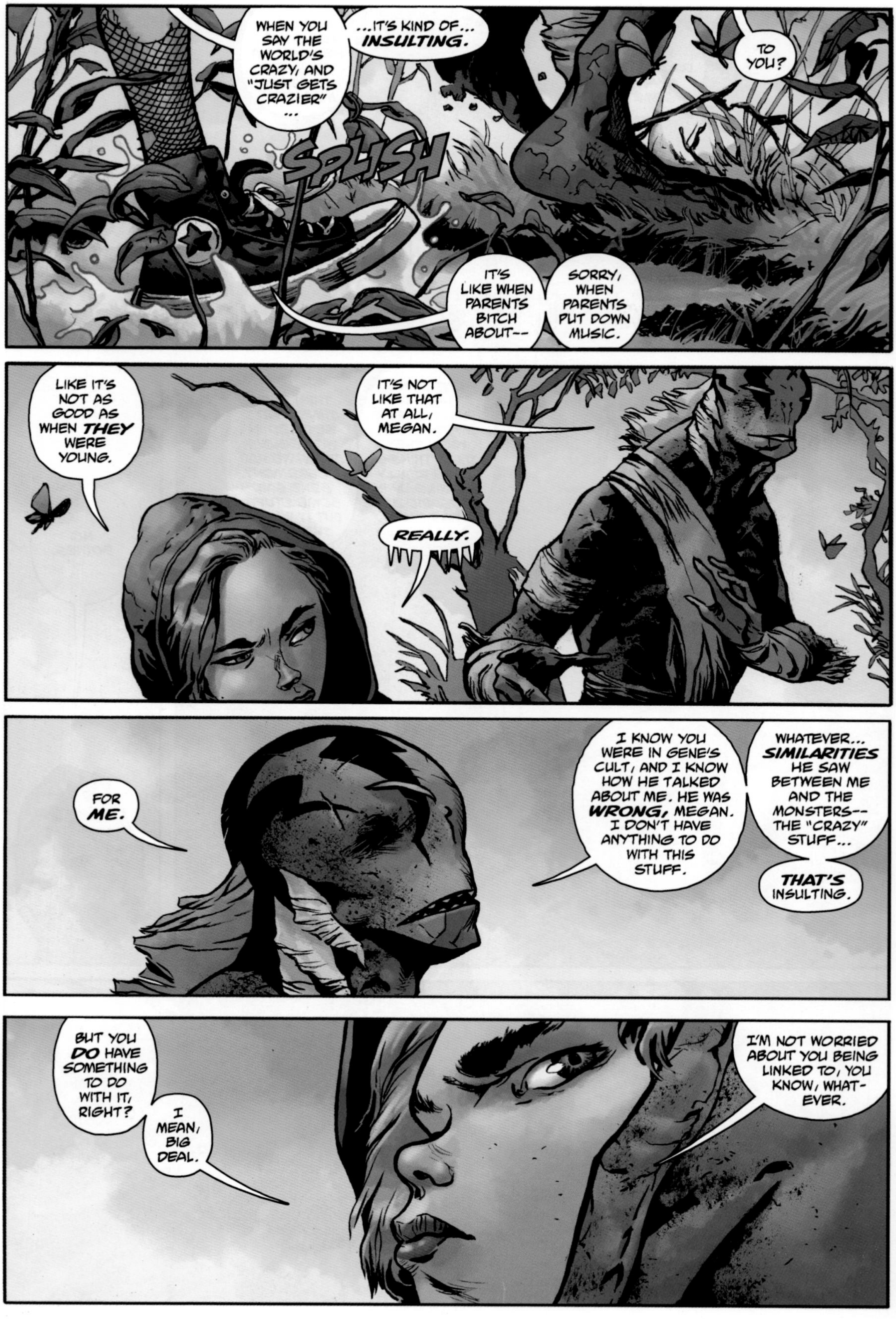
WHEN YOU SAY THE WORLD'S CRAZY, AND "JUST GETS CRAZIER" ...
...IT'S KIND OF... INSULTING.
TO YOU?
SPLISH
IT'S LIKE WHEN PARENTS BITCH ABOUT--
SORRY, WHEN PARENTS PUT DOWN MUSIC.
LIKE IT'S NOT AS GOOD AS WHEN THEY WERE YOUNG.
IT'S NOT LIKE THAT AT ALL, MEGAN.
REALLY.
FOR ME.
I KNOW YOU WERE IN GENE'S CULT, AND I KNOW HOW HE TALKED ABOUT ME. HE WAS WRONG, MEGAN. I DON'T HAVE ANYTHING TO DO WITH THIS STUFF.
WHATEVER... SIMILARITIES HE SAW BETWEEN ME AND THE MONSTERS-- THE "CRAZY" STUFF...
THAT'S INSULTING.
BUT YOU DO HAVE SOMETHING TO DO WITH IT, RIGHT?
I MEAN, BIG DEAL.
I'M NOT WORRIED ABOUT YOU BEING LINKED TO, YOU KNOW, WHAT-EVER.

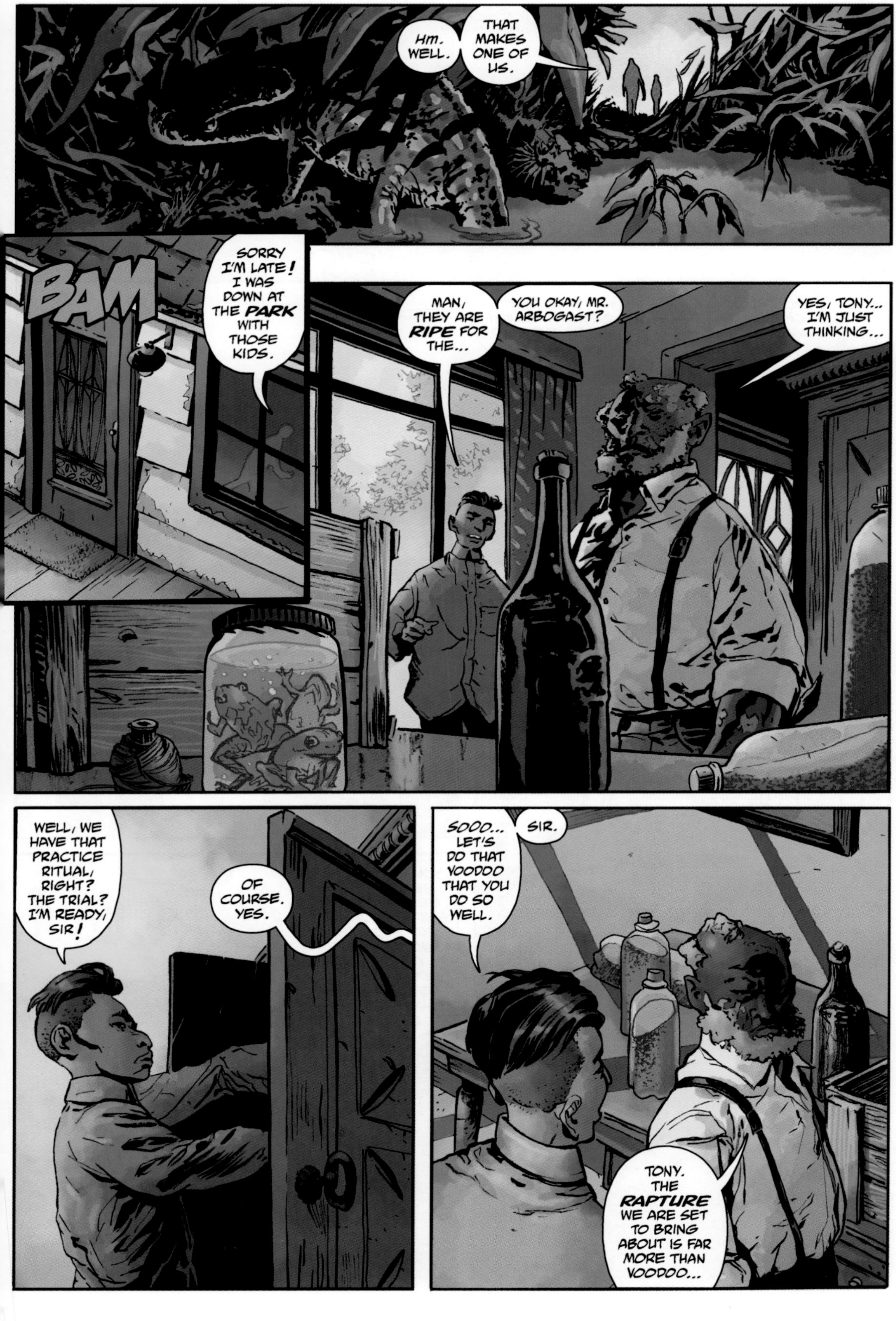
HM. WELL.
THAT MAKES ONE OF US.
BAM
SORRY I'M LATE! I WAS DOWN AT THE PARK WITH THOSE KIDS.
MAN, THEY ARE RIPE FOR THE...
YOU OKAY, MR. ARBOGAST?
YES, TONY... I'M JUST THINKING...
WELL, WE HAVE THAT PRACTICE RITUAL, RIGHT? THE TRIAL? I'M READY, SIR!
OF COURSE. YES.
SOOO... LET'S DO THAT VOODOO THAT YOU DO SO WELL.
SIR.
TONY. THE RAPTURE WE ARE SET TO BRING ABOUT IS FAR MORE THAN VOODOO...

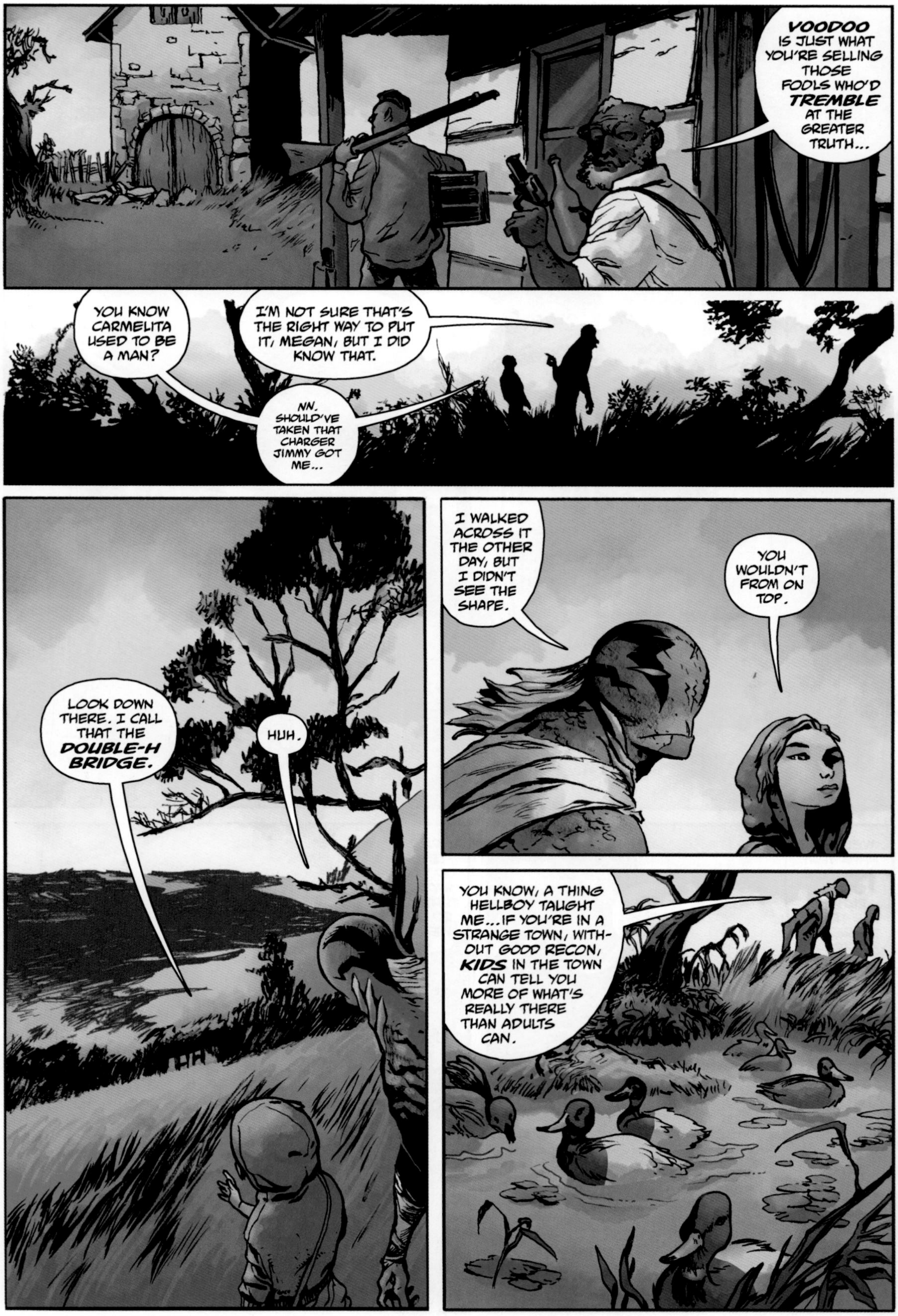
VOODOO IS JUST WHAT YOU'RE SELLING THOSE FOOLS WHO'D TREMBLE AT THE GREATER TRUTH...
YOU KNOW CARMELITA USED TO BE A MAN?
I'M NOT SURE THAT'S THE RIGHT WAY TO PUT IT, MEGAN, BUT I DID KNOW THAT.
NN. SHOULD'VE TAKEN THAT CHARGER JIMMY GOT ME...
LOOK DOWN THERE. I CALL THAT THE DOUBLE-H BRIDGE.
HUH.
I WALKED ACROSS IT THE OTHER DAY, BUT I DIDN'T SEE THE SHAPE.
YOU WOULDN'T FROM ON TOP.
YOU KNOW, A THING HELLBOY TAUGHT ME... IF YOU'RE IN A STRANGE TOWN, WITH-OUT GOOD RECON, KIDS IN THE TOWN CAN TELL YOU MORE OF WHAT'S REALLY THERE THAN ADULTS CAN.

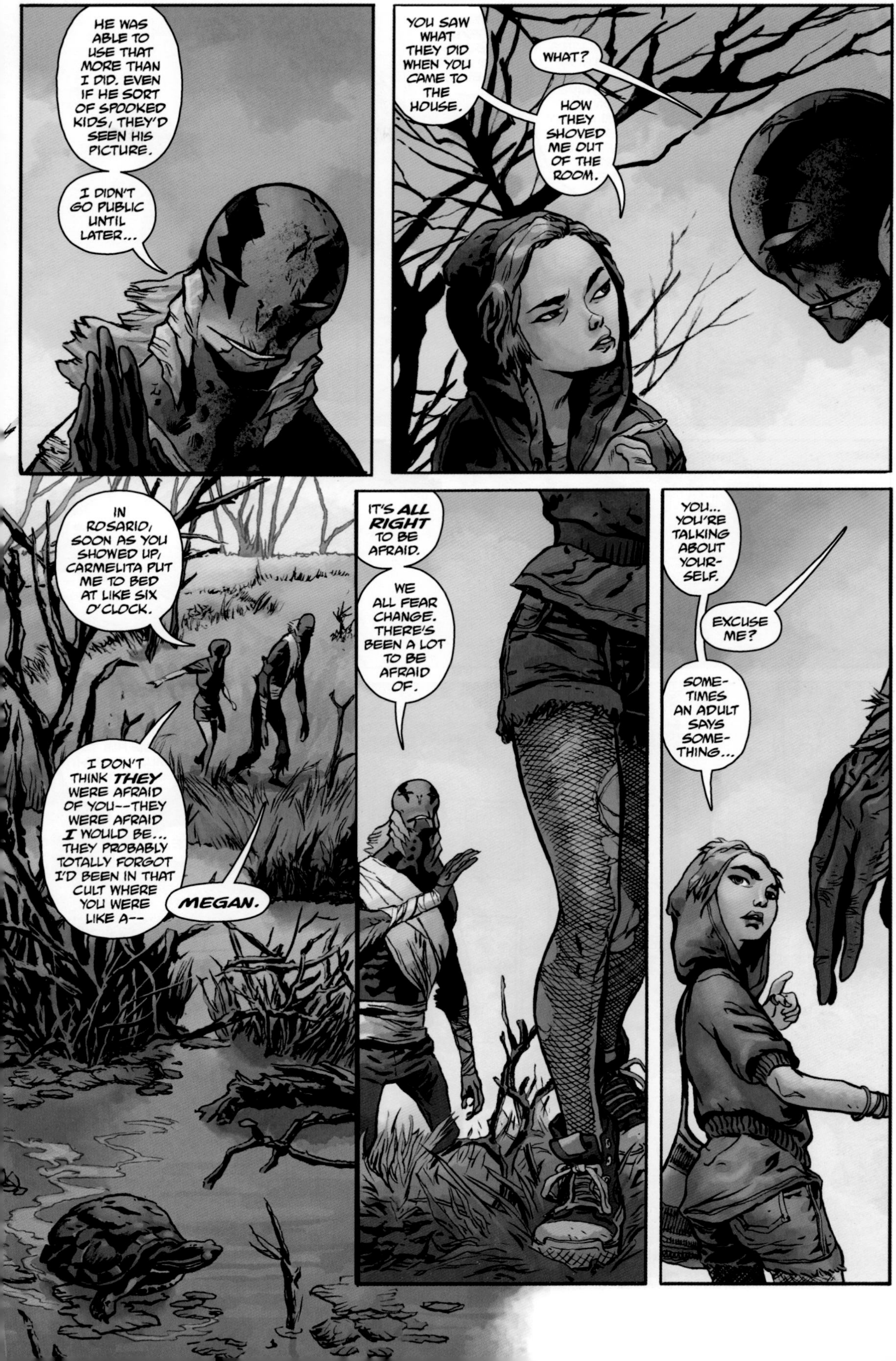
HE WAS ABLE TO USE THAT MORE THAN I DID. EVEN IF HE SORT OF SPOOKED KIDS, THEY'D SEEN HIS PICTURE.
I DIDN'T GO PUBLIC UNTIL LATER...
YOU SAW WHAT THEY DID WHEN YOU CAME TO THE HOUSE.
WHAT?
HOW THEY SHOVED ME OUT OF THE ROOM.
IN ROSARIO, SOON AS YOU SHOWED UP, CARMELITA PUT ME TO BED AT LIKE SIX O'CLOCK.
I DON'T THINK THEY WERE AFRAID OF YOU--THEY WERE AFRAID I WOULD BE... THEY PROBABLY TOTALLY FORGOT I'D BEEN IN THAT CULT WHERE YOU WERE LIKE A--
MEGAN.
IT'S ALL RIGHT TO BE AFRAID.
WE ALL FEAR CHANGE. THERE'S BEEN A LOT TO BE AFRAID OF.
YOU... YOU'RE TALKING ABOUT YOURSELF.
EXCUSE ME?
SOMETIMES AN ADULT SAYS SOMETHING...

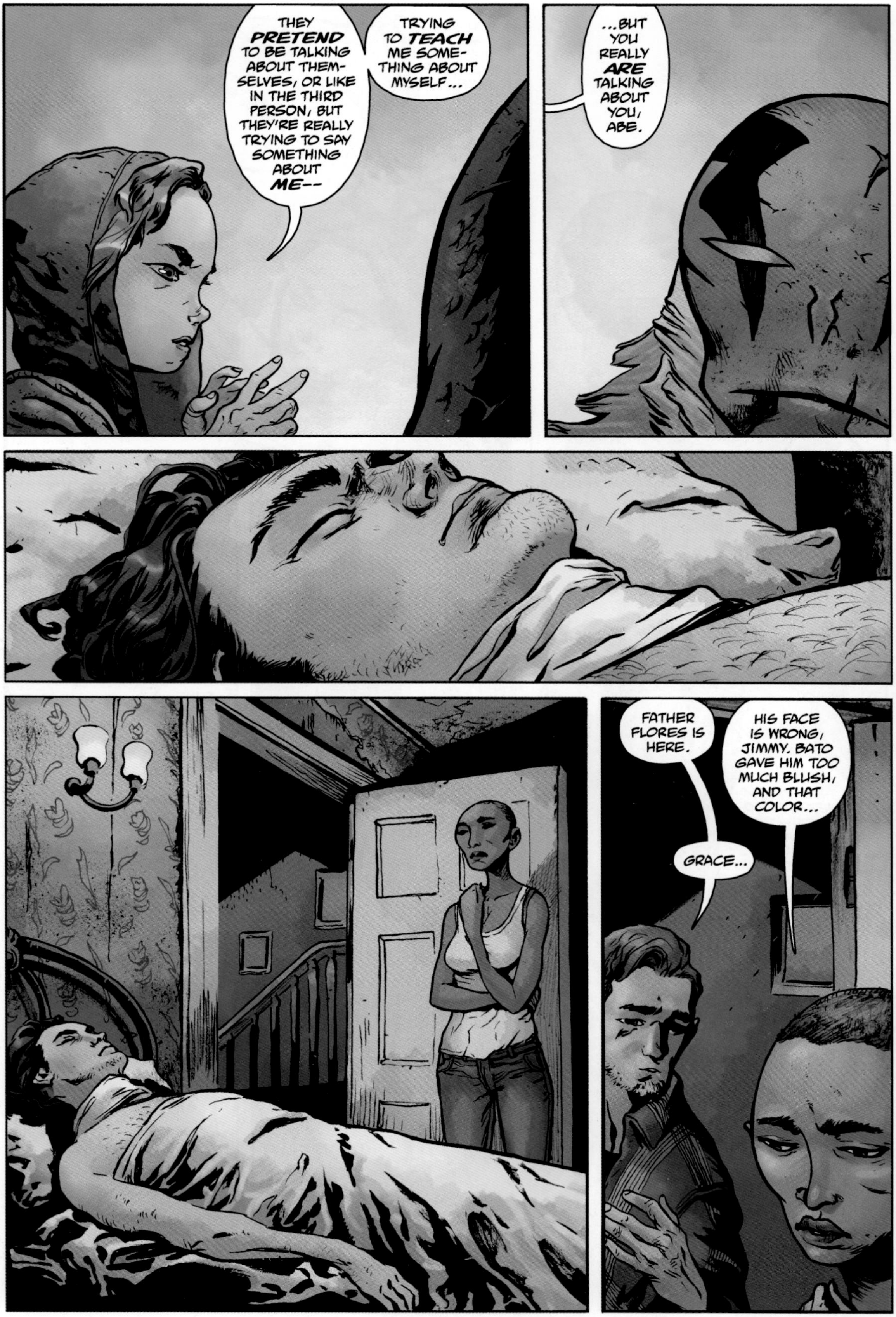
THEY PRETEND TO BE TALKING ABOUT THEMSELVES, OR LIKE IN THE THIRD PERSON, BUT THEY'RE REALLY TRYING TO SAY SOMETHING ABOUT ME--
TRYING TO TEACH ME SOMETHING ABOUT MYSELF...
...BUT YOU REALLY ARE TALKING ABOUT YOU, ABE.
FATHER FLORES IS HERE.
HIS FACE IS WRONG, JIMMY. BATO GAVE HIM TOO MUCH BLUSH, AND THAT COLOR...
GRACE...

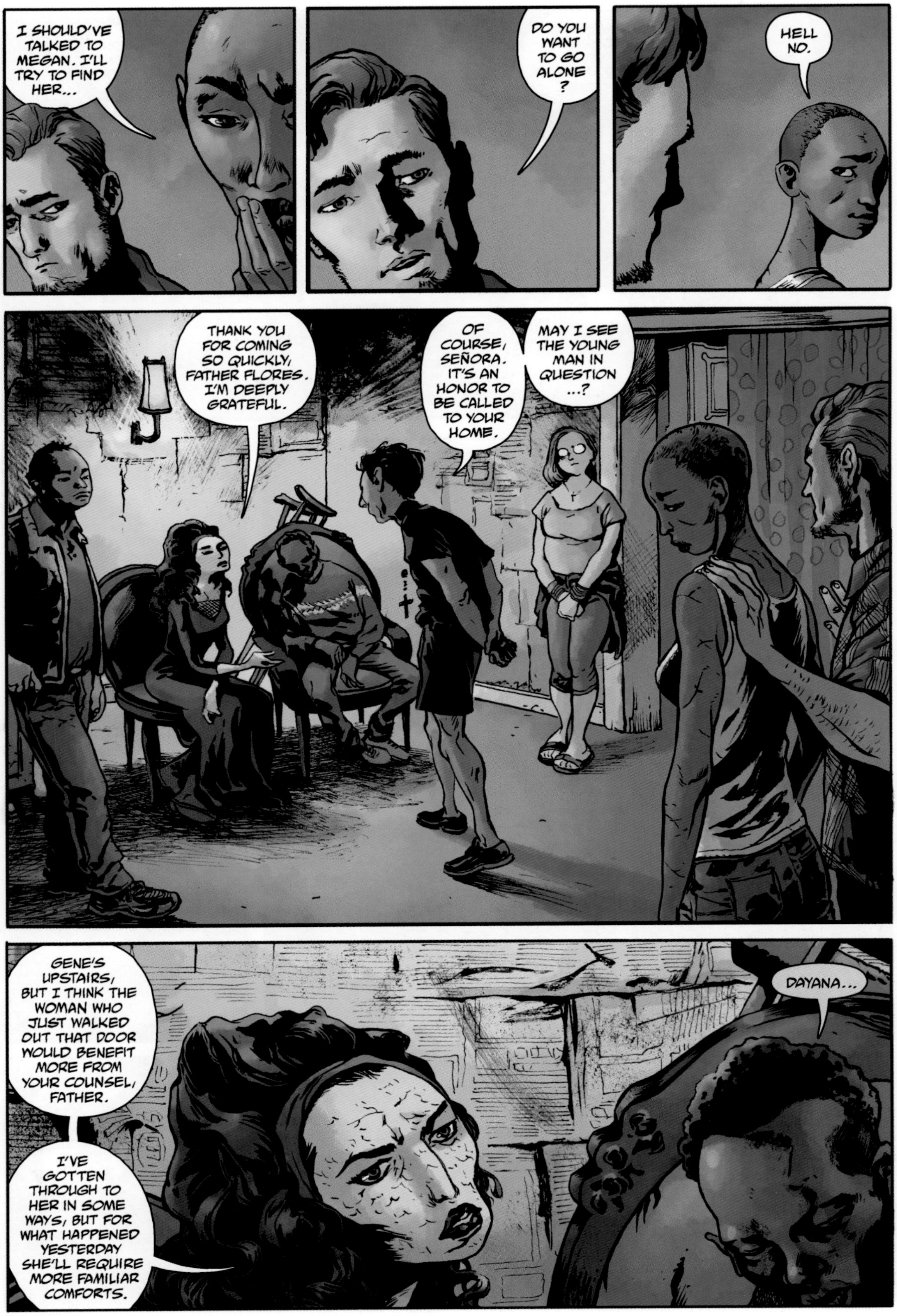
I SHOULD'VE TALKED TO MEGAN. I'LL TRY TO FIND HER...
DO YOU WANT TO GO ALONE ?
HELL NO.
THANK YOU FOR COMING SO QUICKLY, FATHER FLORES. I'M DEEPLY GRATEFUL.
OF COURSE, SEÑORA. IT'S AN HONOR TO BE CALLED TO YOUR HOME.
MAY I SEE THE YOUNG MAN IN QUESTION ...?
GENE'S UPSTAIRS, BUT I THINK THE WOMAN WHO JUST WALKED OUT THAT DOOR WOULD BENEFIT MORE FROM YOUR COUNSEL, FATHER.
I'VE GOTTEN THROUGH TO HER IN SOME WAYS, BUT FOR WHAT HAPPENED YESTERDAY SHE'LL REQUIRE MORE FAMILIAR COMFORTS.
DAYANA...

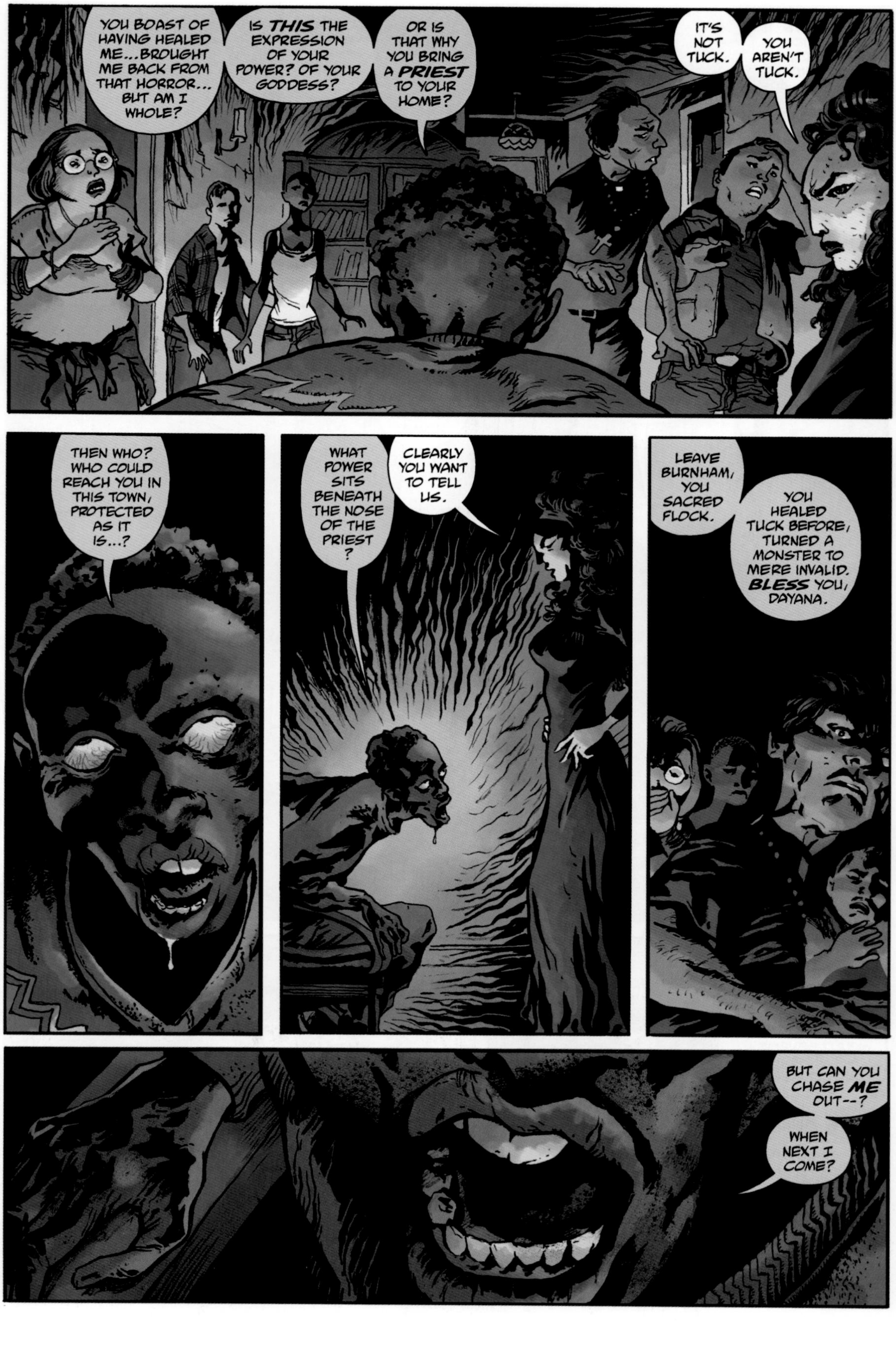
YOU BOAST OF HAVING HEALED ME...BROUGHT ME BACK FROM THAT HORROR... BUT AM I WHOLE?
IS THIS THE EXPRESSION OF YOUR POWER? OF YOUR GODDESS?
OR IS THAT WHY YOU BRING A PRIEST TO YOUR HOME?
IT'S NOT TUCK.
YOU AREN'T TUCK.
THEN WHO? WHO COULD REACH YOU IN THIS TOWN, PROTECTED AS IT IS...?
WHAT POWER SITS BENEATH THE NOSE OF THE PRIEST?
CLEARLY YOU WANT TO TELL US.
LEAVE BURNHAM, YOU SACRED FLOCK.
YOU HEALED TUCK BEFORE, TURNED A MONSTER TO MERE INVALID. BLESS YOU, DAYANA.
BUT CAN YOU CHASE ME OUT--?
WHEN NEXT I COME?

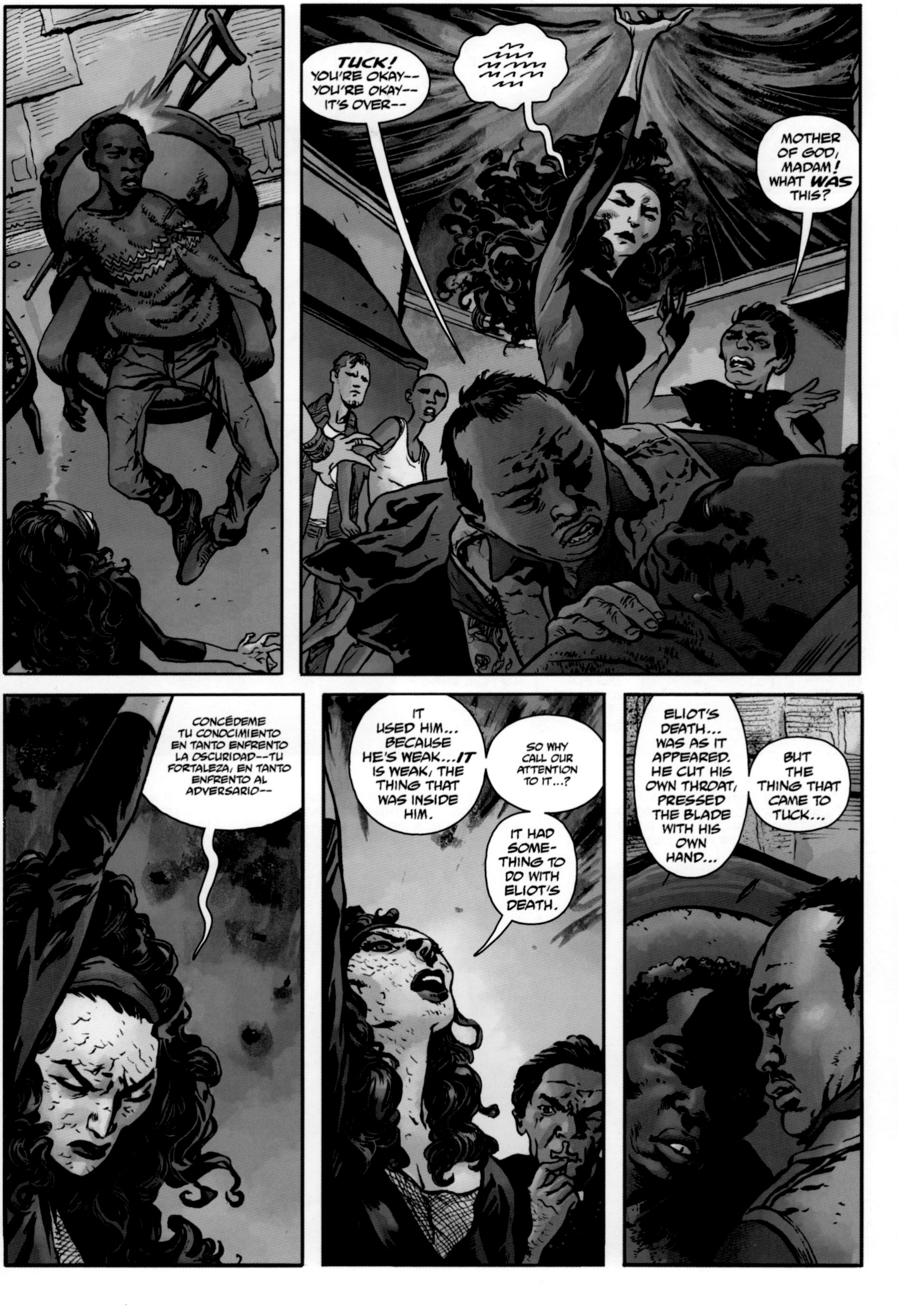
TUCK! YOU'RE OKAY-- YOU'RE OKAY-- IT'S OVER--
MOTHER OF GOD, MADAM! WHAT WAS THIS?
CONCÉDEME TU CONOCIMIENTO EN TANTO ENFRENTO LA OSCURIDAD--TU FORTALEZA, EN TANTO ENFRENTO AL ADVERSARIO--
IT USED HIM... BECAUSE HE'S WEAK...IT IS WEAK, THE THING THAT WAS INSIDE HIM.
SO WHY CALL OUR ATTENTION TO IT...?
IT HAD SOME-THING TO DO WITH ELIOT'S DEATH.
ELIOT'S DEATH... WAS AS IT APPEARED. HE CUT HIS OWN THROAT, PRESSED THE BLADE WITH HIS OWN HAND...
BUT THE THING THAT CAME TO TUCK...

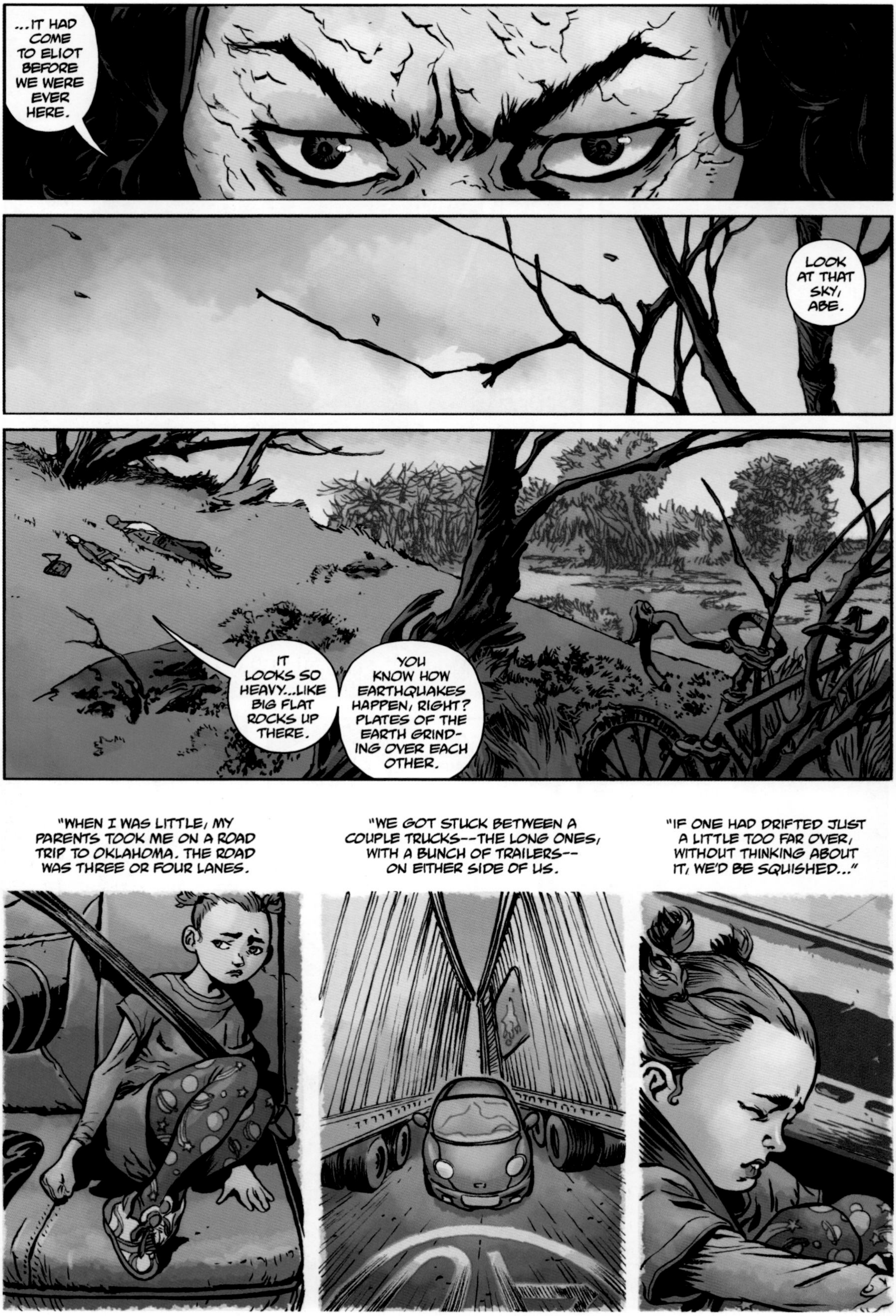
...IT HAD COME TO ELIOT BEFORE WE WERE EVER HERE.
LOOK AT THAT SKY, ABE.
IT LOOKS SO HEAVY...LIKE BIG FLAT ROCKS UP THERE.
YOU KNOW HOW EARTHQUAKES HAPPEN, RIGHT? PLATES OF THE EARTH GRINDING OVER EACH OTHER.
"WHEN I WAS LITTLE, MY PARENTS TOOK ME ON A ROAD TRIP TO OKLAHOMA. THE ROAD WAS THREE OR FOUR LANES.
"WE GOT STUCK BETWEEN A COUPLE TRUCKS--THE LONG ONES, WITH A BUNCH OF TRAILERS--ON EITHER SIDE OF US.
"IF ONE HAD DRIFTED JUST A LITTLE TOO FAR OVER, WITHOUT THINKING ABOUT IT, WE'D BE SQUISHED..."

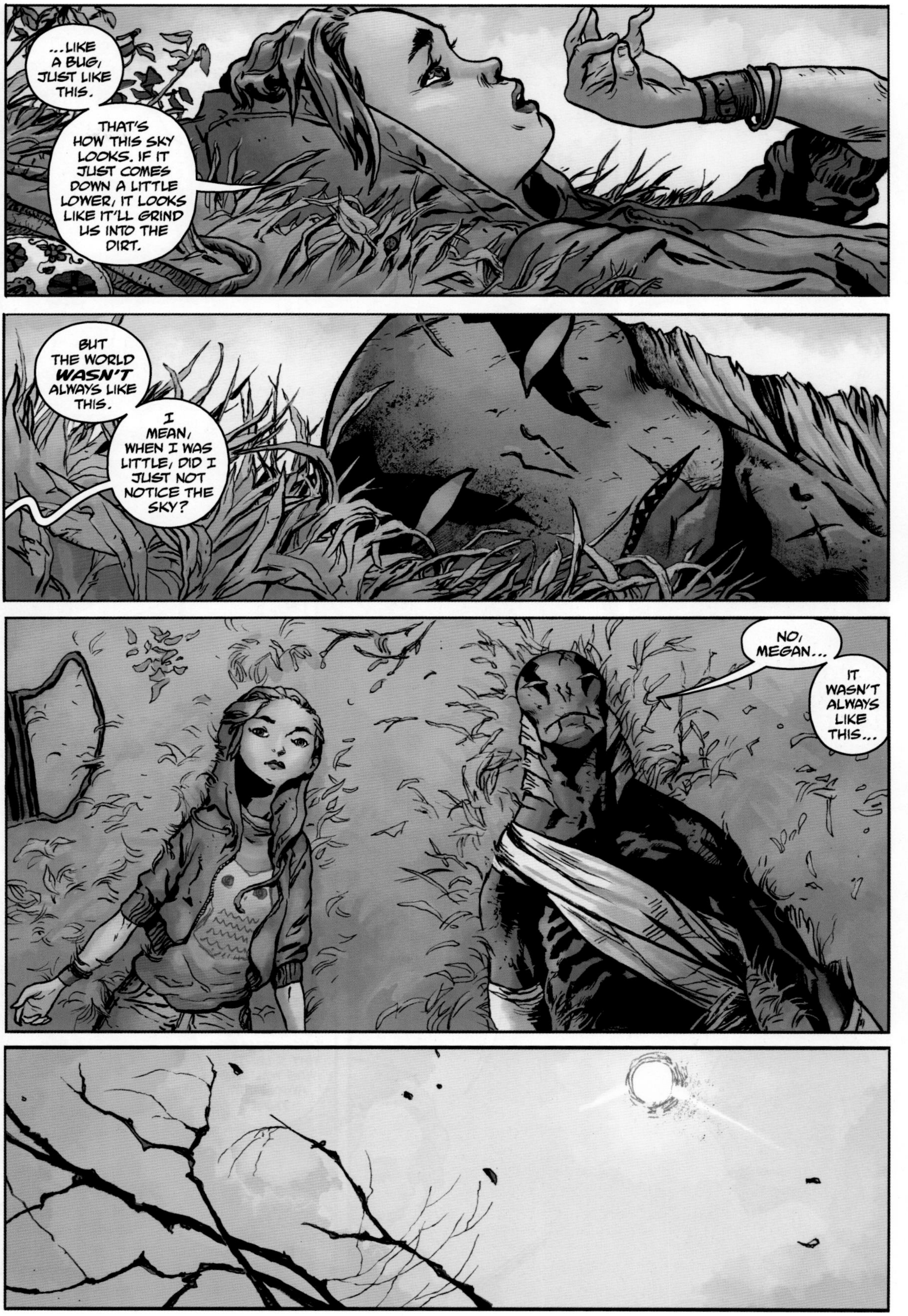
...LIKE A BUG, JUST LIKE THIS.
THAT'S HOW THIS SKY LOOKS. IF IT JUST COMES DOWN A LITTLE LOWER, IT LOOKS LIKE IT'LL GRIND US INTO THE DIRT.
BUT THE WORLD WASN'T ALWAYS LIKE THIS.
I MEAN, WHEN I WAS LITTLE, DID I JUST NOT NOTICE THE SKY?
NO, MEGAN...
IT WASN'T ALWAYS LIKE THIS...

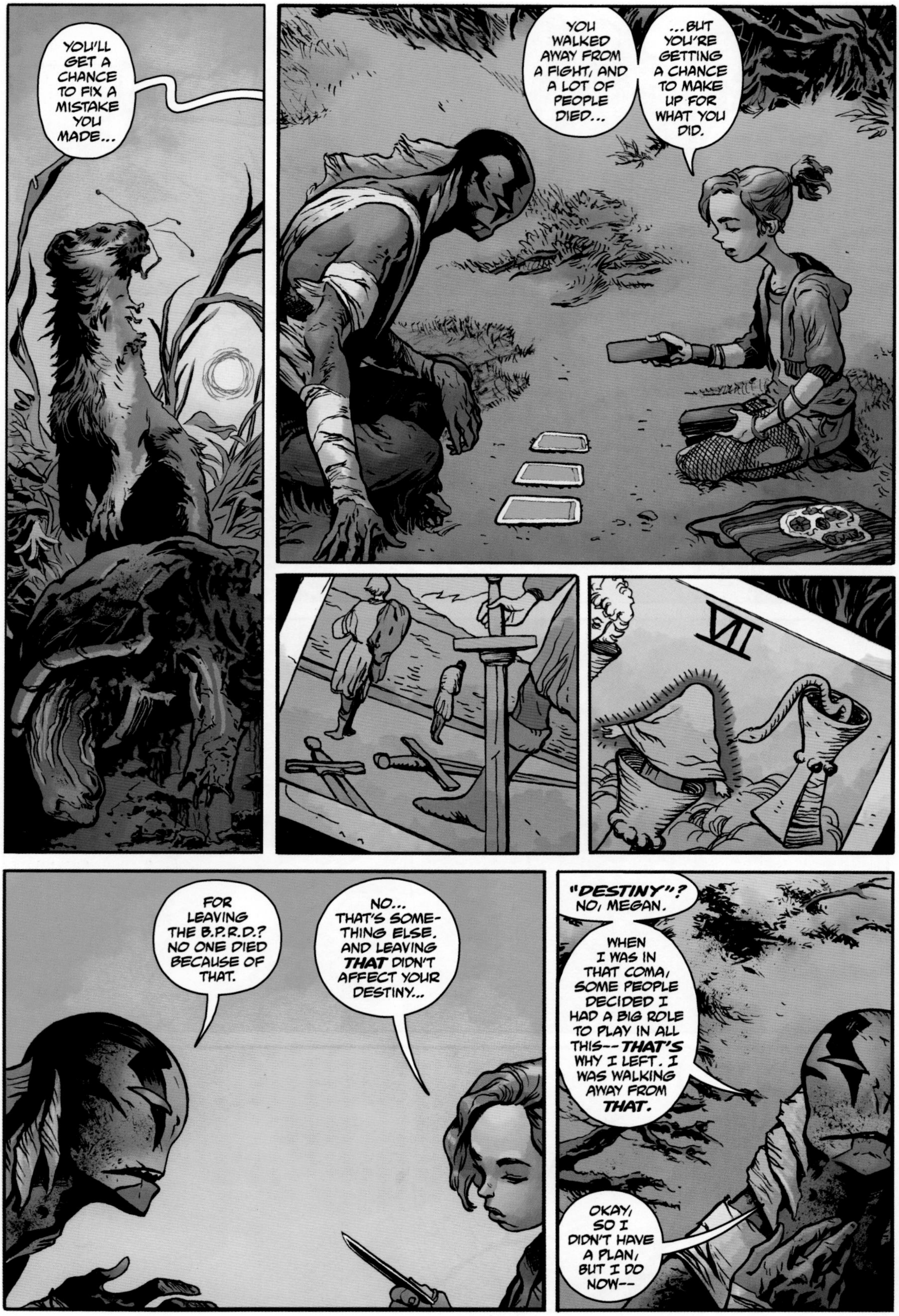
YOU'LL GET A CHANCE TO FIX A MISTAKE YOU MADE...
YOU WALKED AWAY FROM A FIGHT, AND A LOT OF PEOPLE DIED...
...BUT YOU'RE GETTING A CHANCE TO MAKE UP FOR WHAT YOU DID.
VII
FOR LEAVING THE B.P.R.D.? NO ONE DIED BECAUSE OF THAT.
NO... THAT'S SOMETHING ELSE. AND LEAVING **THAT** DIDN'T AFFECT YOUR DESTINY...
"DESTINY"? NO, MEGAN.
WHEN I WAS IN THAT COMA, SOME PEOPLE DECIDED I HAD A BIG ROLE TO PLAY IN ALL THIS--**THAT'S** WHY I LEFT. I WAS WALKING AWAY FROM **THAT**.
OKAY, SO I DIDN'T HAVE A PLAN, BUT I DO NOW--

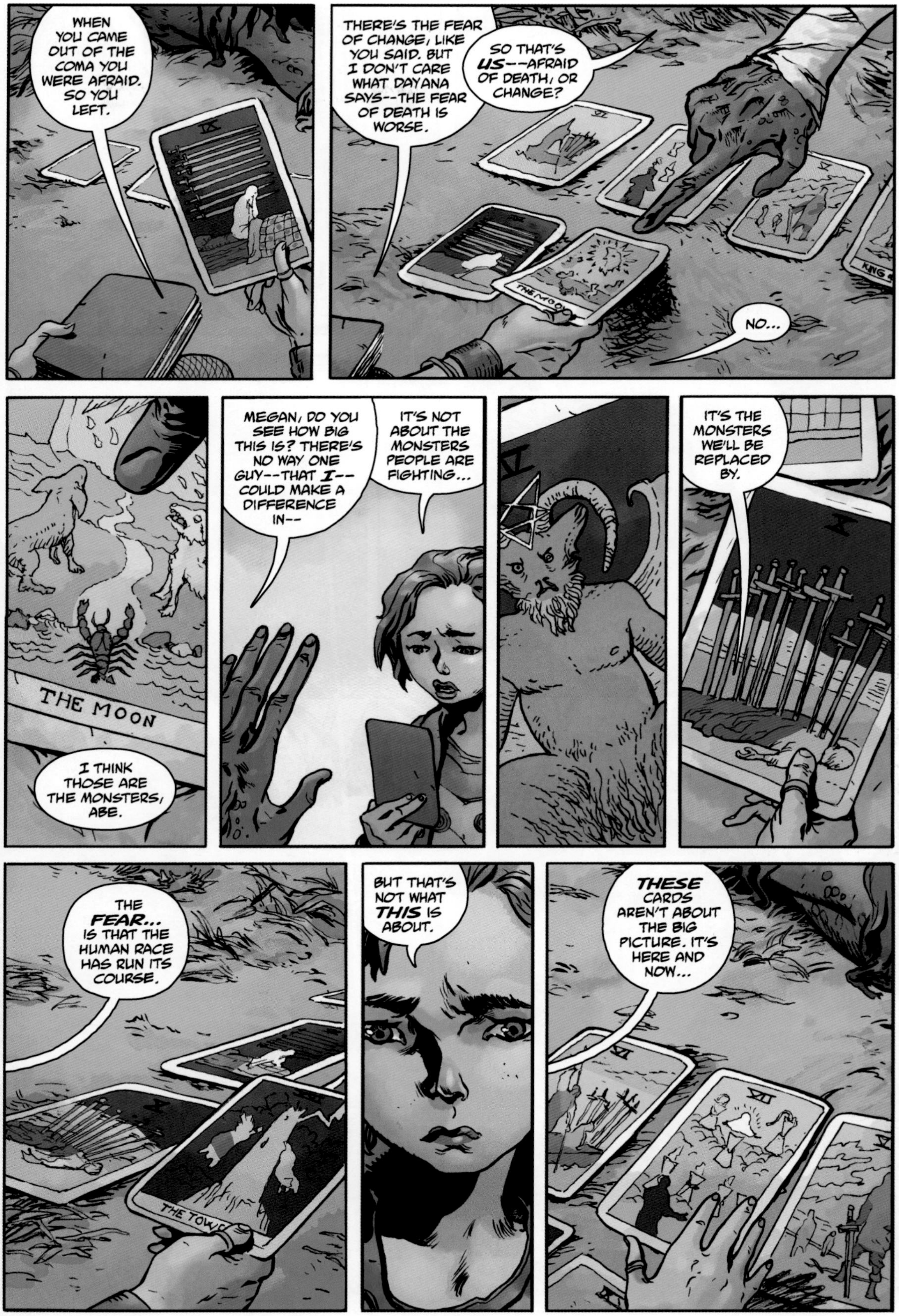
WHEN YOU CAME OUT OF THE COMA YOU WERE AFRAID. SO YOU LEFT.
THERE'S THE FEAR OF CHANGE, LIKE YOU SAID. BUT I DON'T CARE WHAT DAYANA SAYS--THE FEAR OF DEATH IS WORSE.
SO THAT'S *US*--AFRAID OF DEATH, OR CHANGE?
NO...
THE MOON
I THINK THOSE ARE THE MONSTERS, ABE.
MEGAN, DO YOU SEE HOW BIG THIS IS? THERE'S NO WAY ONE GUY--THAT *I*--COULD MAKE A DIFFERENCE IN--
IT'S NOT ABOUT THE MONSTERS PEOPLE ARE FIGHTING...
IT'S THE MONSTERS WE'LL BE REPLACED BY.
THE *FEAR*... IS THAT THE HUMAN RACE HAS RUN ITS COURSE.
BUT THAT'S NOT WHAT *THIS* IS ABOUT.
THESE CARDS AREN'T ABOUT THE BIG PICTURE. IT'S HERE AND NOW...

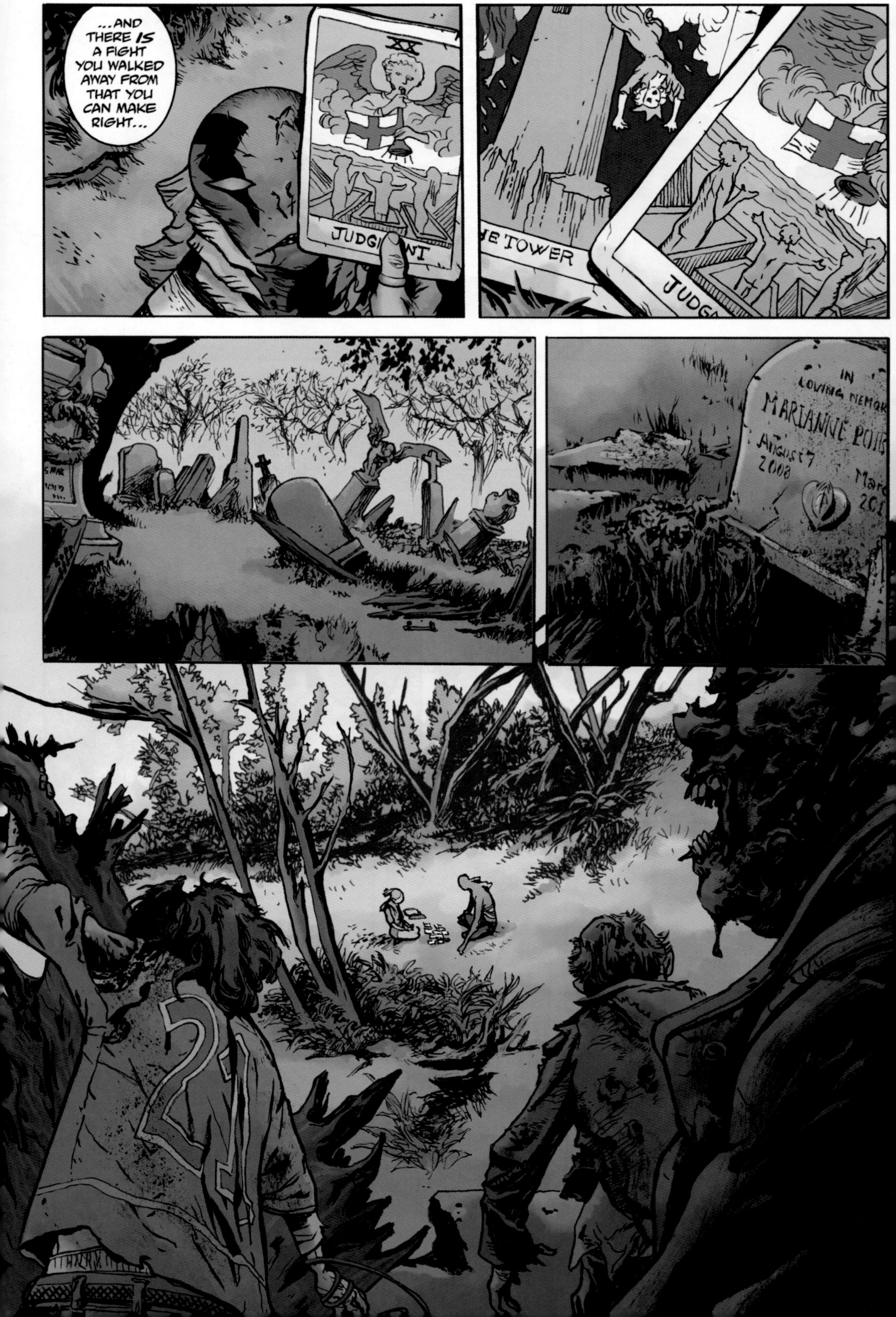
...AND THERE IS A FIGHT YOU WALKED AWAY FROM THAT YOU CAN MAKE RIGHT...
XX
August 7
2008

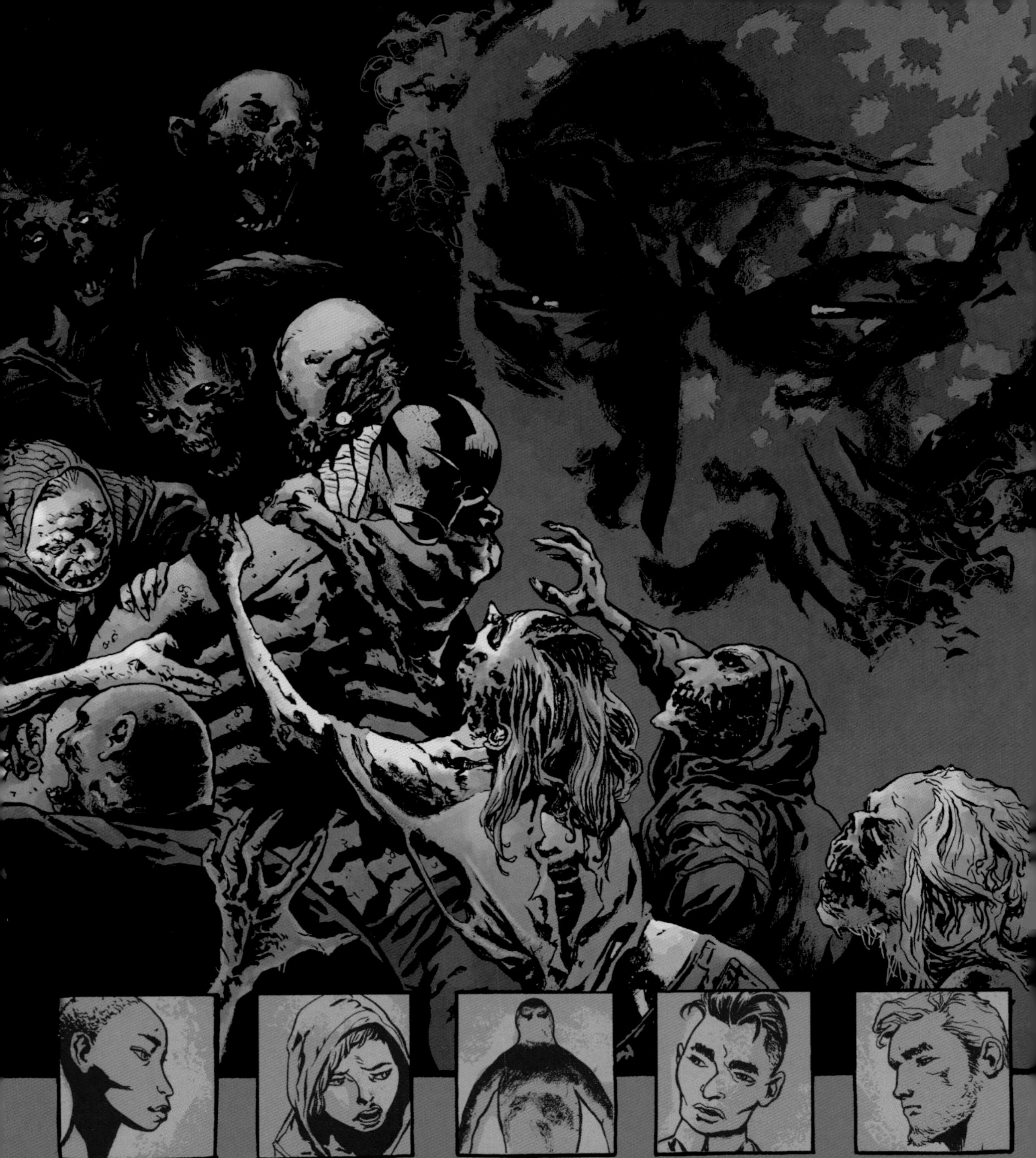

ARBOGAST

Born in 1942 in Lake Charles, Louisiana, Arbogast
has lived in every state on the Gulf Coast from Florida
to Tamaulipas, Mexico, and outlived three wives while
producing no children. His last wife died in her hometown
of Burnham, Texas, where the two met in 1999. Since 2010
he's recruited young people into a secret cult, under a veil
of Haitian voodoo . . .

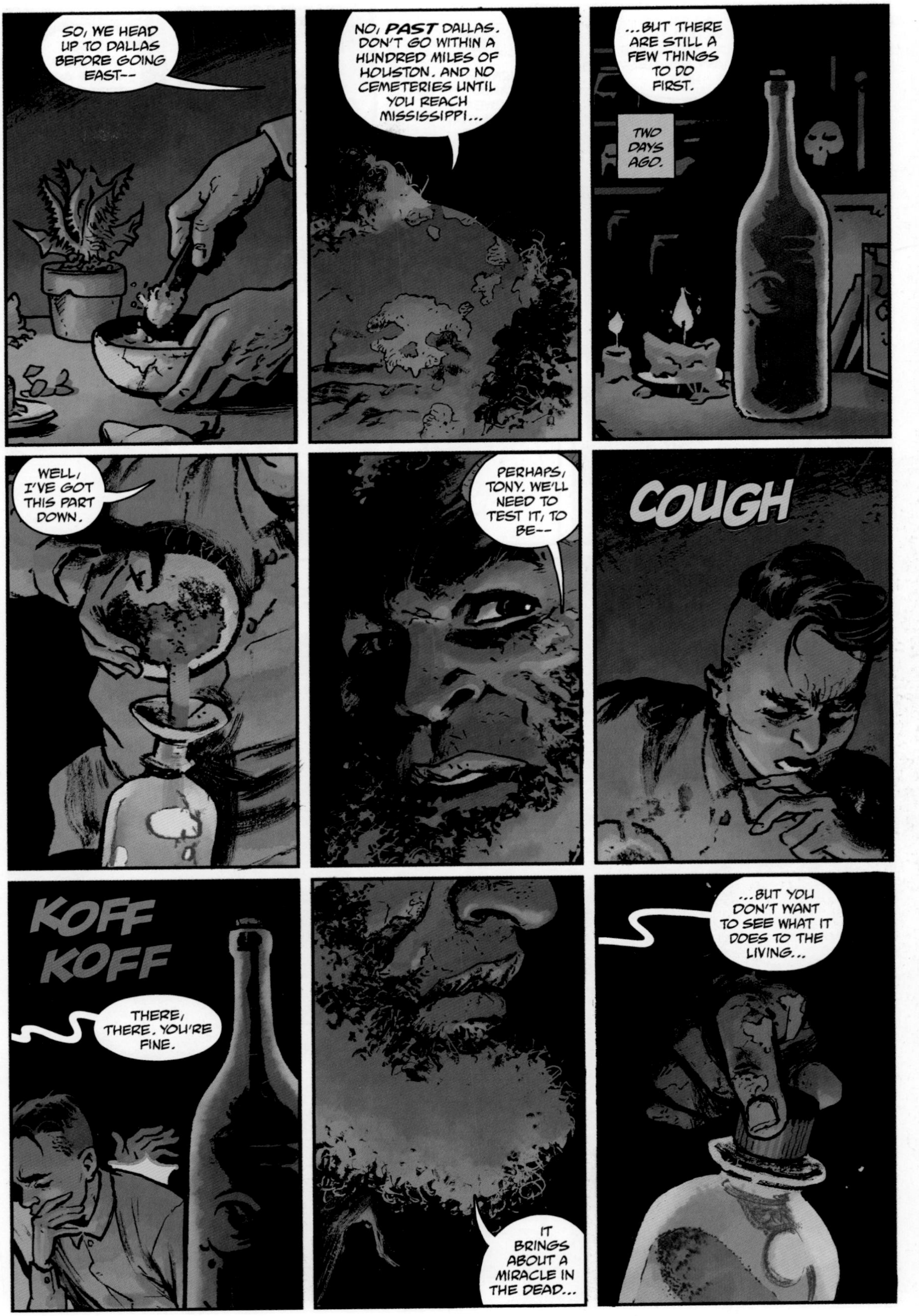
SO, WE HEAD UP TO DALLAS BEFORE GOING EAST--
NO, PAST DALLAS. DON'T GO WITHIN A HUNDRED MILES OF HOUSTON. AND NO CEMETERIES UNTIL YOU REACH MISSISSIPPI...
...BUT THERE ARE STILL A FEW THINGS TO DO FIRST.
TWO DAYS AGO.
WELL, I'VE GOT THIS PART DOWN.
PERHAPS, TONY. WE'LL NEED TO TEST IT, TO BE--
COUGH
KOFF KOFF
THERE, THERE. YOU'RE FINE.
IT BRINGS ABOUT A MIRACLE IN THE DEAD...
...BUT YOU DON'T WANT TO SEE WHAT IT DOES TO THE LIVING...

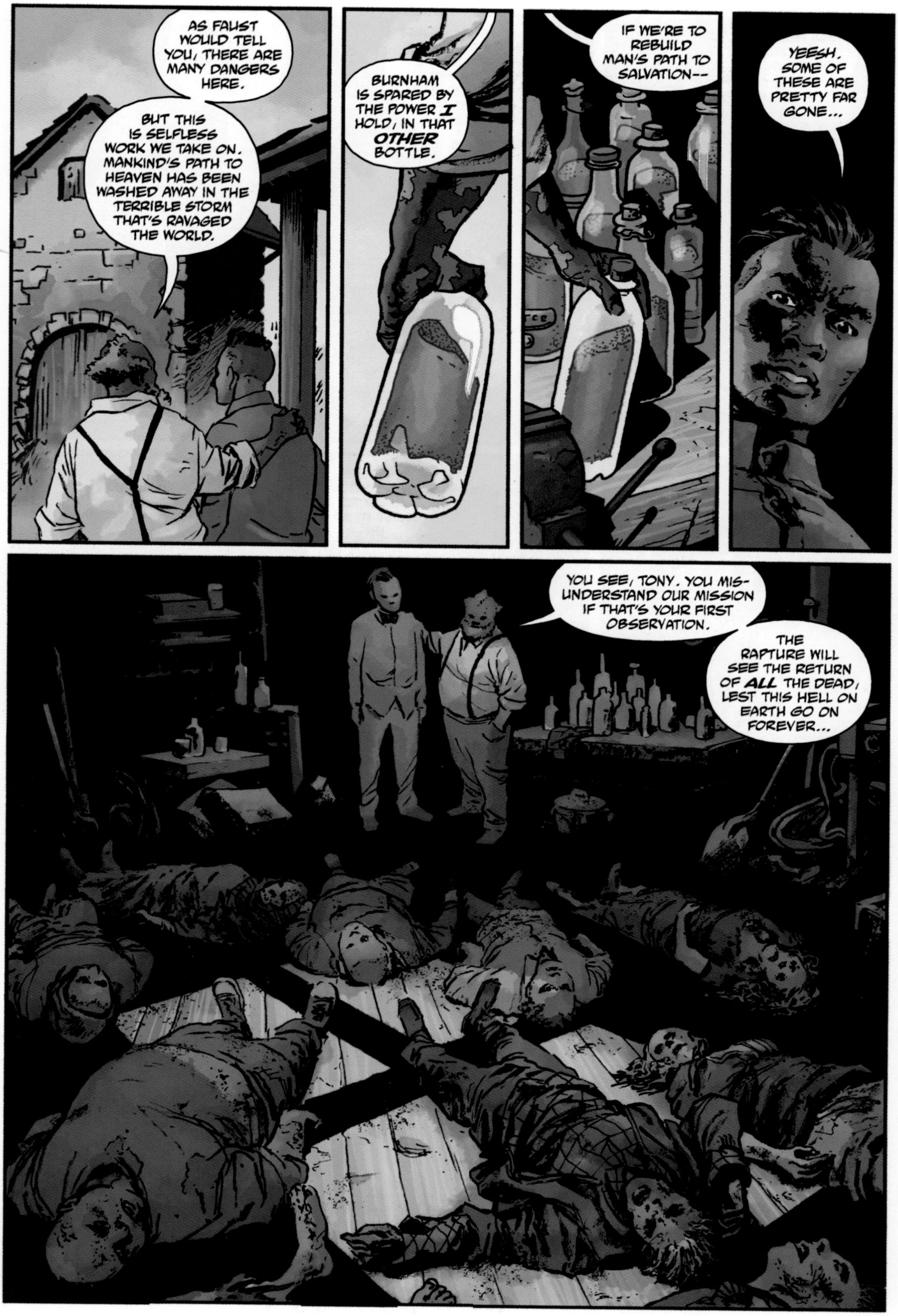
AS FAUST WOULD TELL YOU, THERE ARE MANY DANGERS HERE.
BUT THIS IS SELFLESS WORK WE TAKE ON. MANKIND'S PATH TO HEAVEN HAS BEEN WASHED AWAY IN THE TERRIBLE STORM THAT'S RAVAGED THE WORLD.
BURNHAM IS SPARED BY THE POWER *I* HOLD, IN THAT ***OTHER*** BOTTLE.
IF WE'RE TO REBUILD MAN'S PATH TO SALVATION--
YEESH. SOME OF THESE ARE PRETTY FAR GONE...
YOU SEE, TONY. YOU MISUNDERSTAND OUR MISSION IF THAT'S YOUR FIRST OBSERVATION.
THE RAPTURE WILL SEE THE RETURN OF ***ALL*** THE DEAD, LEST THIS HELL ON EARTH GO ON FOREVER...

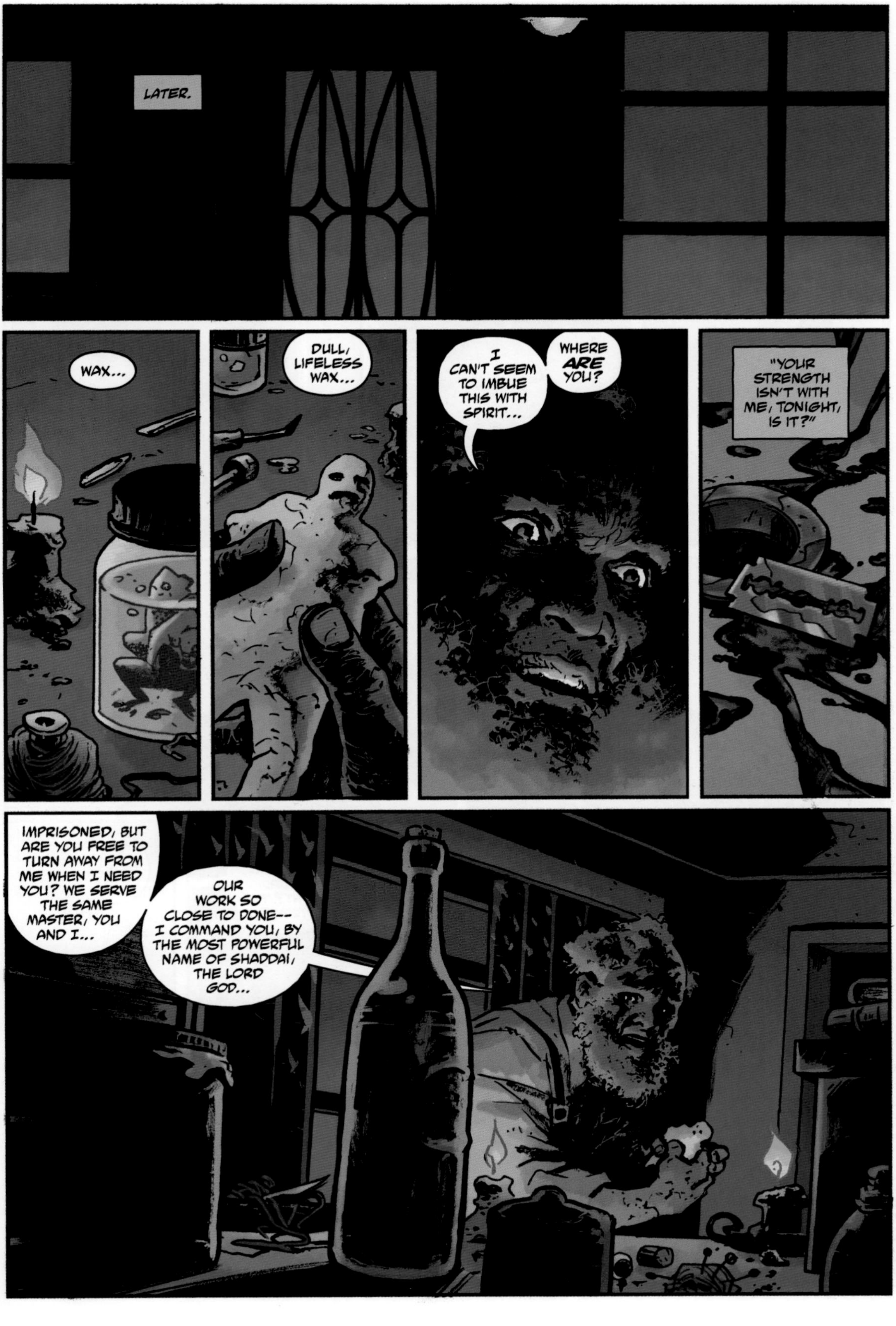
LATER.
WAX...
DULL, LIFELESS WAX...
I CAN'T SEEM TO IMBUE THIS WITH SPIRIT...
WHERE ARE YOU?
"YOUR STRENGTH ISN'T WITH ME, TONIGHT, IS IT?"
IMPRISONED, BUT ARE YOU FREE TO TURN AWAY FROM ME WHEN I NEED YOU? WE SERVE THE SAME MASTER, YOU AND I...
OUR WORK SO CLOSE TO DONE-- I COMMAND YOU, BY THE MOST POWERFUL NAME OF SHADDAI, THE LORD GOD...

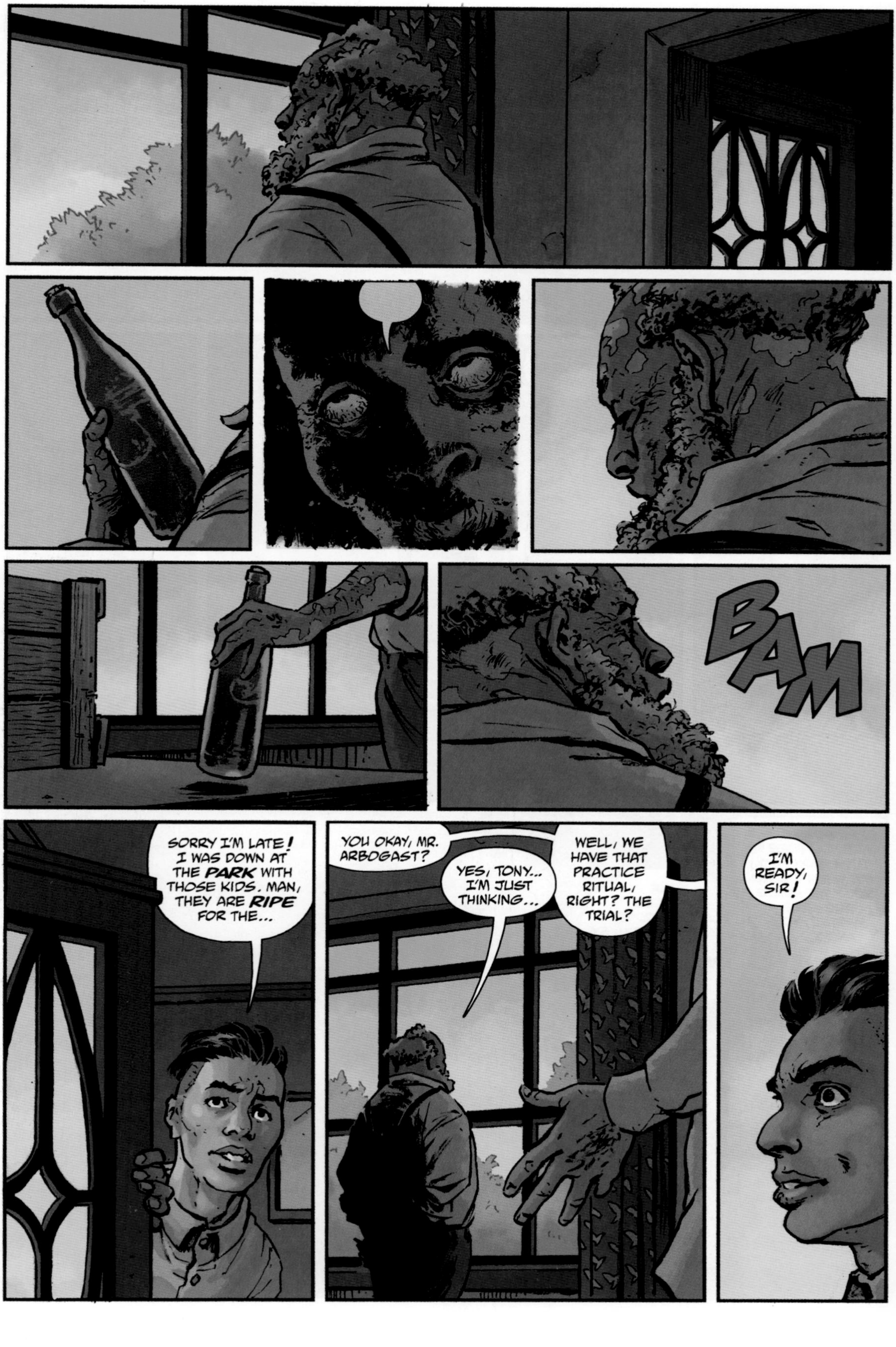
BAM
SORRY I'M LATE! I WAS DOWN AT THE PARK WITH THOSE KIDS. MAN, THEY ARE RIPE FOR THE...
YOU OKAY, MR. ARBOGAST?
YES, TONY... I'M JUST THINKING...
WELL, WE HAVE THAT PRACTICE RITUAL, RIGHT? THE TRIAL?
I'M READY, SIR!

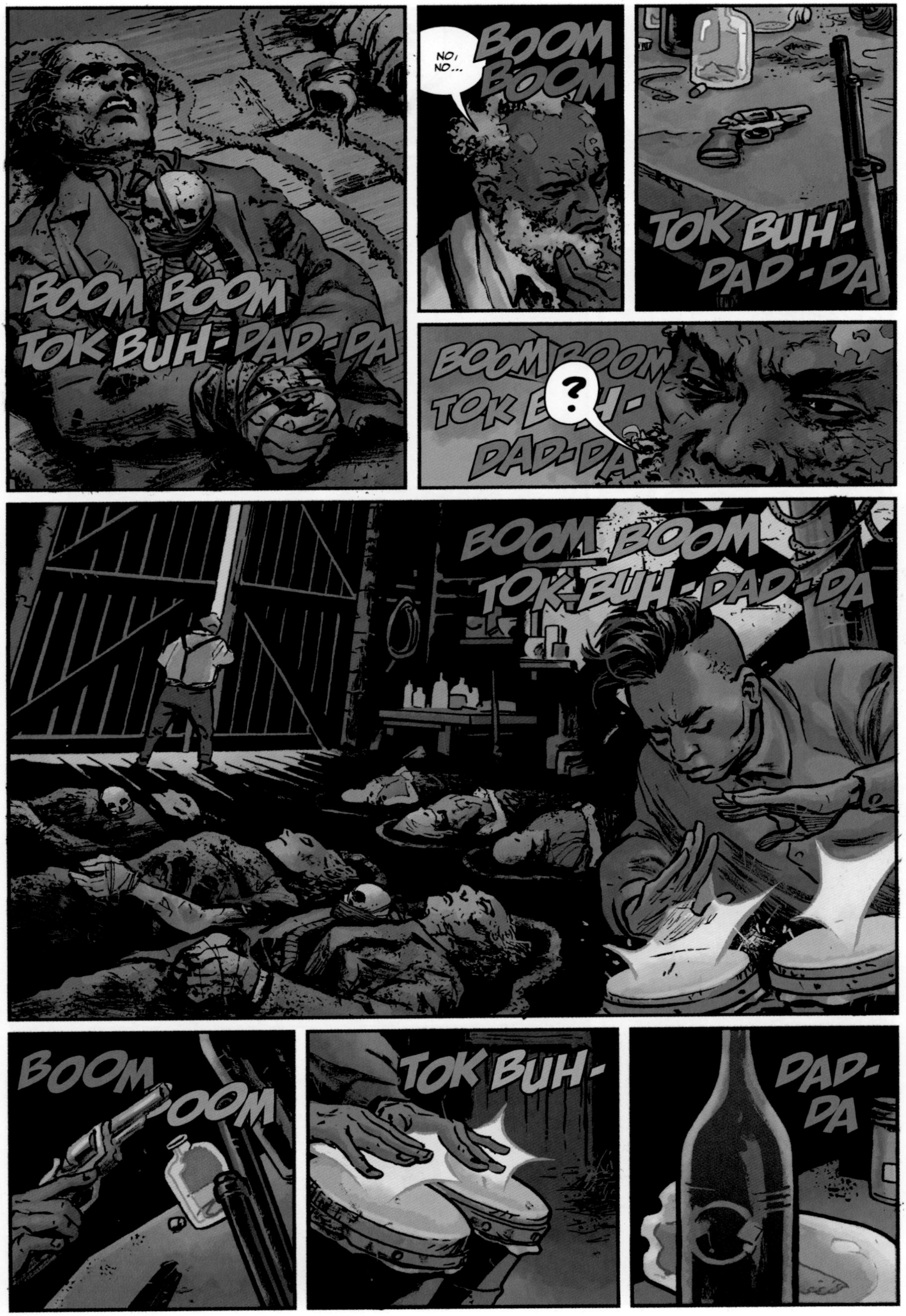
BOOM BOOM
TOK BUH-DAD-DA
NO, NO...
BOOM BOOM
TOK BUH-DAD-DA
BOOM BOOM
?
TOK BUH-DAD-DA
BOOM BOOM
TOK-BUH-DAD-DA
BOOM BOOM
TOK BUH-
DAD-DA

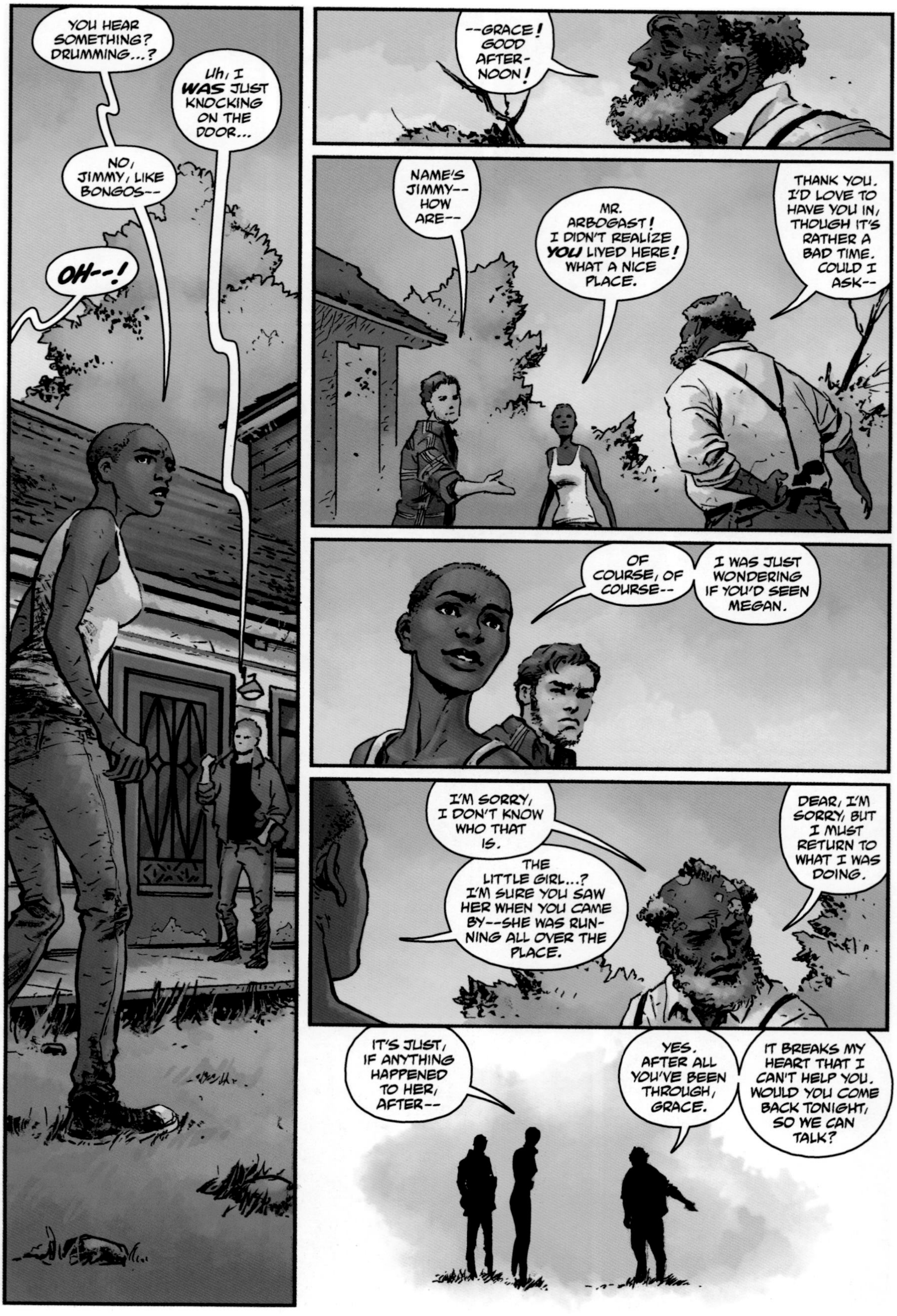
YOU HEAR SOMETHING? DRUMMING...?
UH, I WAS JUST KNOCKING ON THE DOOR...
NO, JIMMY, LIKE BONGOS--
OH--!
--GRACE! GOOD AFTER-NOON!
NAME'S JIMMY-- HOW ARE--
MR. ARBOGAST! I DIDN'T REALIZE YOU LIVED HERE! WHAT A NICE PLACE.
THANK YOU. I'D LOVE TO HAVE YOU IN, THOUGH IT'S RATHER A BAD TIME. COULD I ASK--
OF COURSE, OF COURSE--
I WAS JUST WONDERING IF YOU'D SEEN MEGAN.
I'M SORRY, I DON'T KNOW WHO THAT IS.
THE LITTLE GIRL...? I'M SURE YOU SAW HER WHEN YOU CAME BY--SHE WAS RUN-NING ALL OVER THE PLACE.
DEAR, I'M SORRY, BUT I MUST RETURN TO WHAT I WAS DOING.
IT'S JUST, IF ANYTHING HAPPENED TO HER, AFTER--
YES. AFTER ALL YOU'VE BEEN THROUGH, GRACE.
IT BREAKS MY HEART THAT I CAN'T HELP YOU. WOULD YOU COME BACK TONIGHT, SO WE CAN TALK?

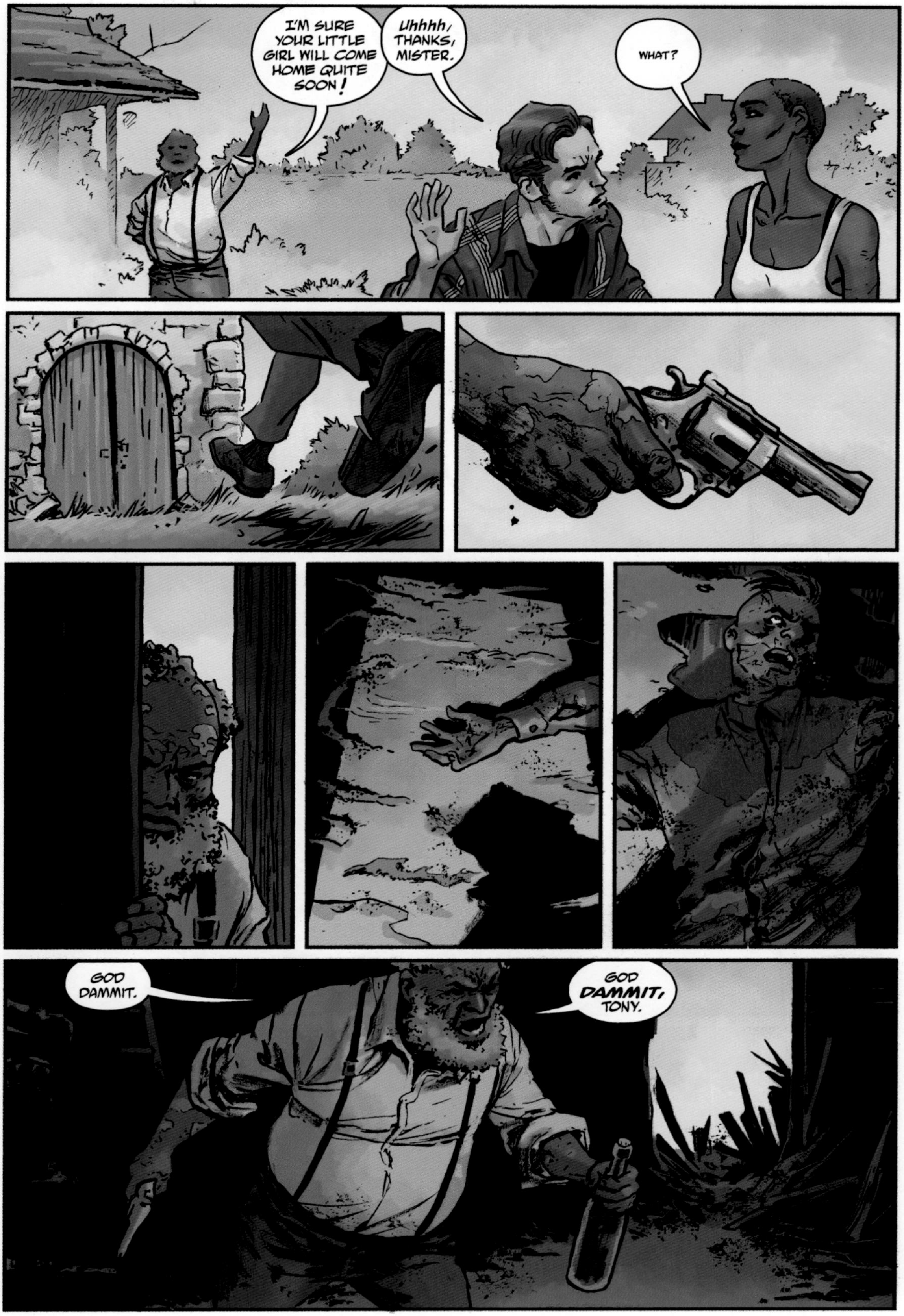
I'M SURE YOUR LITTLE GIRL WILL COME HOME QUITE SOON!
Uhhhh, THANKS, MISTER.
WHAT?
GOD DAMMIT.
GOD DAMMIT, TONY.

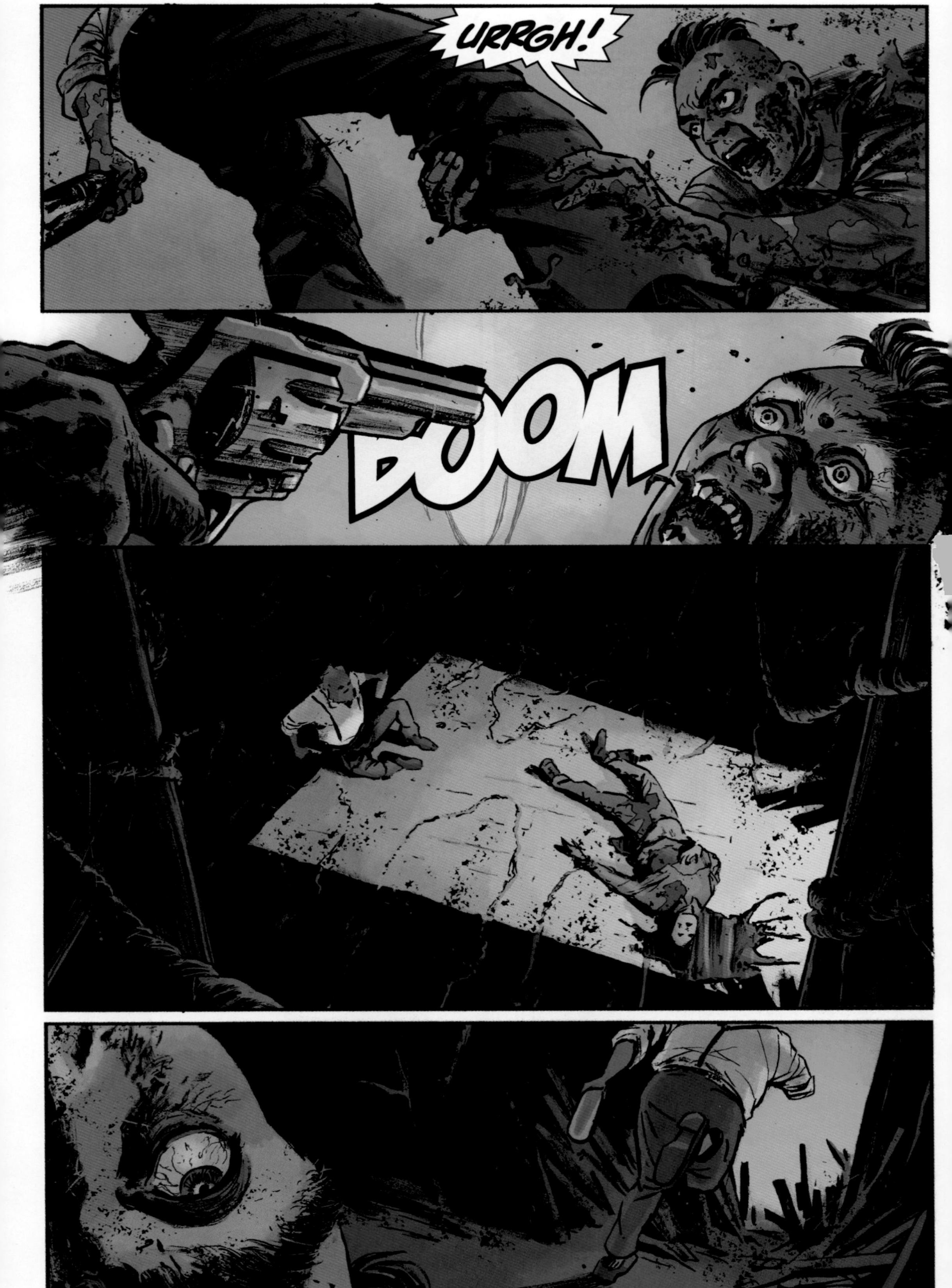
URRGH!
BOOM

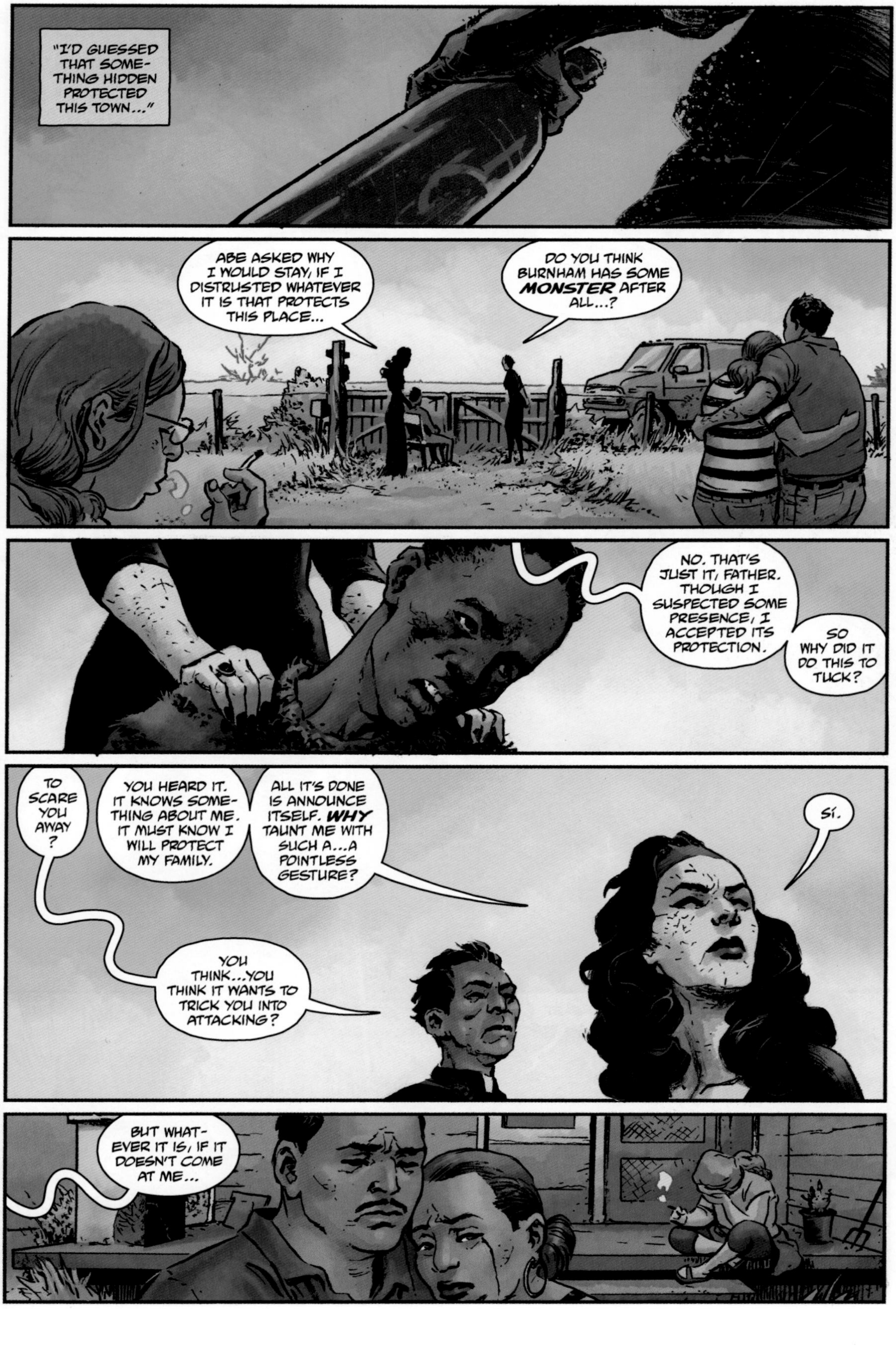
"I'D GUESSED THAT SOME-THING HIDDEN PROTECTED THIS TOWN..."
ABE ASKED WHY I WOULD STAY, IF I DISTRUSTED WHATEVER IT IS THAT PROTECTS THIS PLACE...
DO YOU THINK BURNHAM HAS SOME MONSTER AFTER ALL...?
NO. THAT'S JUST IT, FATHER. THOUGH I SUSPECTED SOME PRESENCE, I ACCEPTED ITS PROTECTION.
SO WHY DID IT DO THIS TO TUCK?
TO SCARE YOU AWAY?
YOU HEARD IT. IT KNOWS SOME-THING ABOUT ME. IT MUST KNOW I WILL PROTECT MY FAMILY.
ALL IT'S DONE IS ANNOUNCE ITSELF. WHY TAUNT ME WITH SUCH A...A POINTLESS GESTURE?
SÍ.
YOU THINK...YOU THINK IT WANTS TO TRICK YOU INTO ATTACKING?
BUT WHAT-EVER IT IS, IF IT DOESN'T COME AT ME...

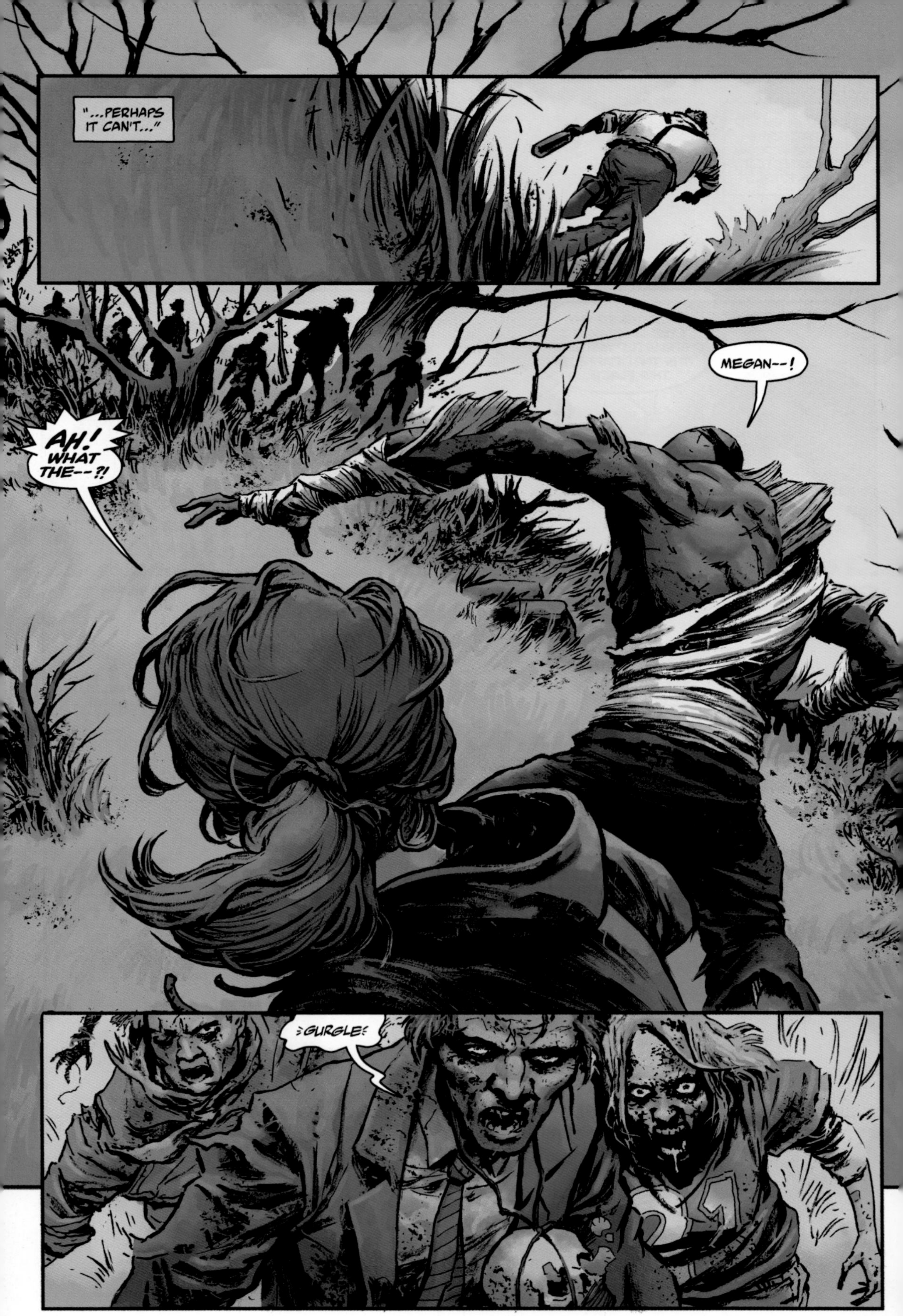
"...PERHAPS IT CAN'T..."
MEGAN--!
AH! WHAT THE--?!
GURGLE

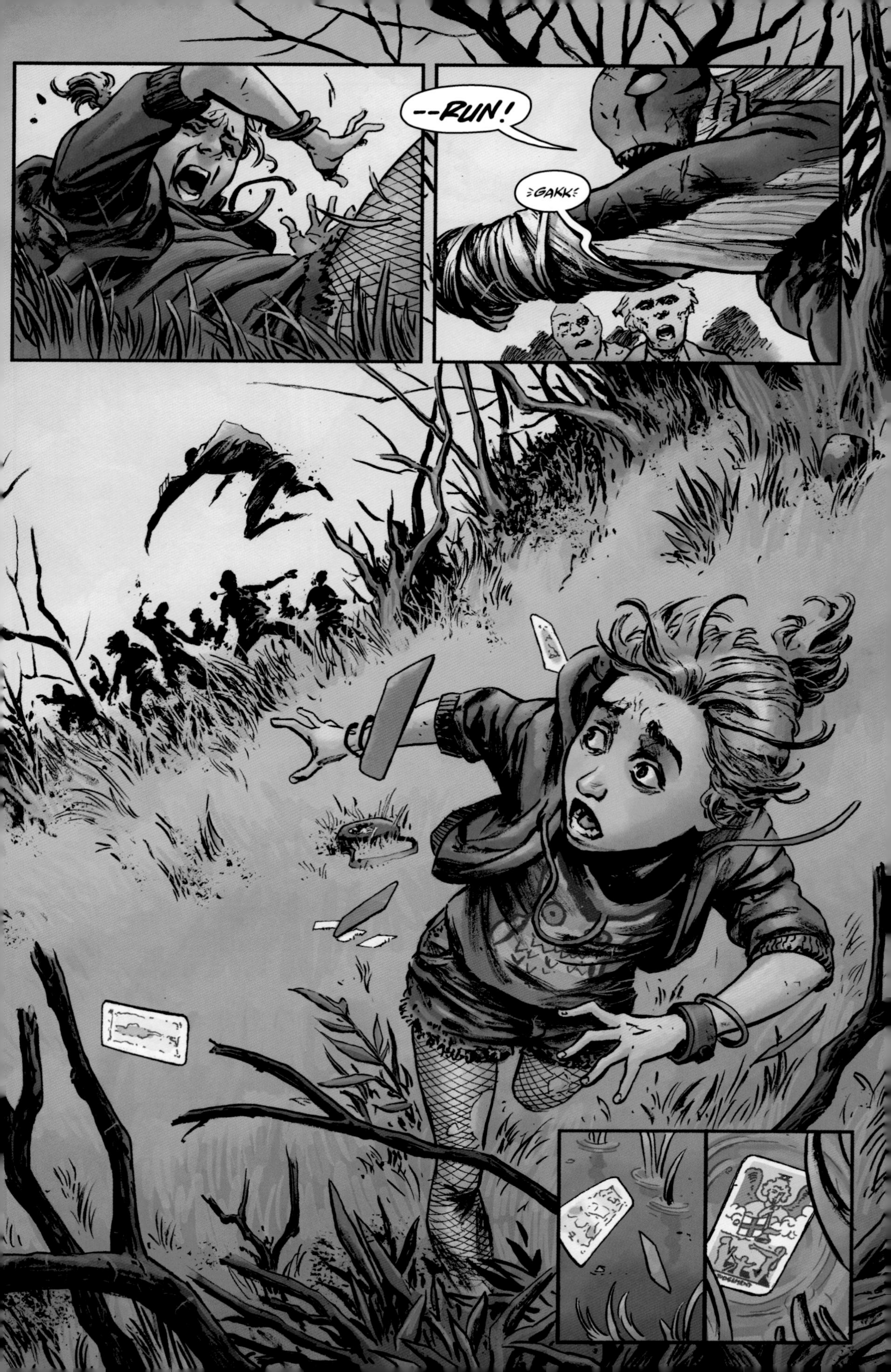
--RUN!
GAKK

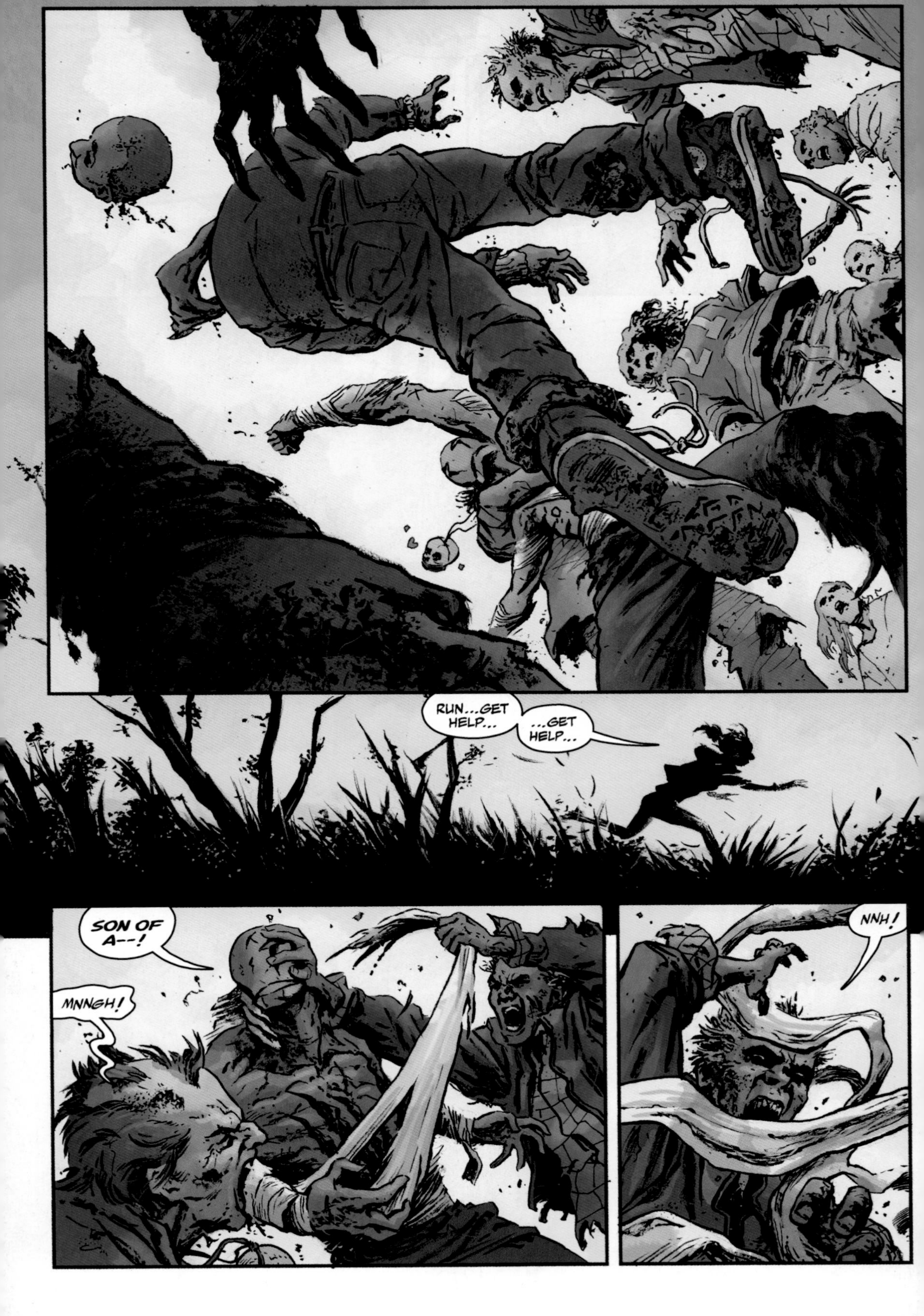
RUN...GET HELP...
...GET HELP...
SON OF A--!
MNNGH!
NNH!

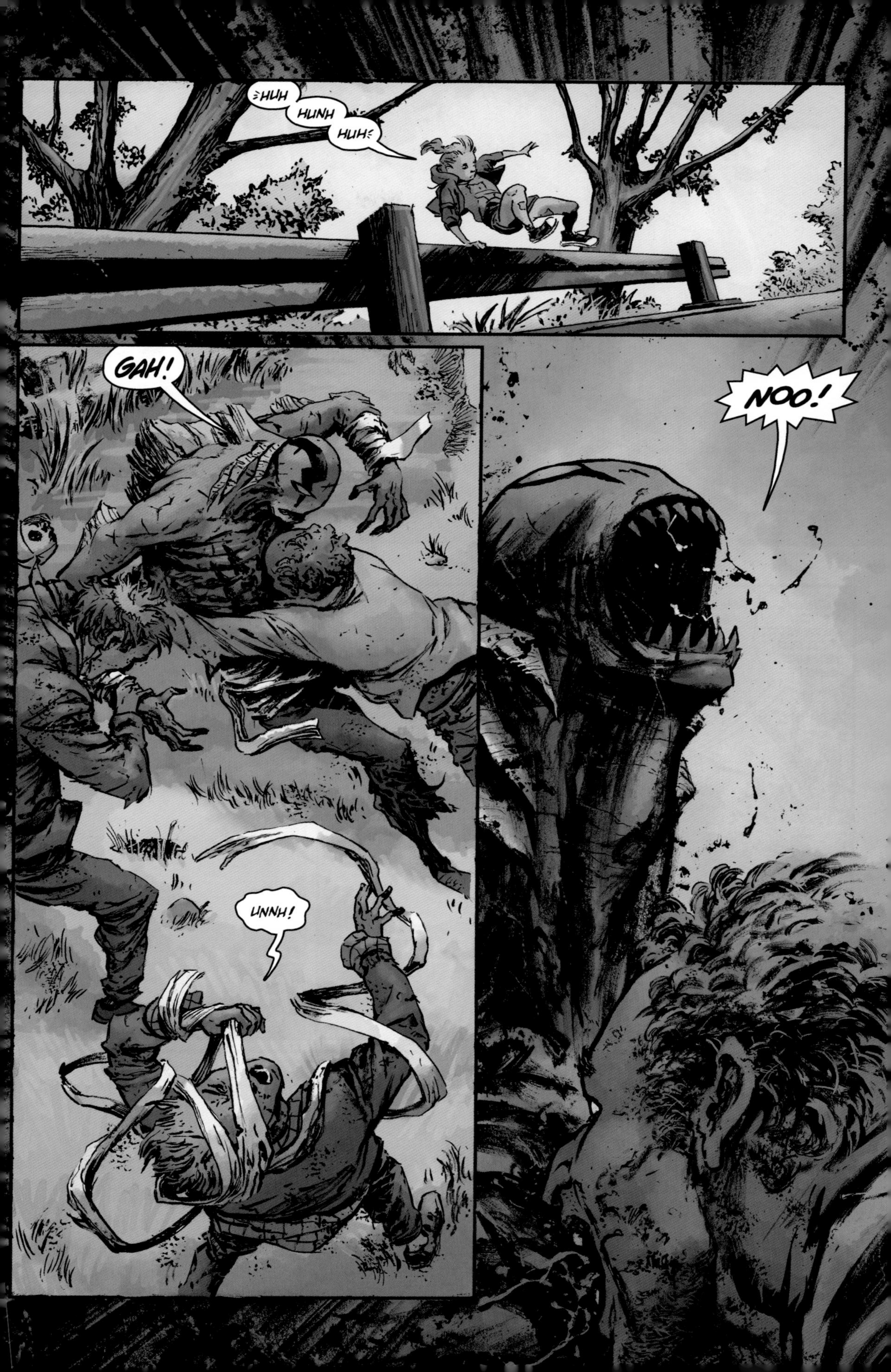
HUH
HUNH
HUH
GAH!
UNNH!
NOO!

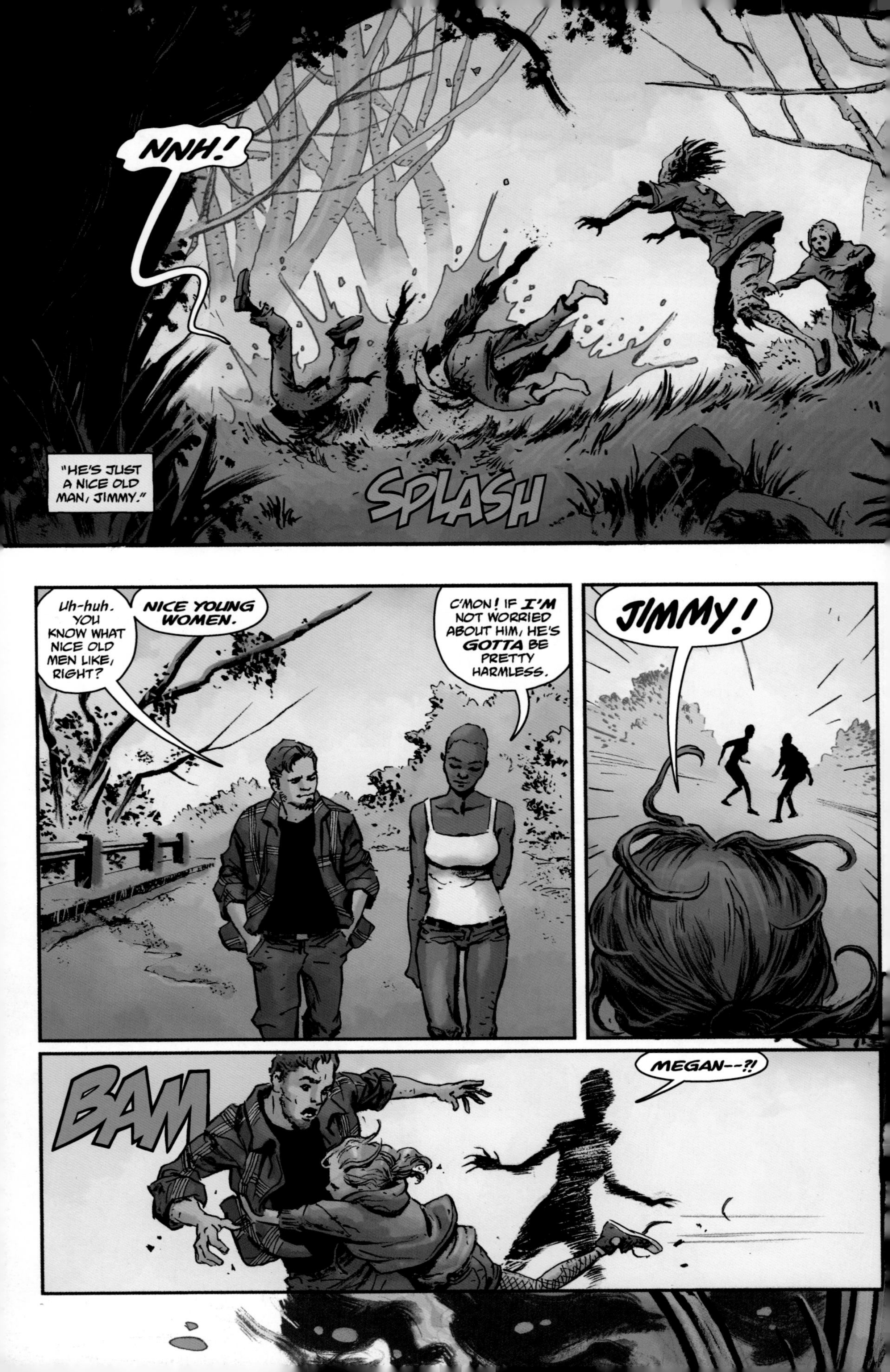
NNH!
"HE'S JUST A NICE OLD MAN, JIMMY."
SPLASH
Uh-huh. YOU KNOW WHAT NICE OLD MEN LIKE, RIGHT?
NICE YOUNG WOMEN.
C'MON! IF I'M NOT WORRIED ABOUT HIM, HE'S GOTTA BE PRETTY HARMLESS.
JIMMY!
BAM
MEGAN--?!

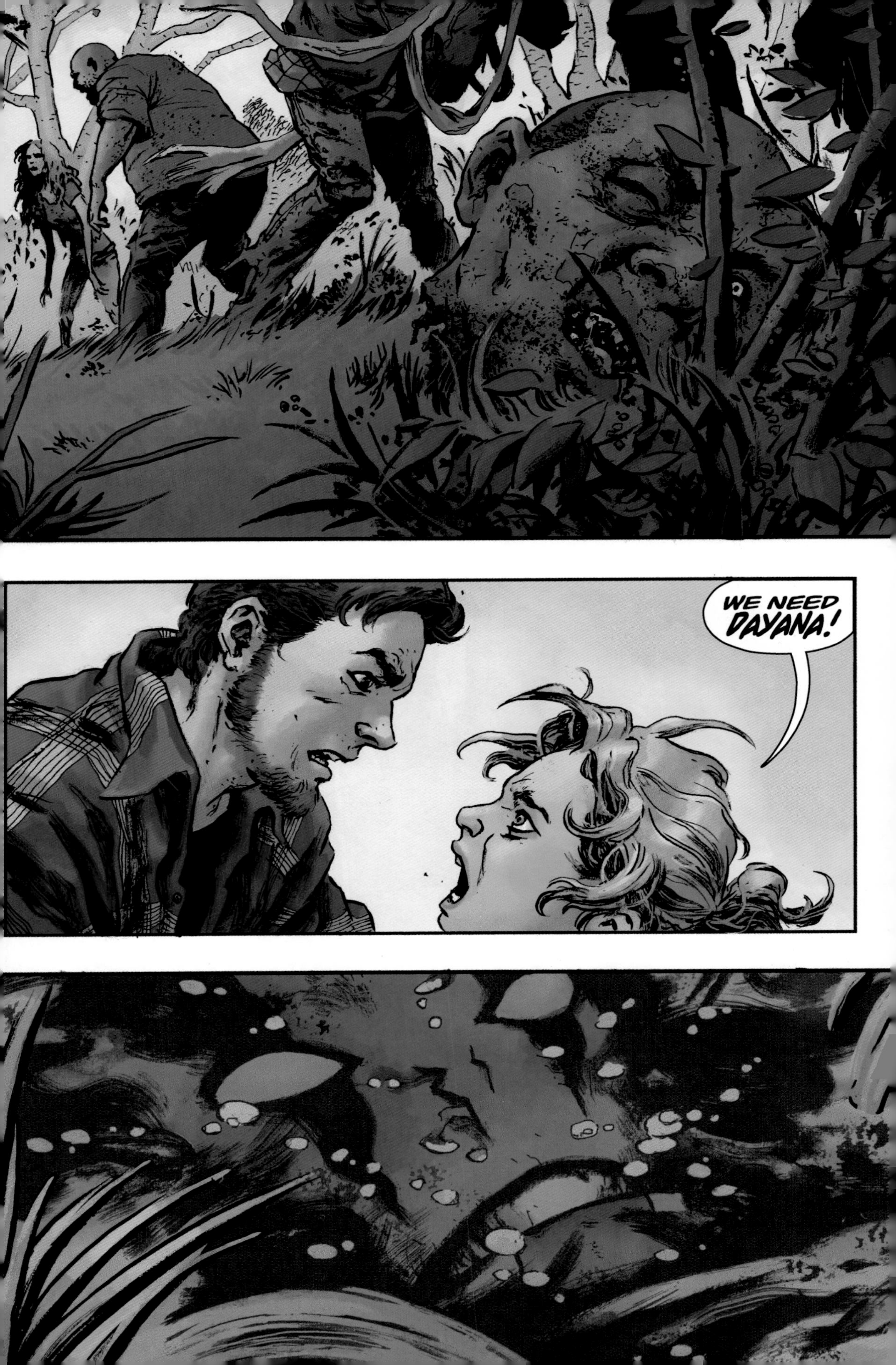
WE NEED DAYANA!

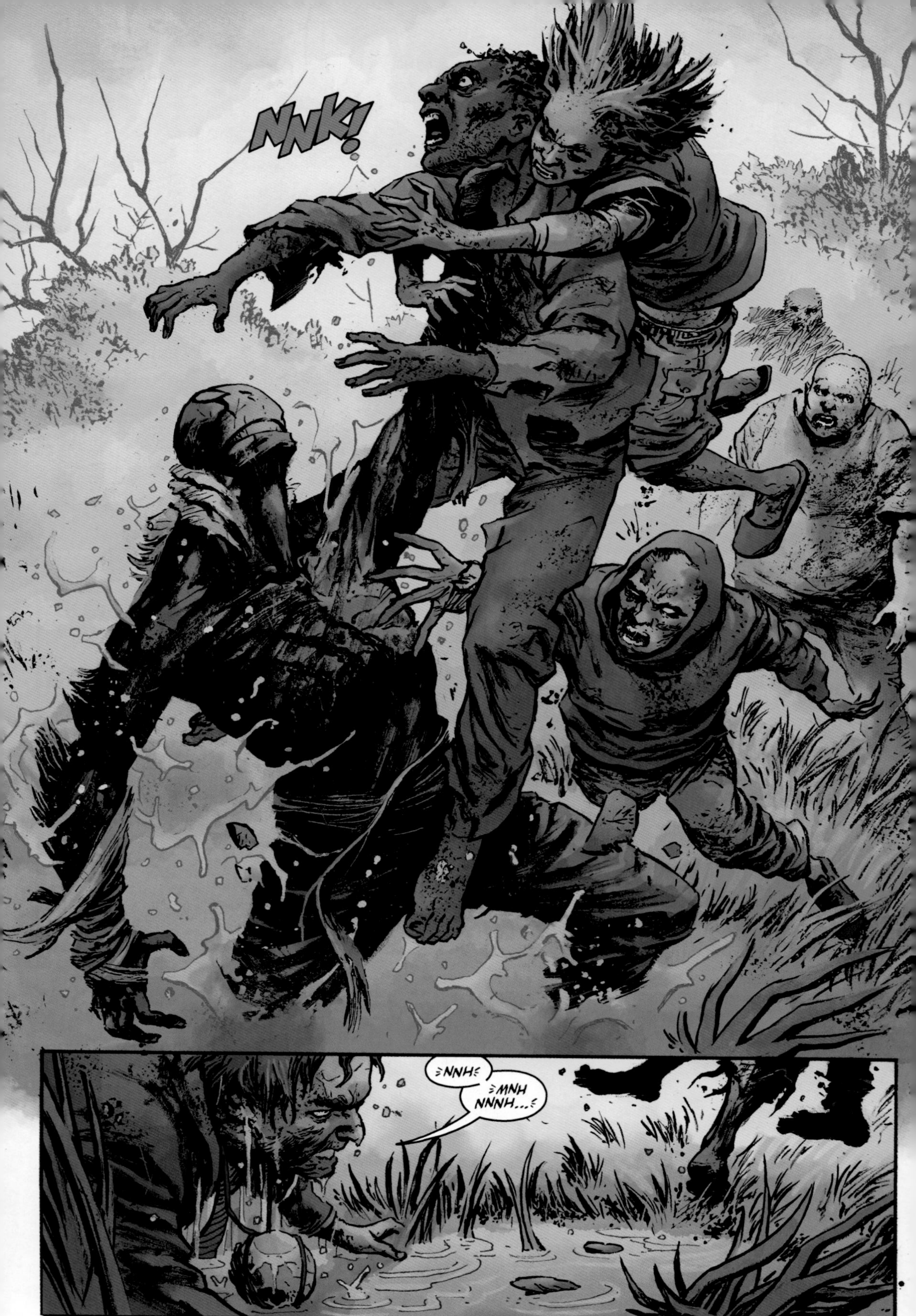
NNK!
NNH
MNH NNNH...

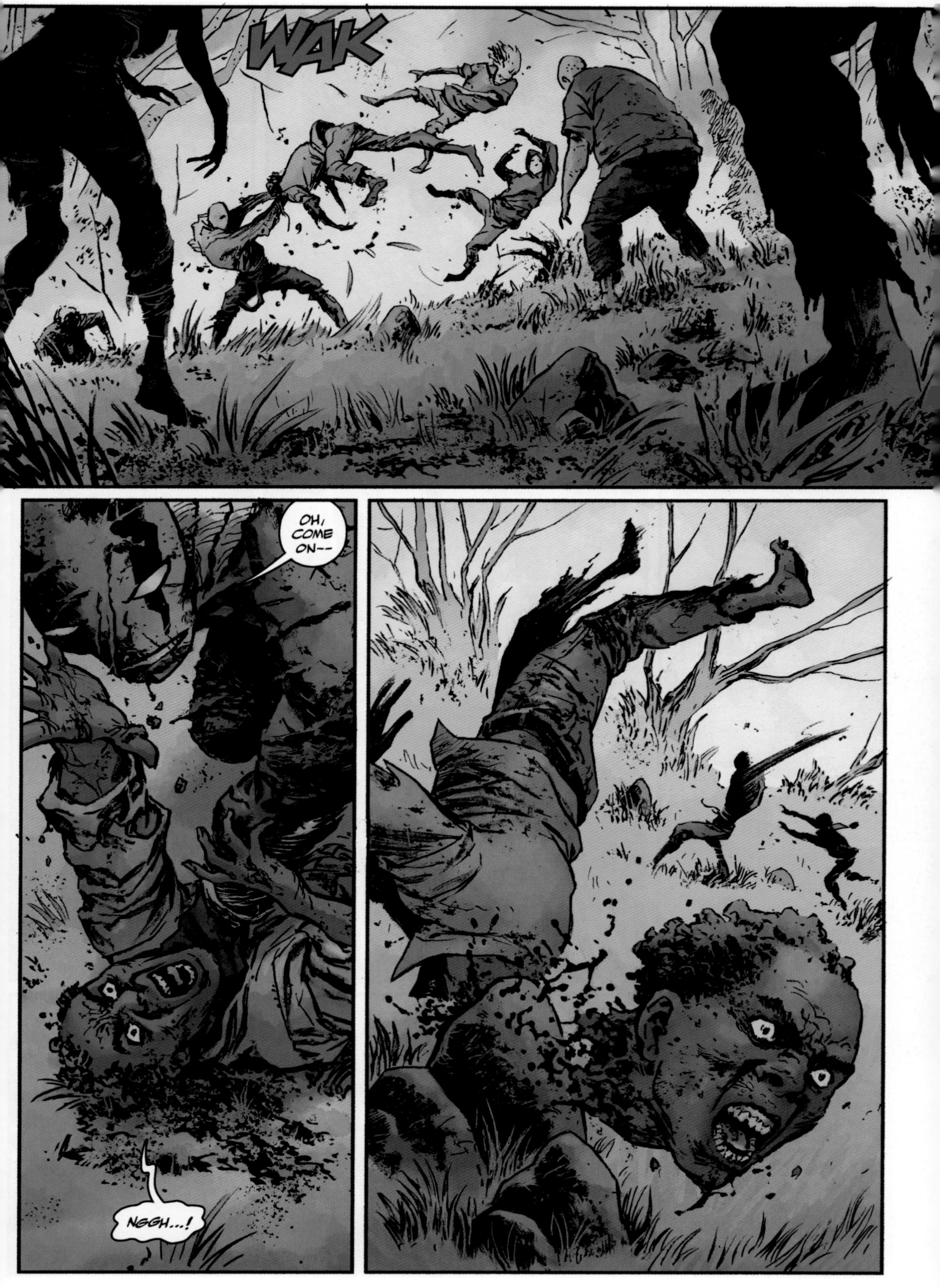
WAK
OH, COME ON--
NGGH...!

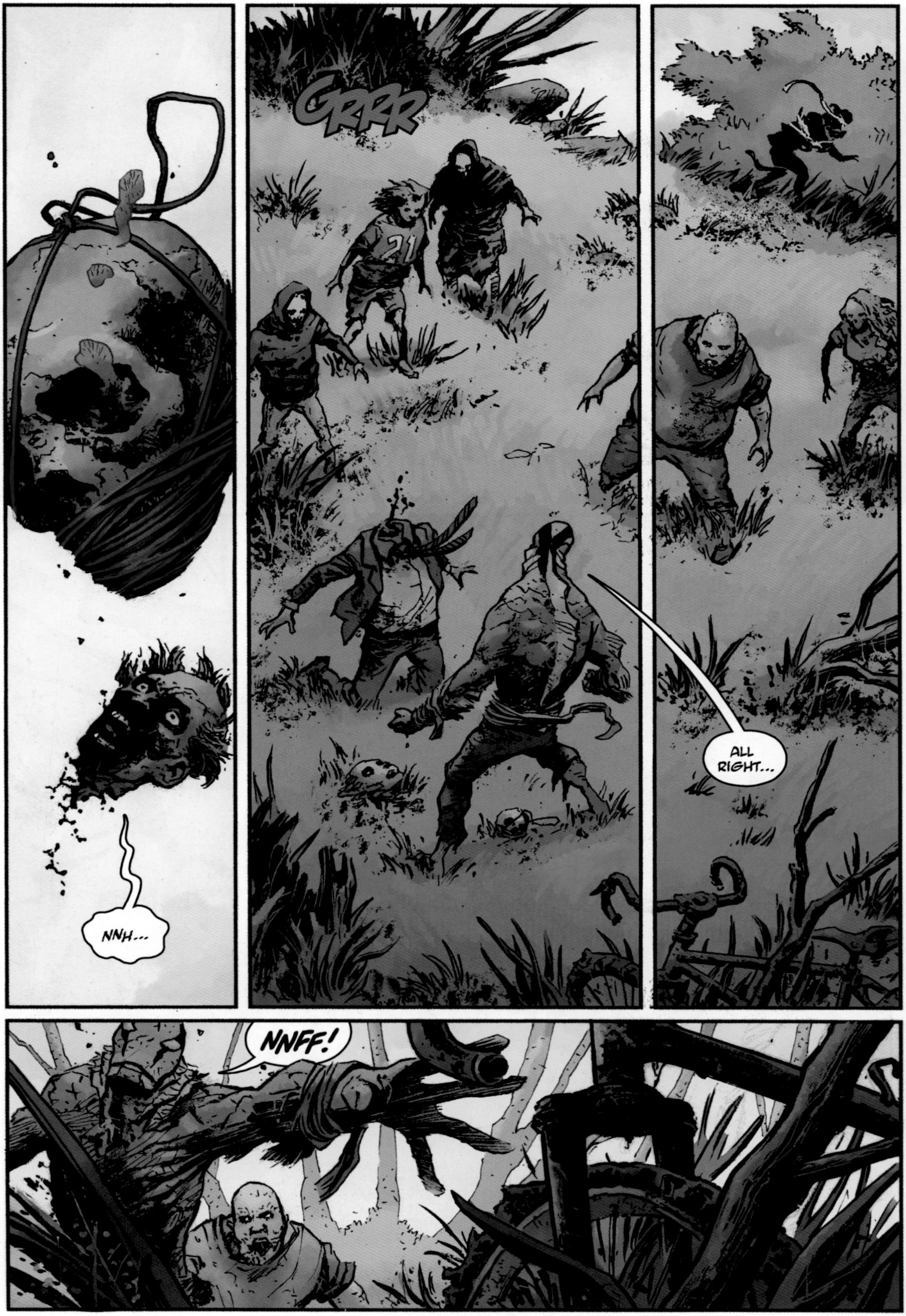
NNH...
GRRR
ALL RIGHT...
NNFF!

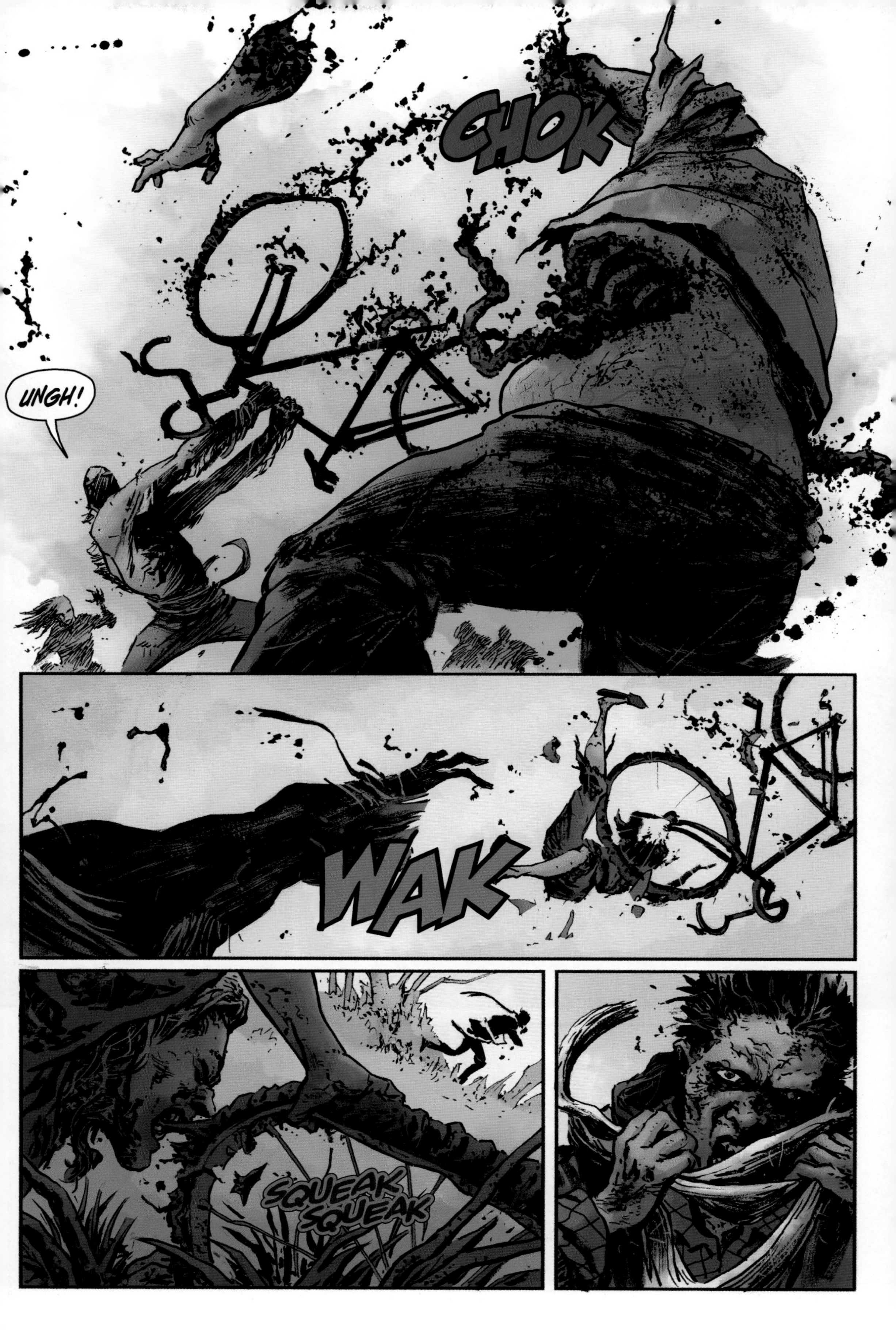
CHOK
UNGH!
WAK
SQUEAK
SQUEAK

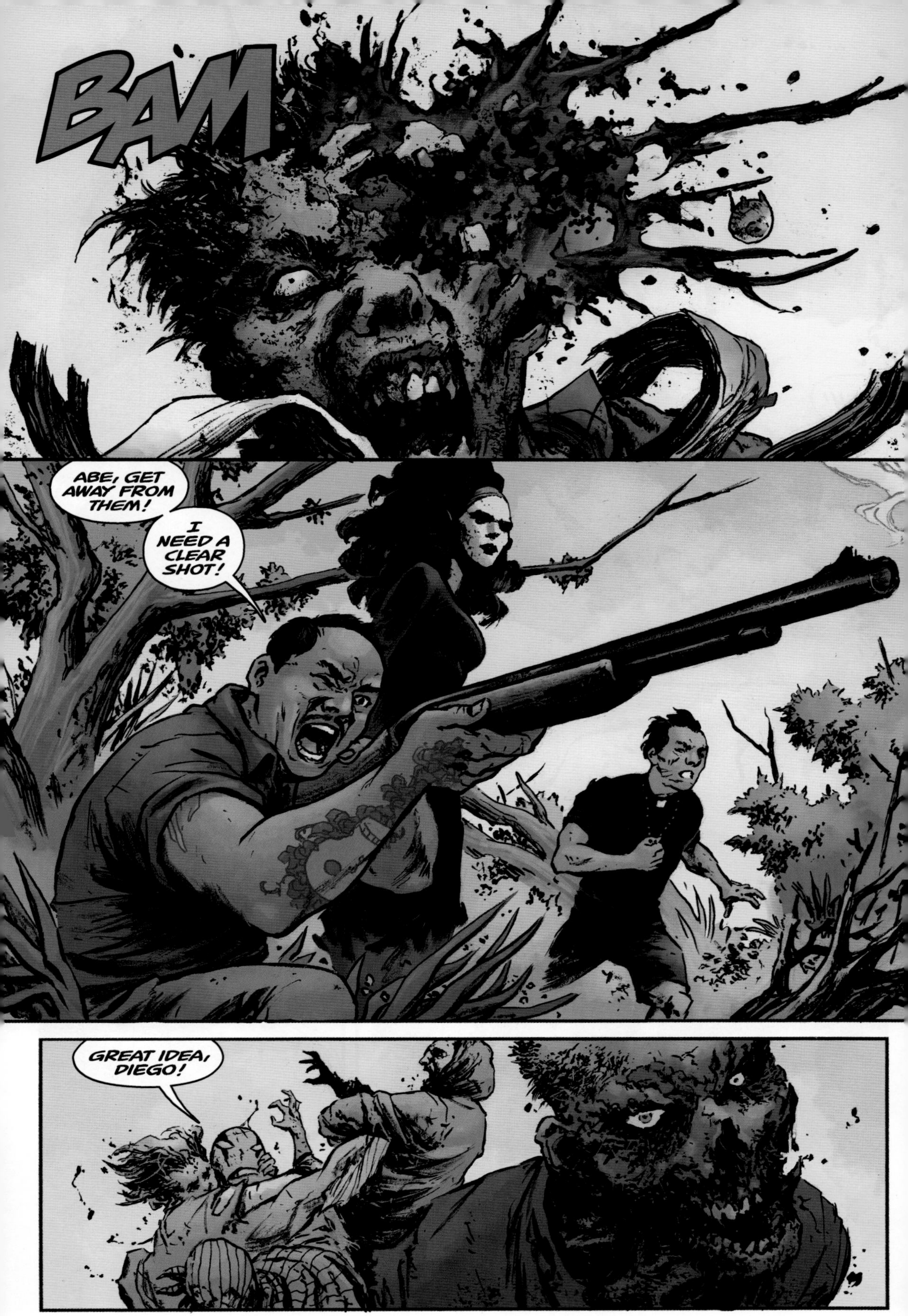
BAM
ABE, GET AWAY FROM THEM!
I NEED A CLEAR SHOT!
GREAT IDEA, DIEGO!

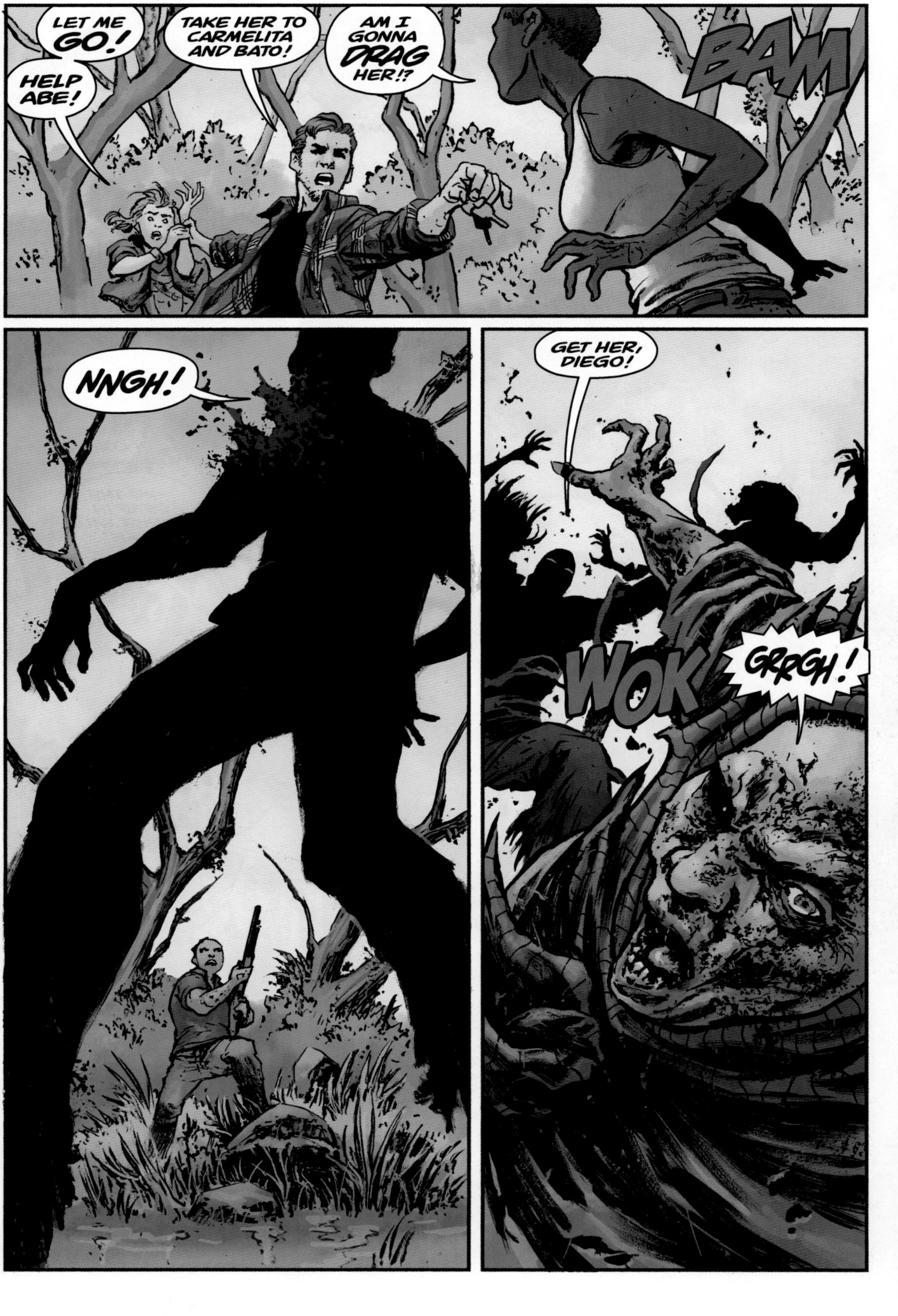
LET ME GO!
HELP ABE!
TAKE HER TO CARMELITA AND BATO!
AM I GONNA DRAG HER!?
BAM
NNGH!
GET HER, DIEGO!
WOK
GRRGH!

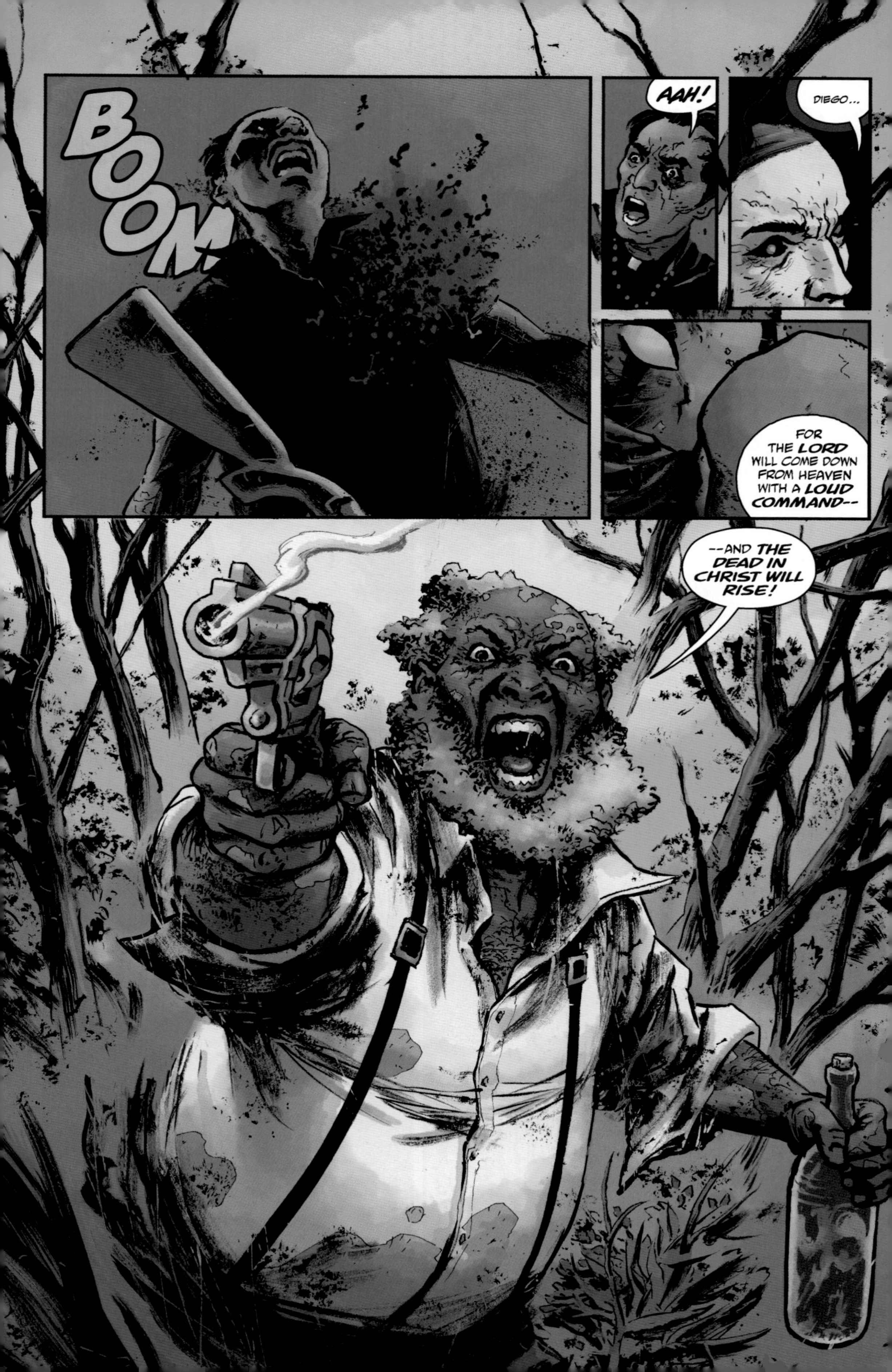
BOOM
AAH!
DIEGO...
FOR THE LORD WILL COME DOWN FROM HEAVEN WITH A LOUD COMMAND--
--AND THE DEAD IN CHRIST WILL RISE!

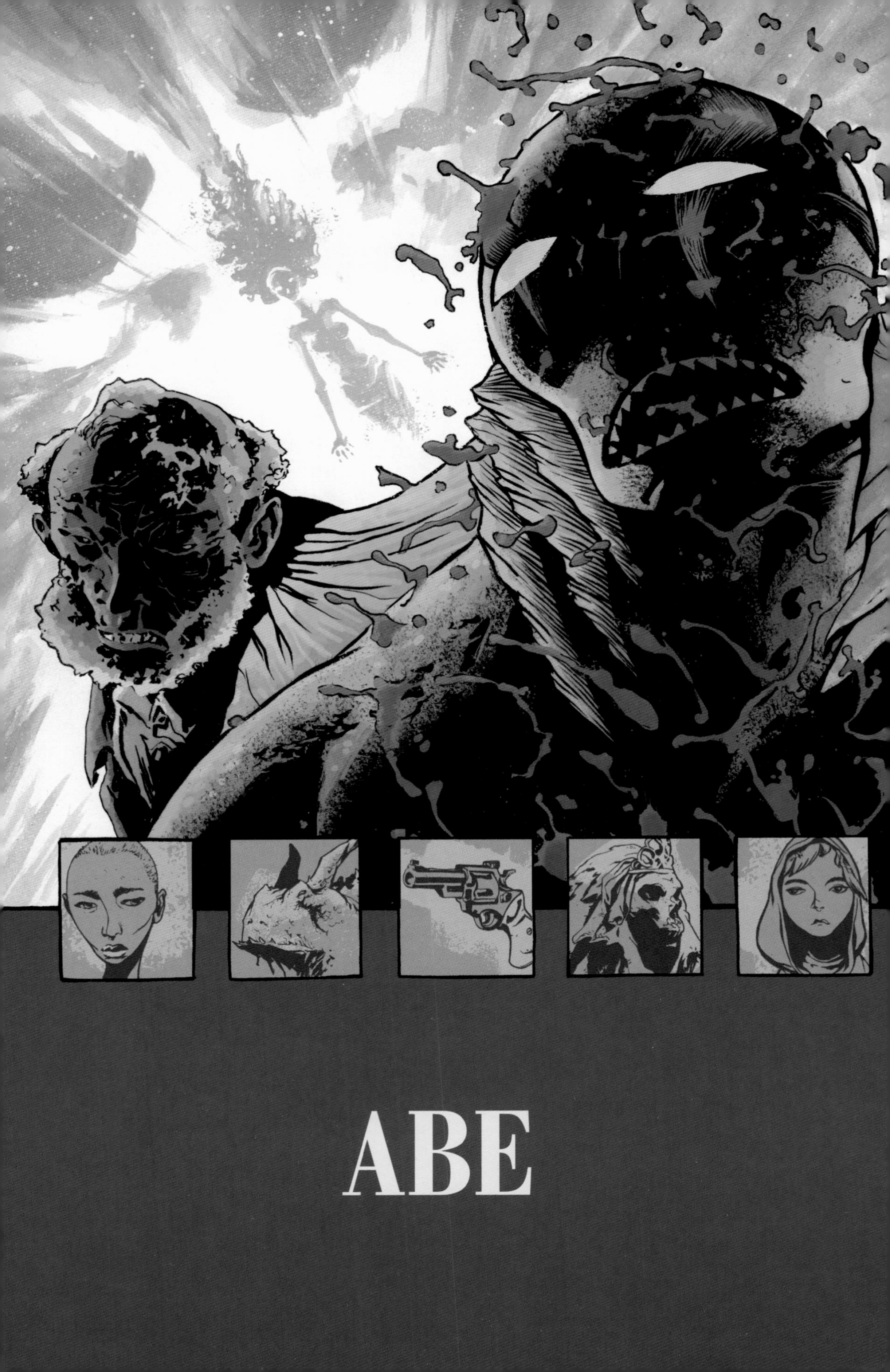

ABE

Abe Sapien was an agent with the BPRD for over twenty
years before uncovering his origins as a Civil War–era
scientist transformed by an undersea relic. As strange
creatures spread across the earth, questions arose about
similarities between Abe and the new monsters. Running
from those suspicions, Abe took up with a Santa Muerte
cult in Texas, settling in a peaceful coastal town harboring
horrible secrets . . .

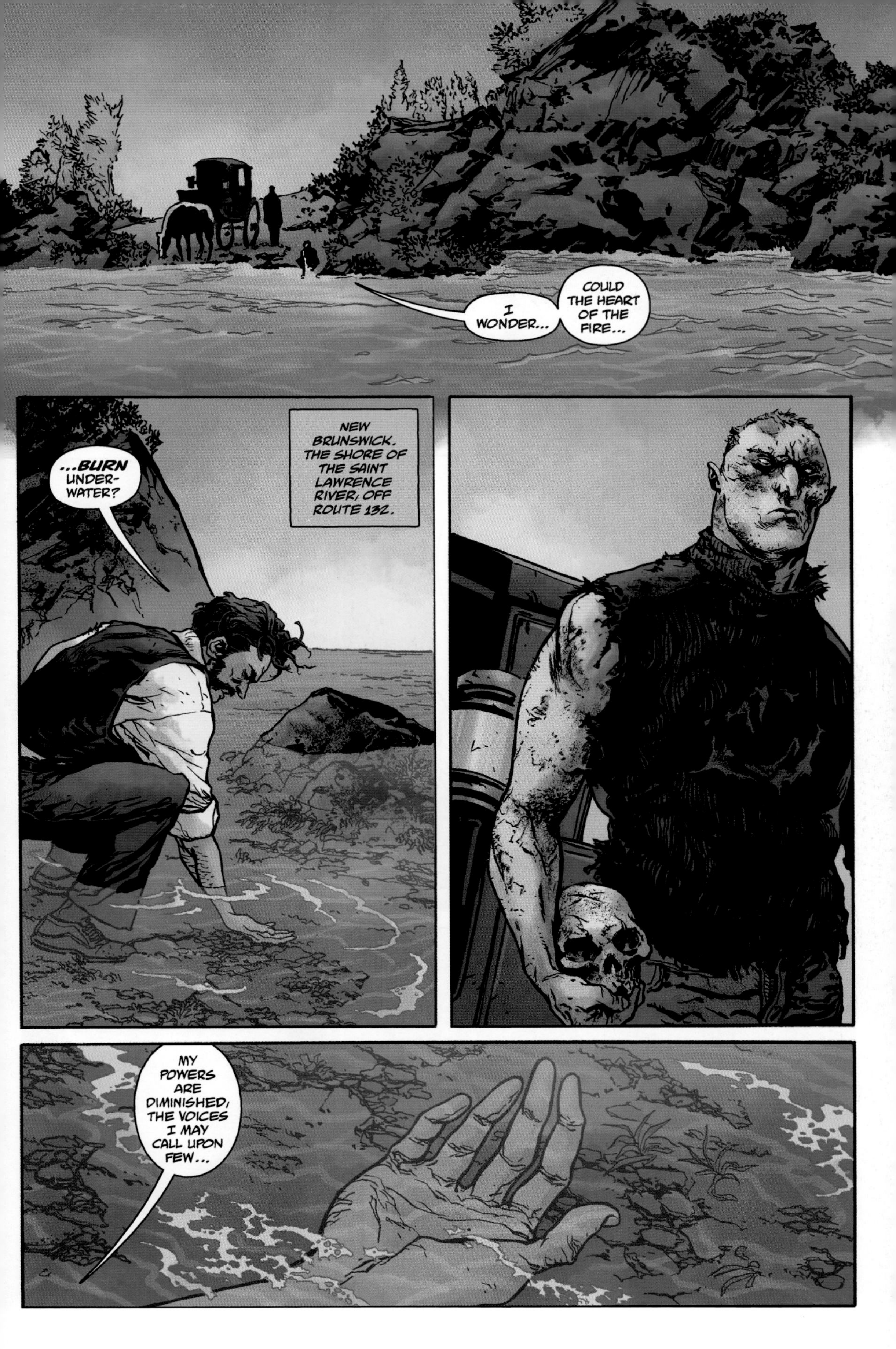
I WONDER...
COULD THE HEART OF THE FIRE...
NEW BRUNSWICK. THE SHORE OF THE SAINT LAWRENCE RIVER, OFF ROUTE 132.
...BURN UNDER-WATER?
MY POWERS ARE DIMINISHED, THE VOICES I MAY CALL UPON FEW...

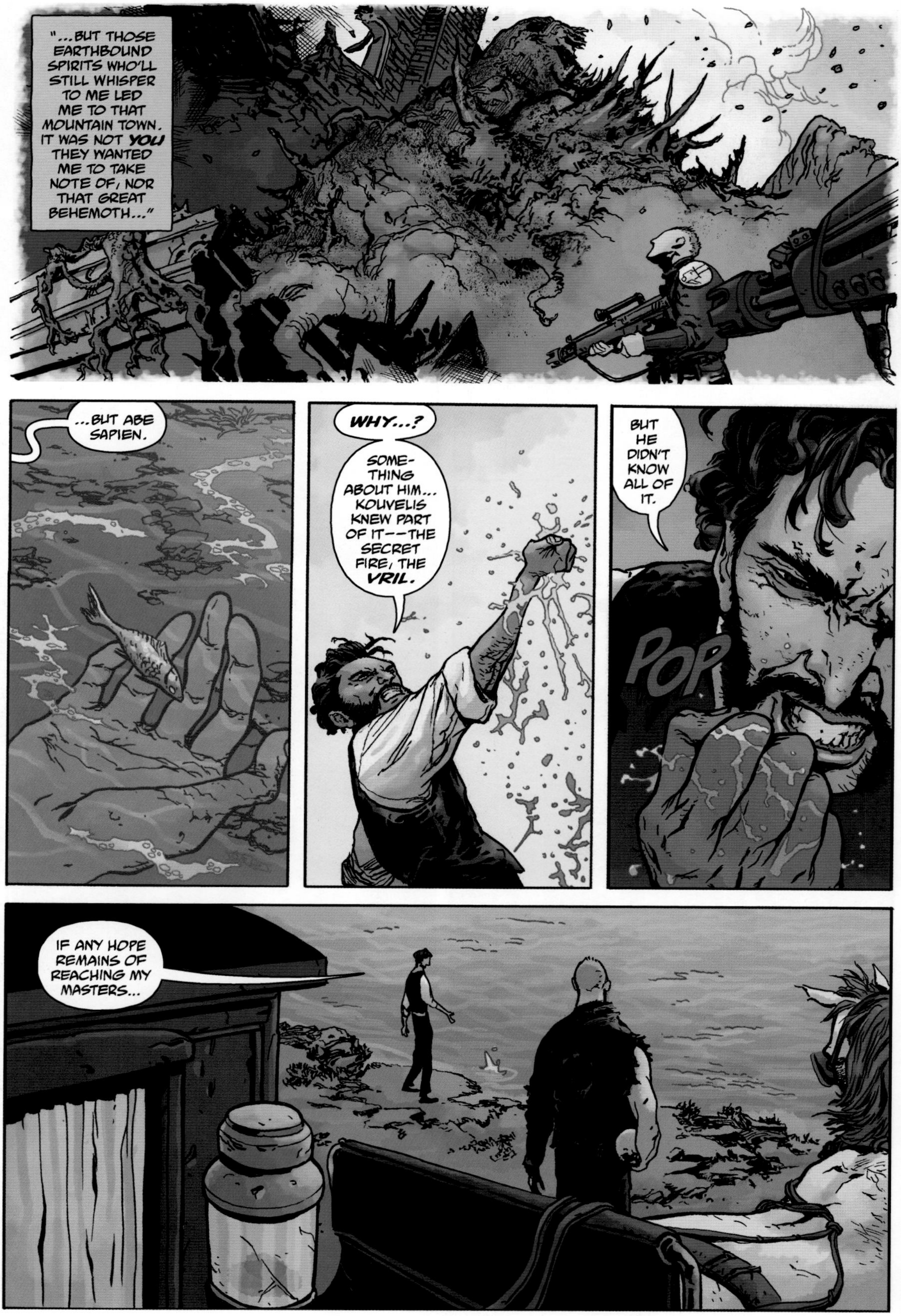
"...BUT THOSE EARTHBOUND SPIRITS WHO'LL STILL WHISPER TO ME LED ME TO THAT MOUNTAIN TOWN. IT WAS NOT **YOU** THEY WANTED ME TO TAKE NOTE OF, NOR THAT GREAT BEHEMOTH..."
...BUT ABE SAPIEN.
WHY...?
SOMETHING ABOUT HIM... KOUVELIS KNEW PART OF IT--THE SECRET FIRE, THE **VRIL.**
BUT HE DIDN'T KNOW ALL OF IT.
POP
IF ANY HOPE REMAINS OF REACHING MY MASTERS...

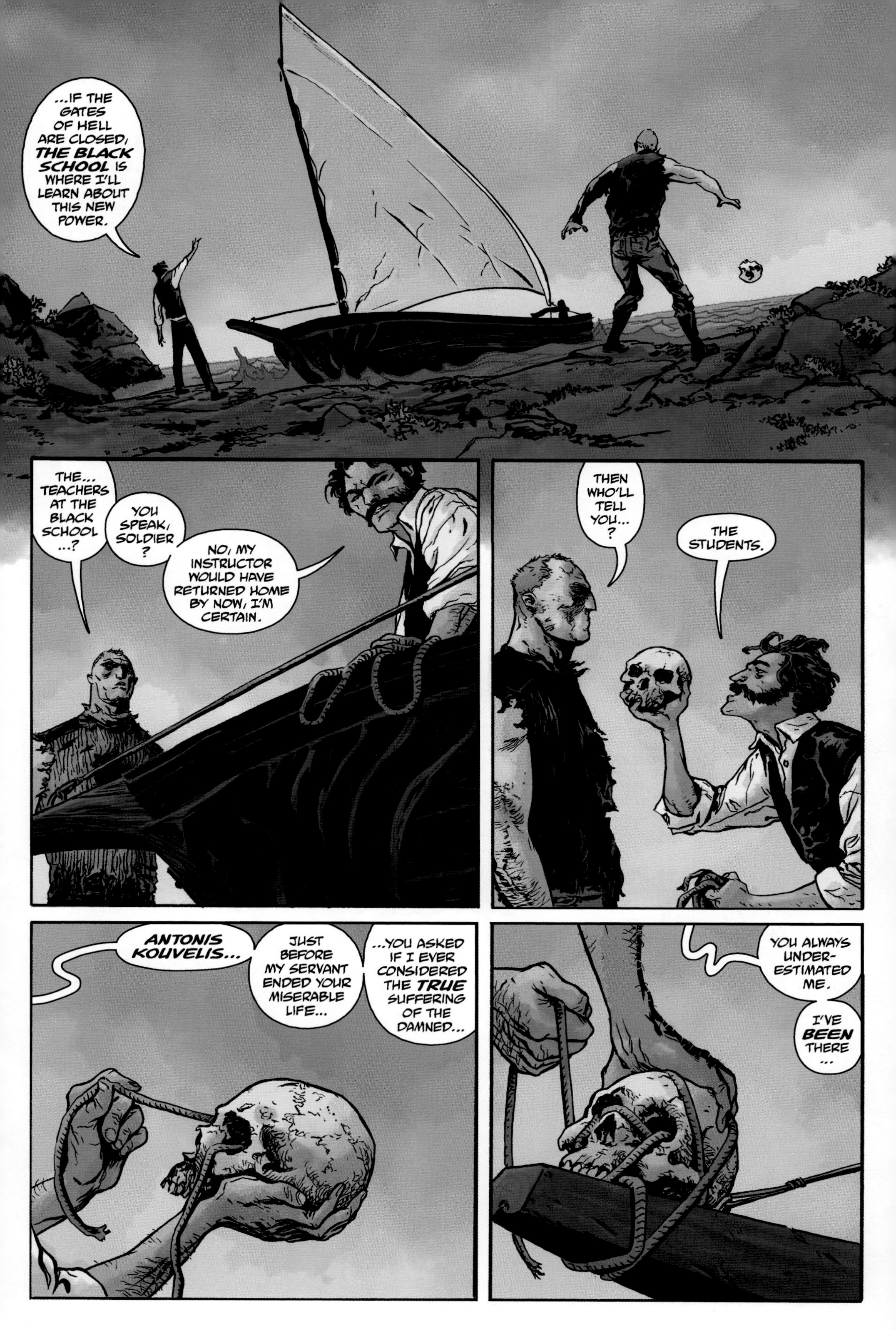
...IF THE GATES OF HELL ARE CLOSED, **THE BLACK SCHOOL** IS WHERE I'LL LEARN ABOUT THIS NEW POWER.
THE... TEACHERS AT THE BLACK SCHOOL ...?
YOU SPEAK, SOLDIER ?
NO, MY INSTRUCTOR WOULD HAVE RETURNED HOME BY NOW, I'M CERTAIN.
THEN WHO'LL TELL YOU... ?
THE STUDENTS.
ANTONIS KOUVELIS...
JUST BEFORE MY SERVANT ENDED YOUR MISERABLE LIFE...
...YOU ASKED IF I EVER CONSIDERED THE ***TRUE*** SUFFERING OF THE DAMNED...
YOU ALWAYS UNDER-ESTIMATED ME.
I'VE ***BEEN*** THERE ...

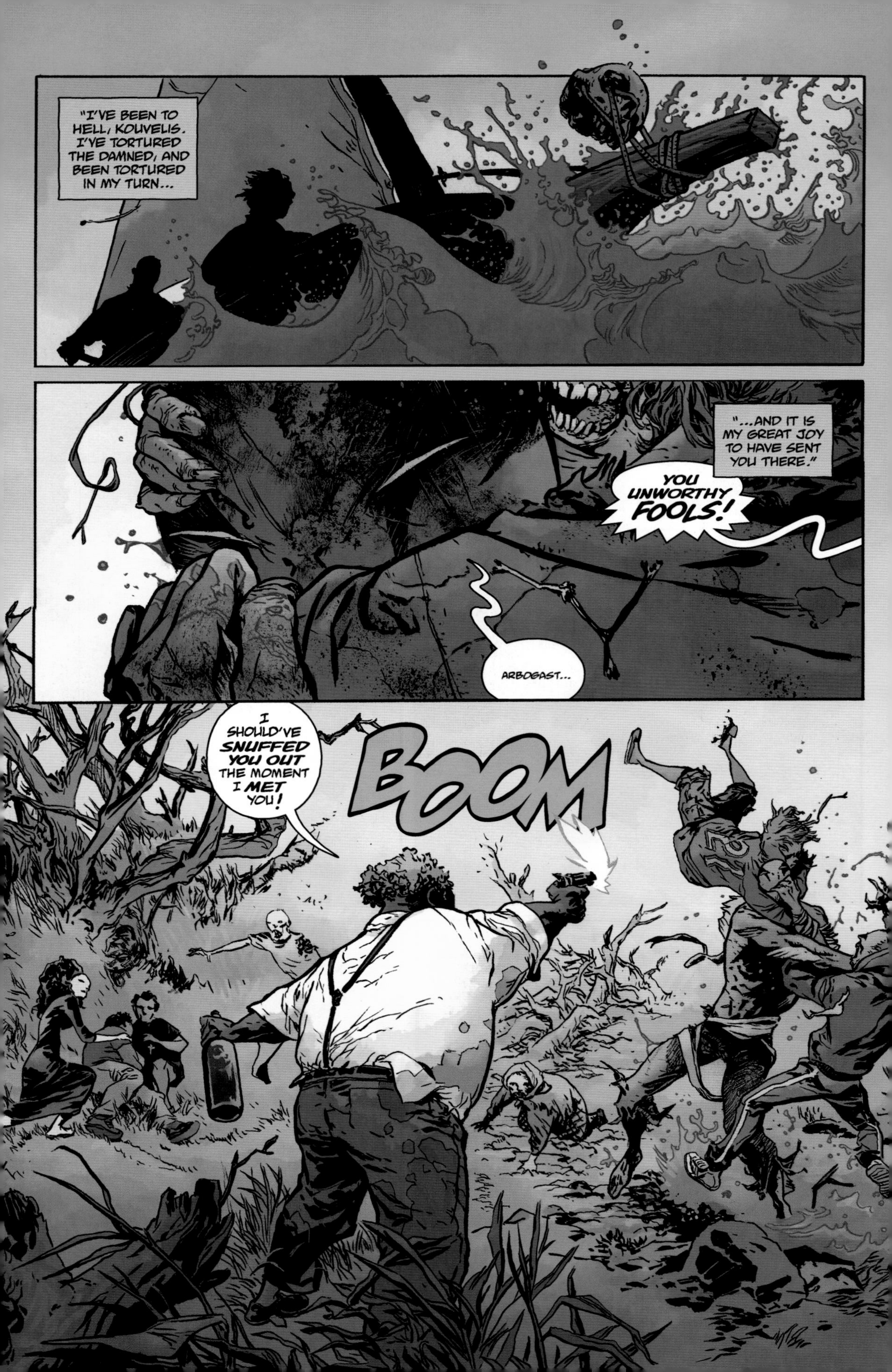
"I'VE BEEN TO HELL, KOUVELIS. I'VE TORTURED THE DAMNED, AND BEEN TORTURED IN MY TURN...
"...AND IT IS MY GREAT JOY TO HAVE SENT YOU THERE."
YOU UNWORTHY FOOLS!
ARBOGAST...
I SHOULD'VE SNUFFED YOU OUT THE MOMENT I MET YOU!
BOOM

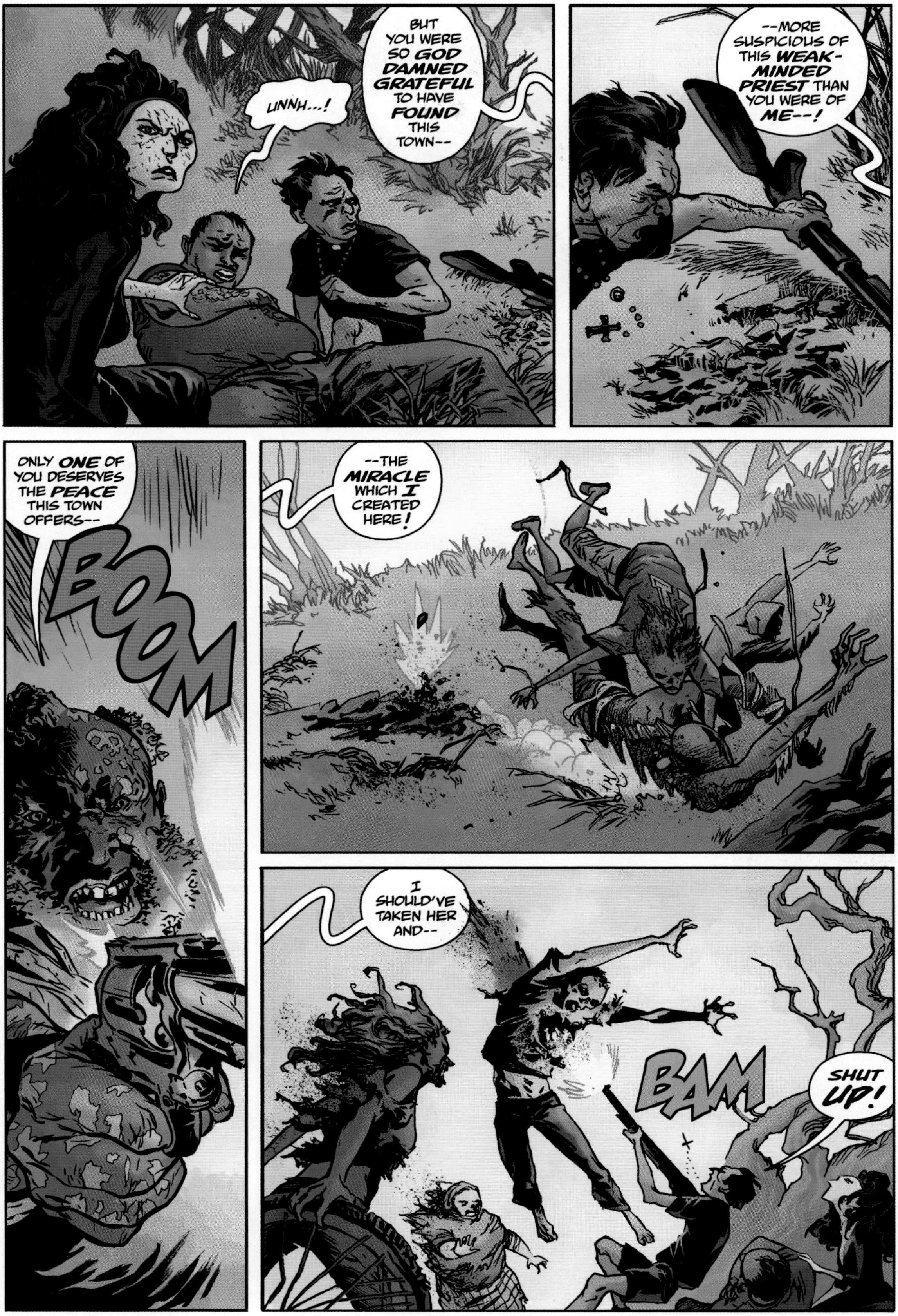
UNNH...!
BUT YOU WERE SO GOD DAMNED GRATEFUL TO HAVE FOUND THIS TOWN--
--MORE SUSPICIOUS OF THIS WEAK-MINDED PRIEST THAN YOU WERE OF ME--!
ONLY ONE OF YOU DESERVES THE PEACE THIS TOWN OFFERS--
BOOM
--THE MIRACLE WHICH I CREATED HERE!
I SHOULD'VE TAKEN HER AND--
BAM
SHUT UP!

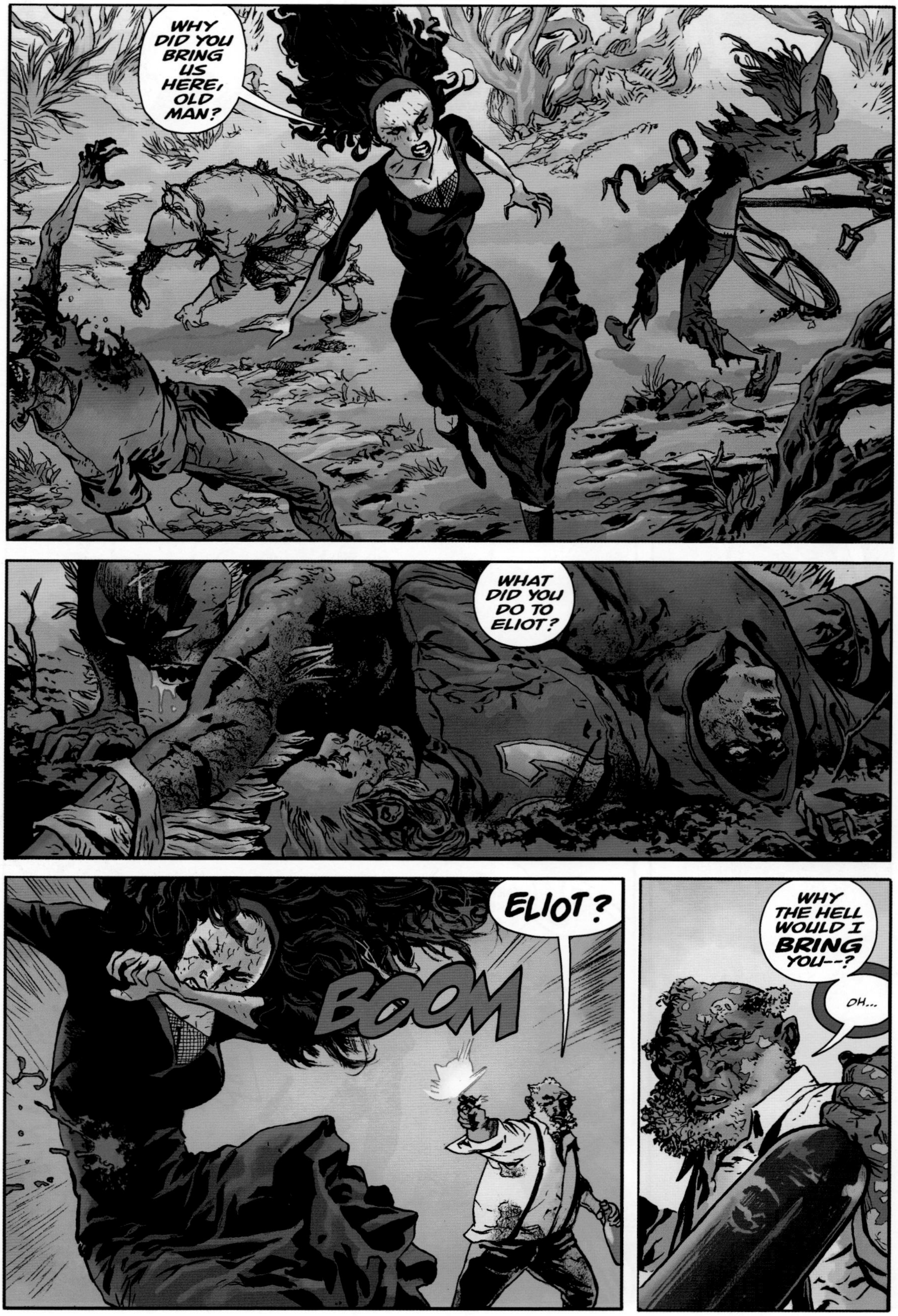
WHY DID YOU BRING US HERE, OLD MAN?
WHAT DID YOU DO TO ELIOT?
ELIOT?
BOOM
WHY THE HELL WOULD I BRING YOU--?
OH...

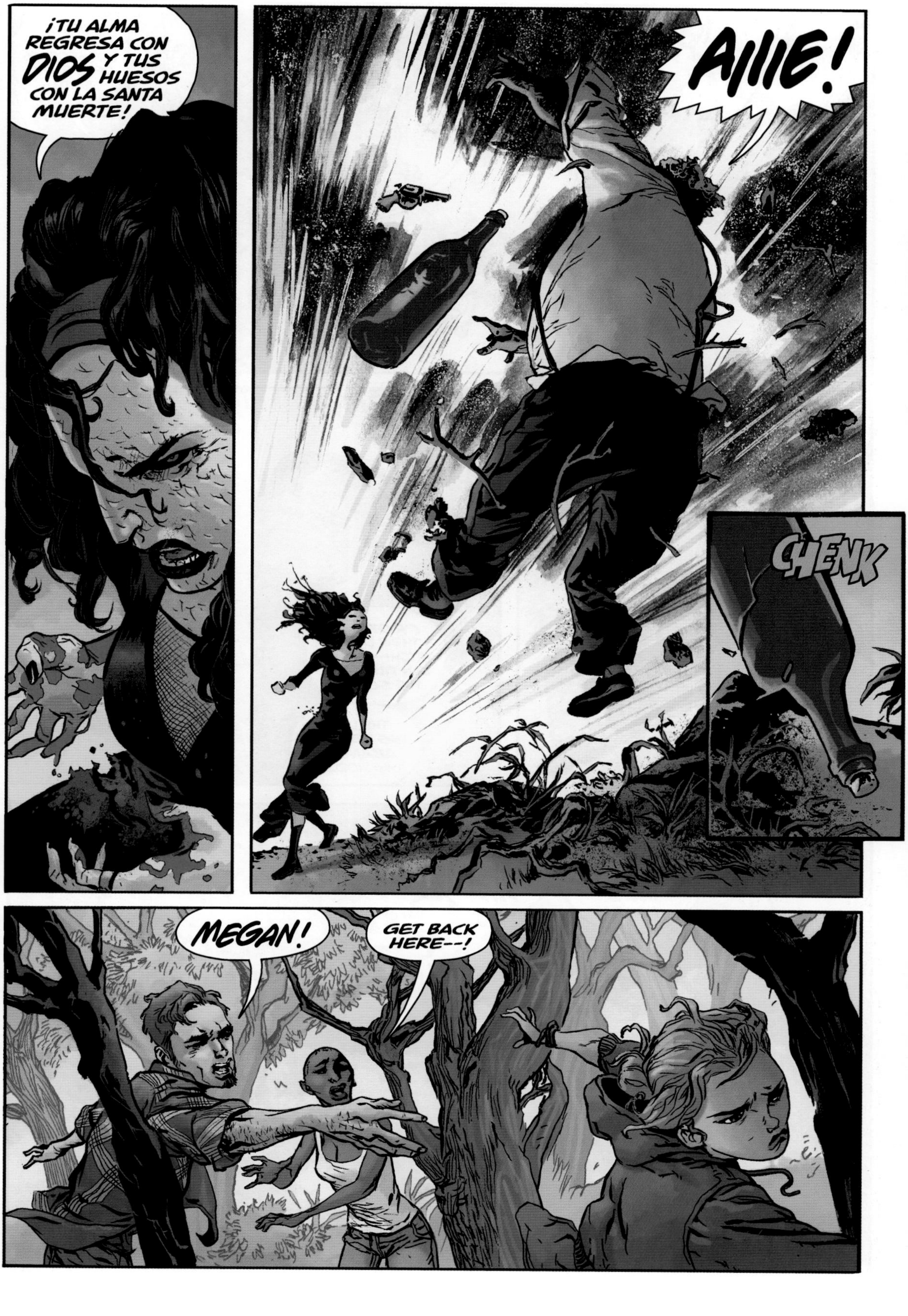
¡TU ALMA REGRESA CON DIOS Y TUS HUESOS CON LA SANTA MUERTE!
AIIIE!
CHENK
MEGAN!
GET BACK HERE--!

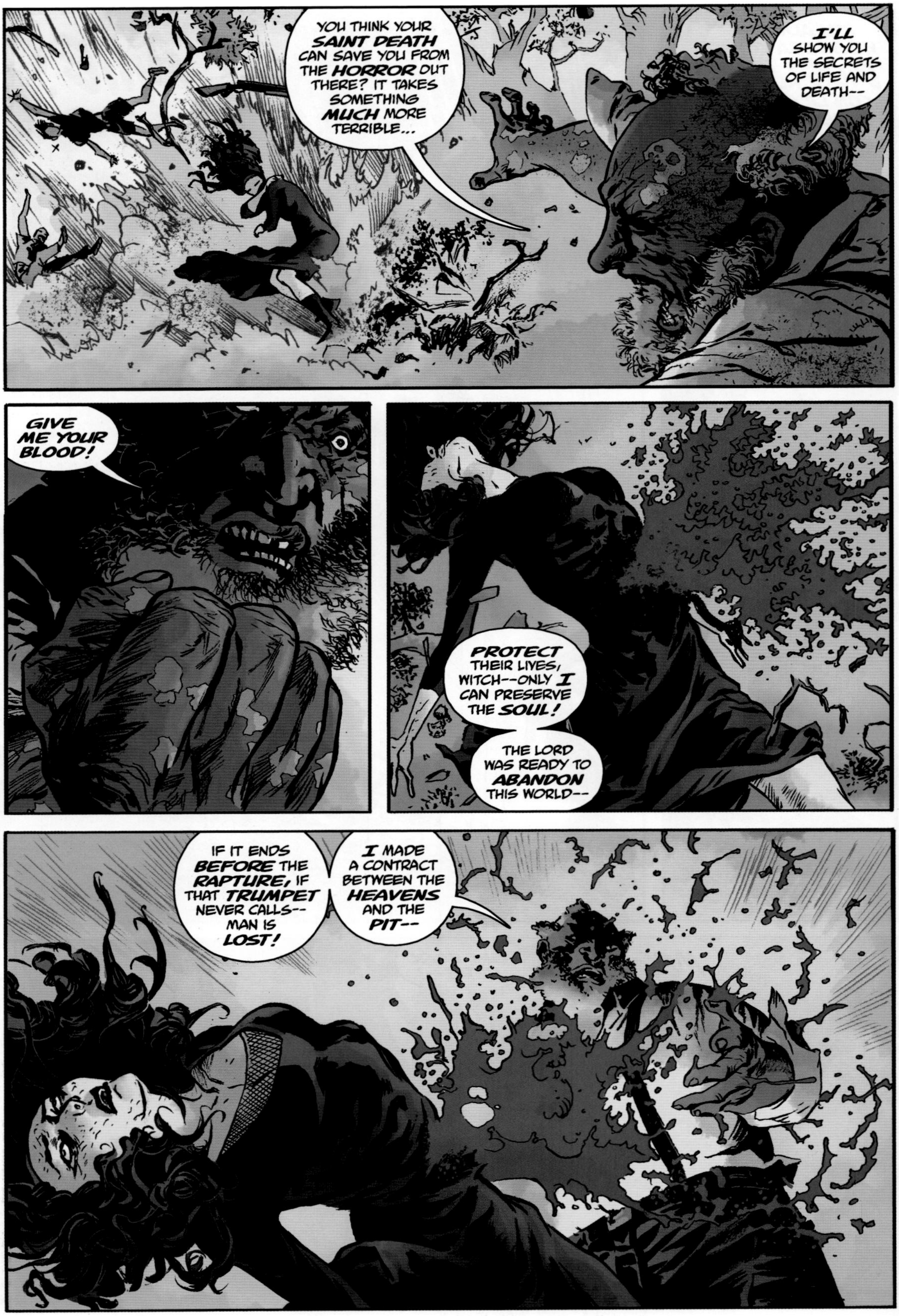
YOU THINK YOUR SAINT DEATH CAN SAVE YOU FROM THE HORROR OUT THERE? IT TAKES SOMETHING MUCH MORE TERRIBLE...
I'LL SHOW YOU THE SECRETS OF LIFE AND DEATH--
GIVE ME YOUR BLOOD!
PROTECT THEIR LIVES, WITCH--ONLY I CAN PRESERVE THE SOUL!
THE LORD WAS READY TO ABANDON THIS WORLD--
IF IT ENDS BEFORE THE RAPTURE, IF THAT TRUMPET NEVER CALLS--MAN IS LOST!
I MADE A CONTRACT BETWEEN THE HEAVENS AND THE PIT--

I HAVEN'T ONLY SAVED **THIS** TOWN.

I'VE EMBRACED A POWER *YOU'RE* TOO TIMID TO FACE-- RAISING *THE DEAD* TO DRAW GOD'S ATTENTION SO THE *WORTHY* WILL BE CAUGHT UP TOGETHER IN THE CLOUDS--

GRACE...

GRACE-- *YOU* ARE WORTHY...

YOU HAVE SEEN HELL FIRSTHAND.

WE SUFFER--

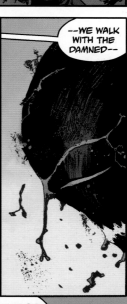

--WE WALK WITH THE DAMNED--

WHY, GRACE!?

WHY NOT BE *REUNITED* WITH *THOSE WE HAVE LOST!*

THOSE WE *LOVE!*

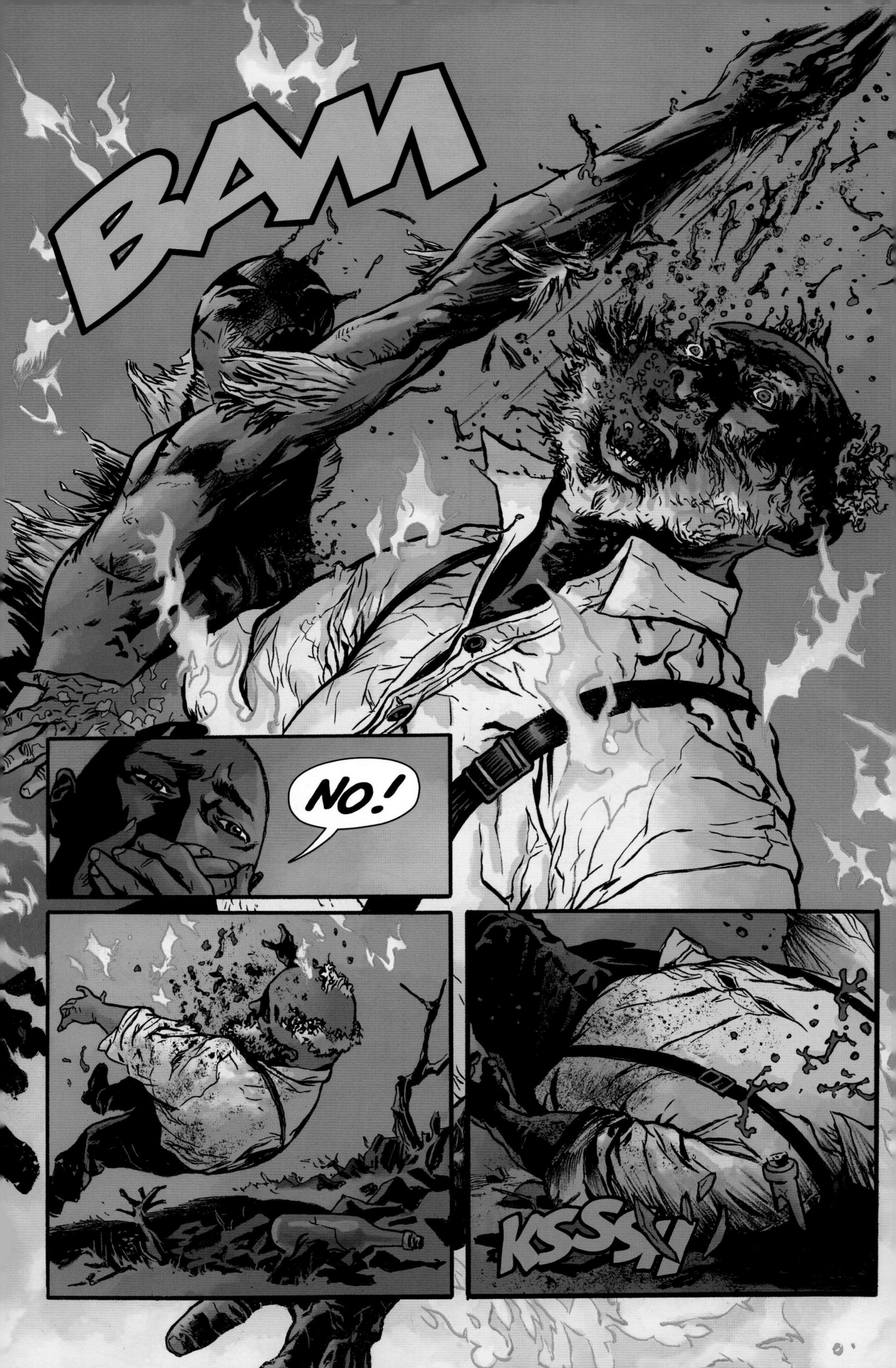
BAM
NO!
KSSSH!

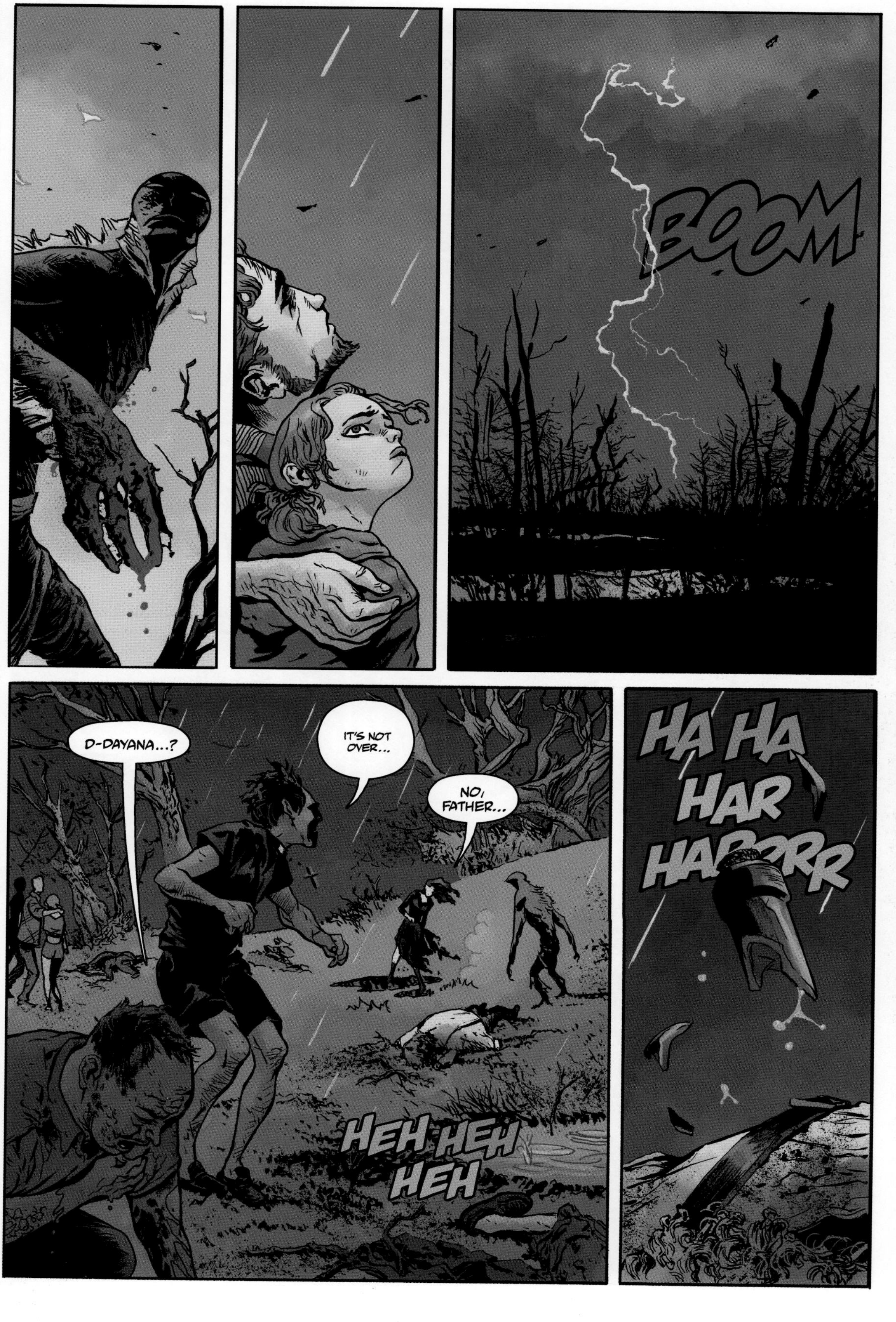
BOOM
D-DAYANA...?
IT'S NOT OVER...
NO, FATHER...
HEH HEH HEH
HA HA HAR HARRRR

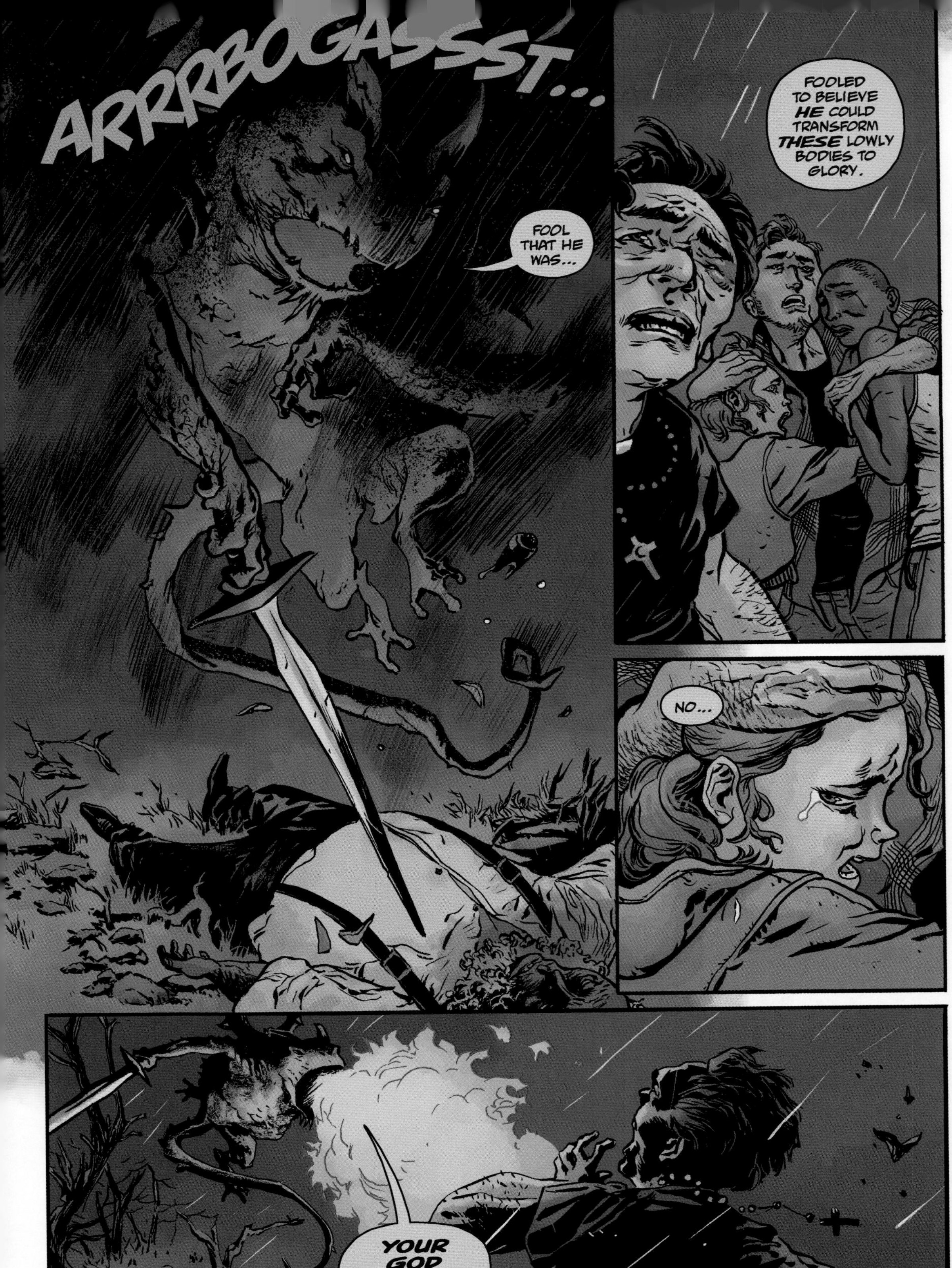
ARRRBOGASSST...
FOOL THAT HE WAS...
FOOLED TO BELIEVE HE COULD TRANSFORM THESE LOWLY BODIES TO GLORY.
NO...
YOUR GOD FORSAKES YOU!

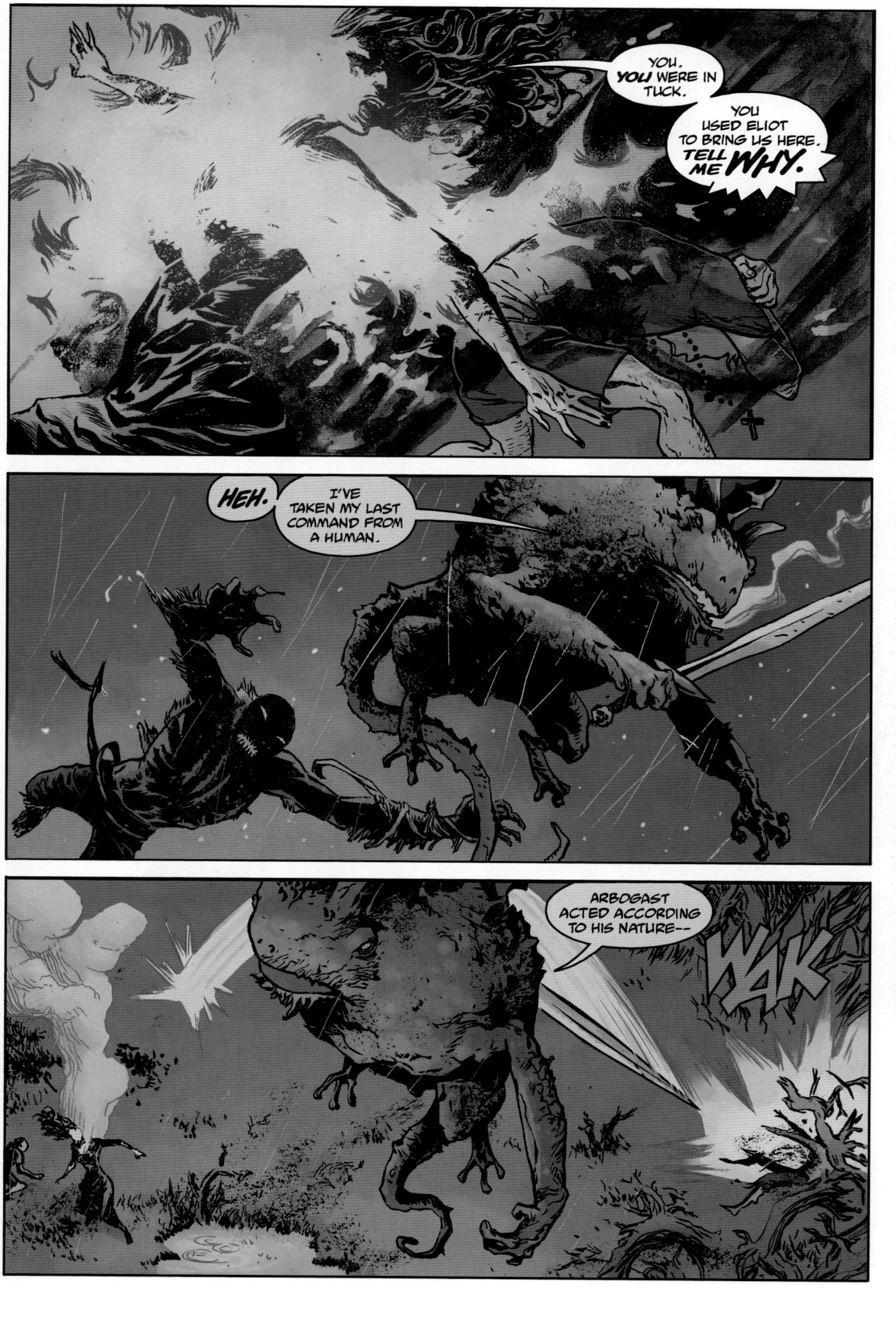

YOU. YOU WERE IN TUCK.
YOU USED ELIOT TO BRING US HERE. TELL ME WHY.
HEH.
I'VE TAKEN MY LAST COMMAND FROM A HUMAN.
ARBOGAST ACTED ACCORDING TO HIS NATURE--
YAK

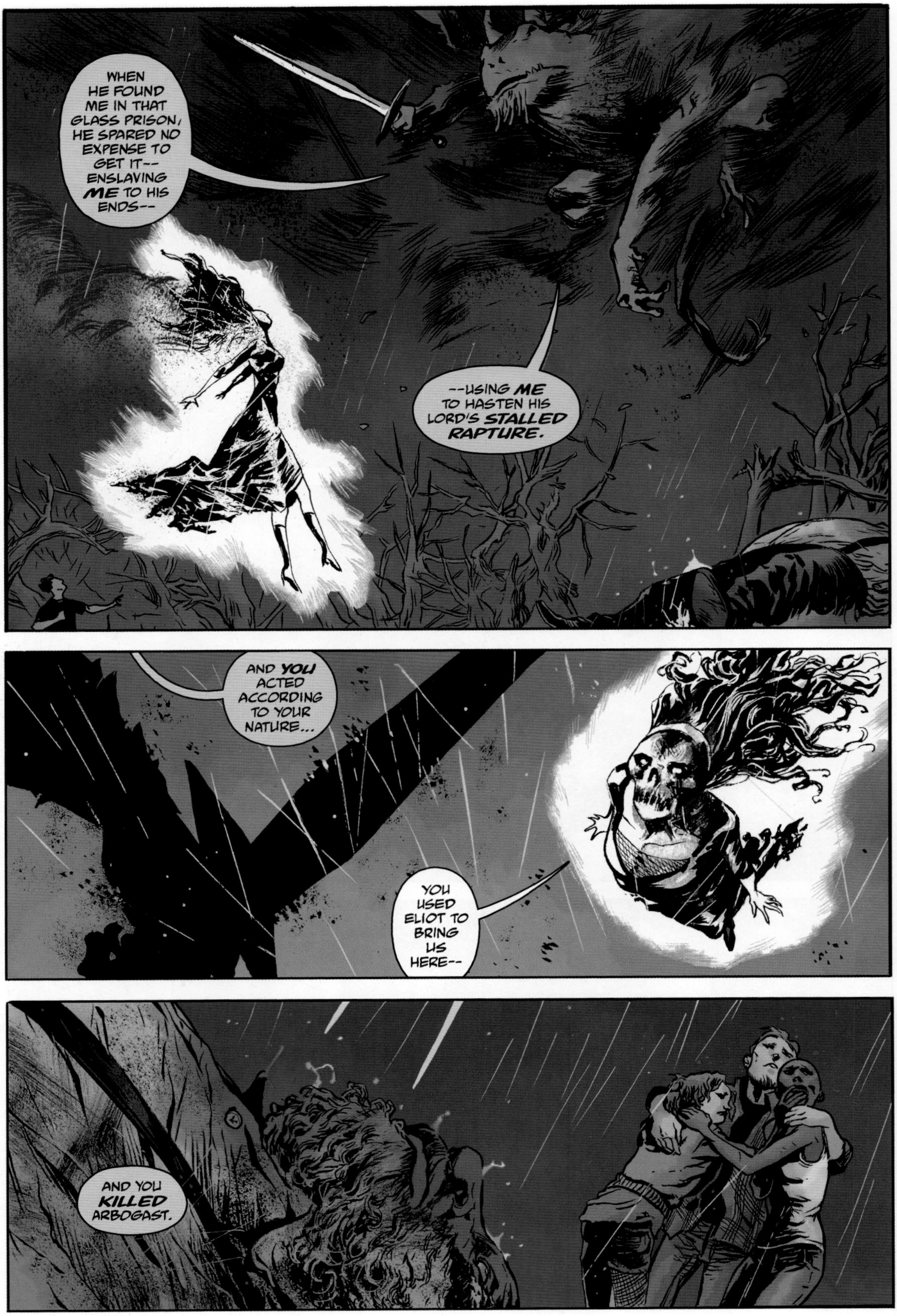
WHEN HE FOUND ME IN THAT GLASS PRISON, HE SPARED NO EXPENSE TO GET IT-- ENSLAVING **ME** TO HIS ENDS--
--USING **ME** TO HASTEN HIS LORD'S **STALLED RAPTURE.**
AND **YOU** ACTED ACCORDING TO YOUR NATURE...
YOU USED ELIOT TO BRING US HERE--
AND YOU **KILLED** ARBOGAST.

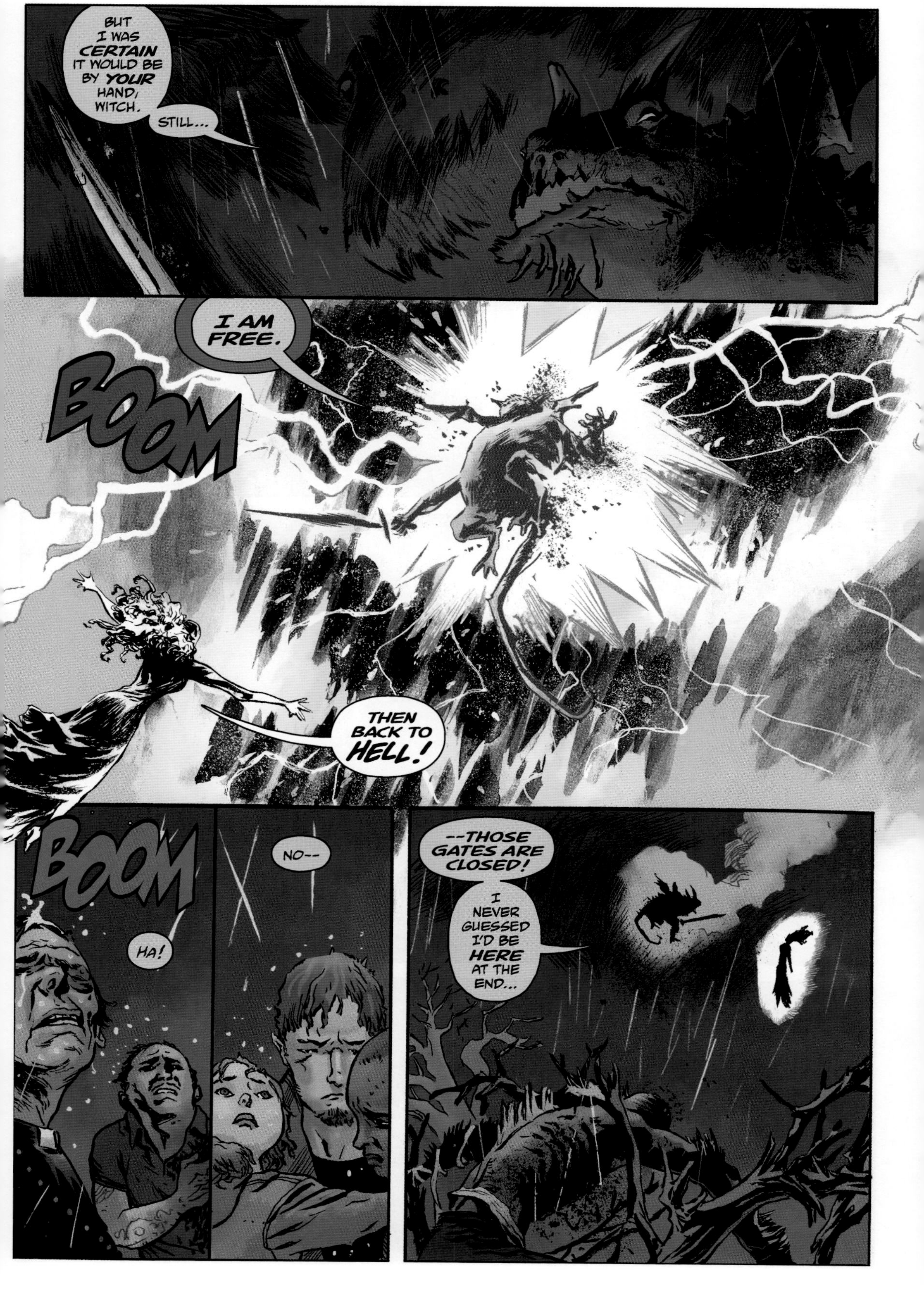

BUT I WAS CERTAIN IT WOULD BE BY YOUR HAND, WITCH.
STILL...
I AM FREE.
BOOM
THEN BACK TO HELL!
BOOM
HA!
NO--
--THOSE GATES ARE CLOSED!
I NEVER GUESSED I'D BE HERE AT THE END...

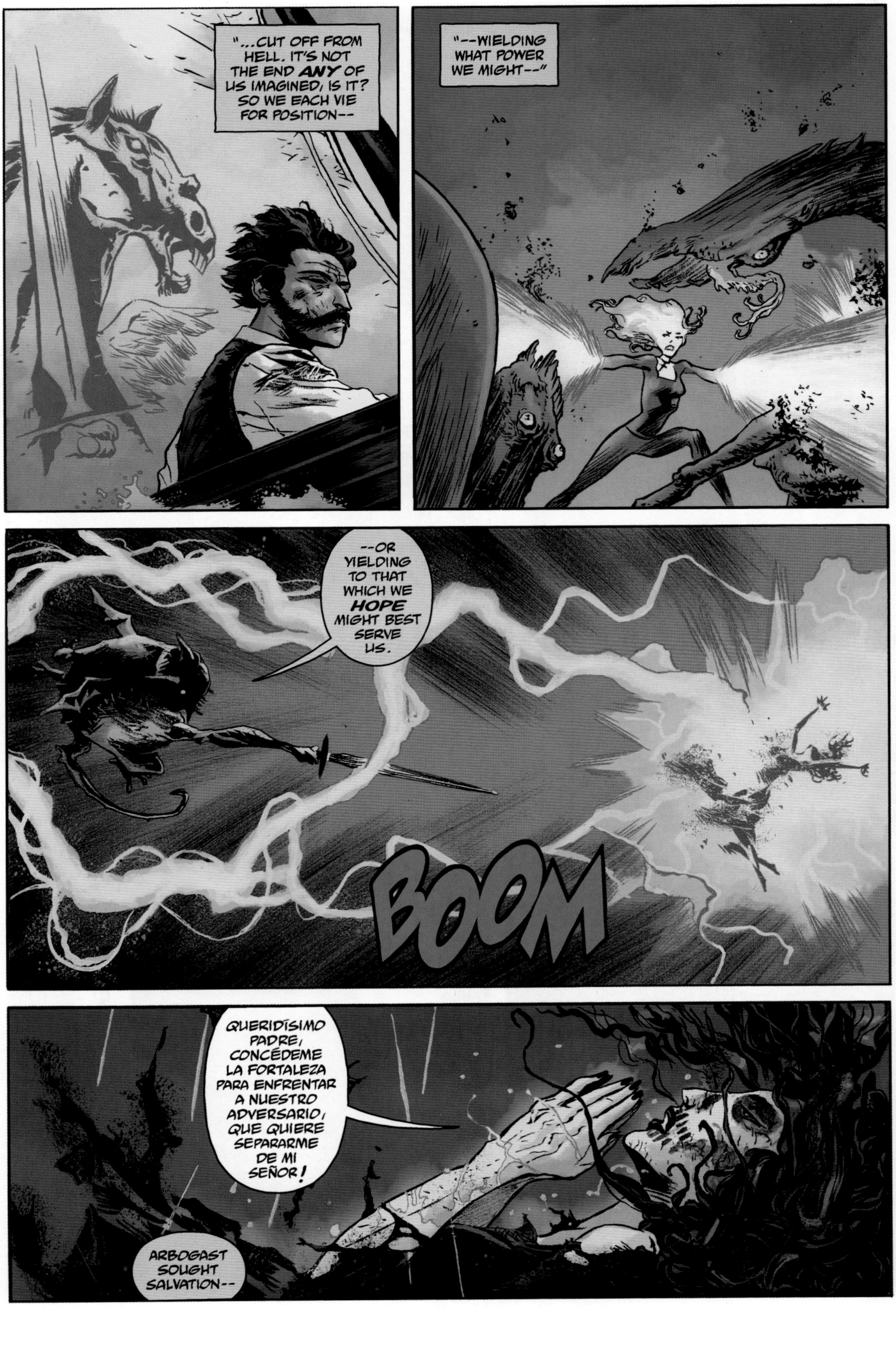
"...CUT OFF FROM HELL. IT'S NOT THE END ANY OF US IMAGINED, IS IT? SO WE EACH VIE FOR POSITION--
"--WIELDING WHAT POWER WE MIGHT--"
--OR YIELDING TO THAT WHICH WE HOPE MIGHT BEST SERVE US.
BOOM
QUERIDÍSIMO PADRE, CONCÉDEME LA FORTALEZA PARA ENFRENTAR A NUESTRO ADVERSARIO, QUE QUIERE SEPARARME DE MI SEÑOR!
ARBOGAST SOUGHT SALVATION--

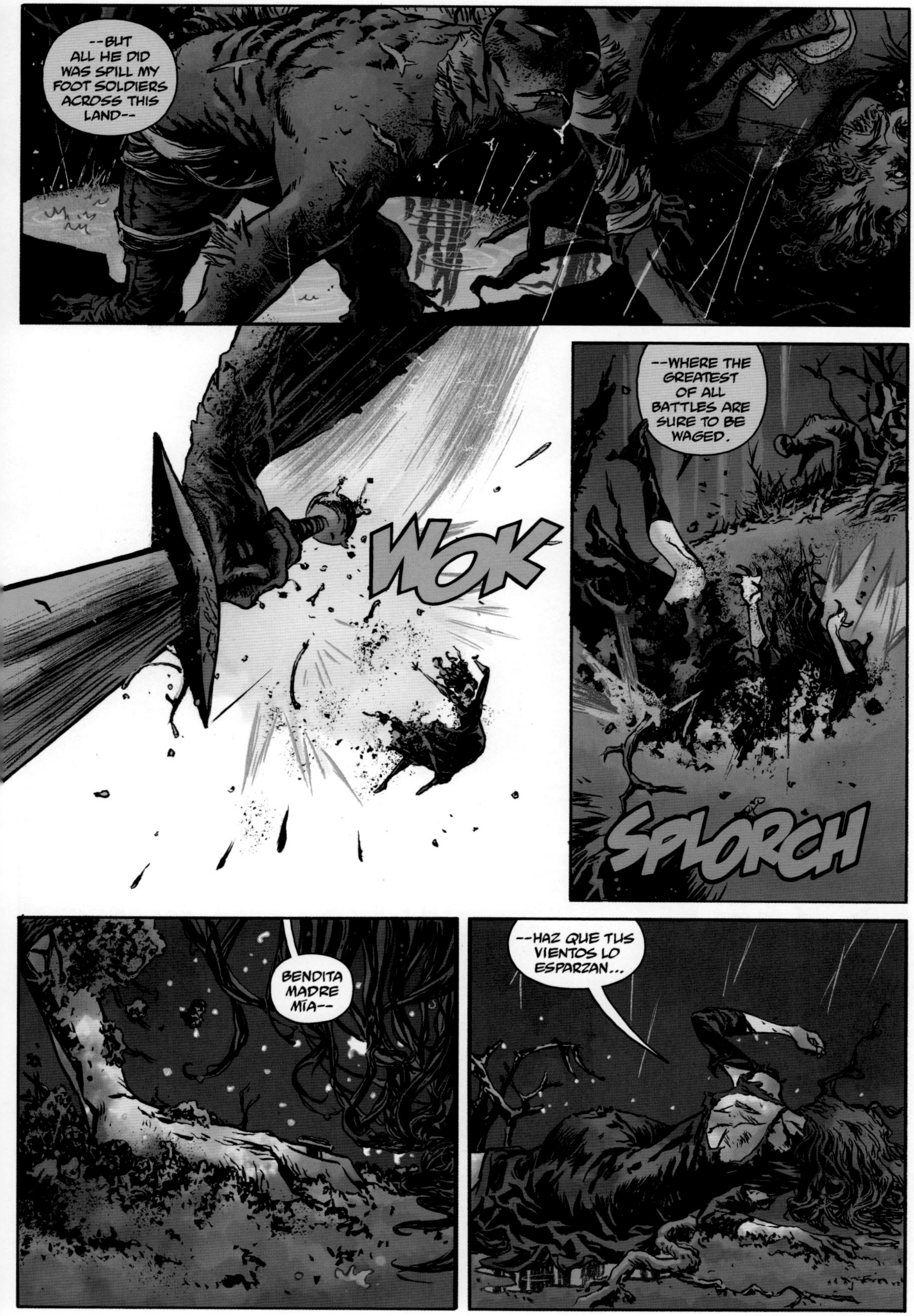
--BUT ALL HE DID WAS SPILL MY FOOT SOLDIERS ACROSS THIS LAND--
WOK
--WHERE THE GREATEST OF ALL BATTLES ARE SURE TO BE WAGED.
SPLORCH
BENDITA MADRE MÍA--
--HAZ QUE TUS VIENTOS LO ESPARZAN...

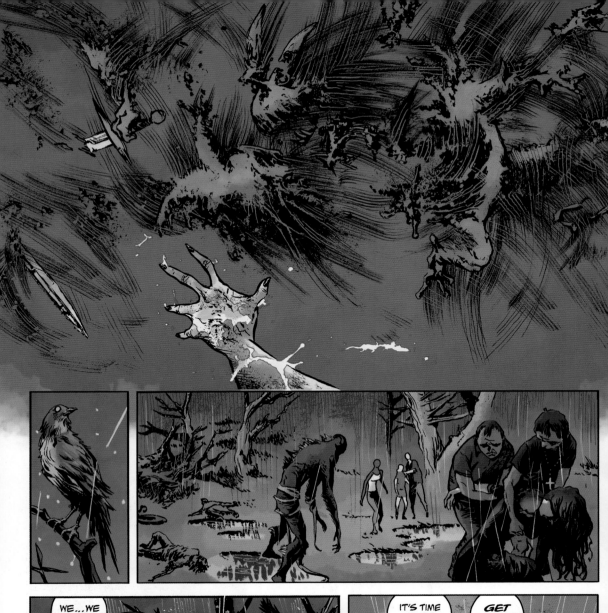

WE...WE HAVE TO GO.

IT WON'T BE SAFE HERE ANY-MORE...

IT'S TIME TO GO NORTH--

GET AWAY FROM ME!

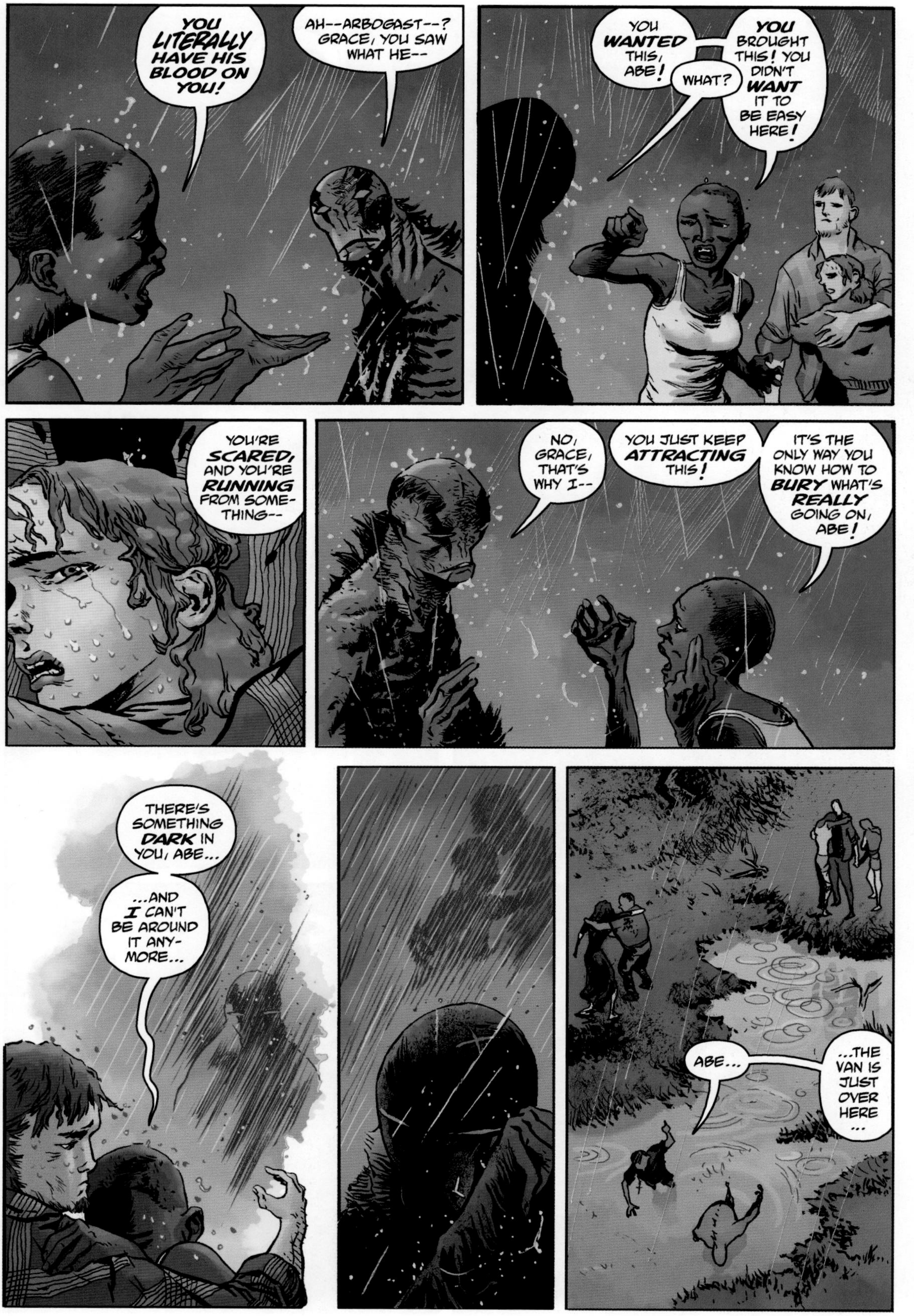
YOU LITERALLY HAVE HIS BLOOD ON YOU!
AH--ARBOGAST--? GRACE, YOU SAW WHAT HE--
YOU WANTED THIS, ABE!
WHAT?
YOU BROUGHT THIS! YOU DIDN'T WANT IT TO BE EASY HERE!
YOU'RE SCARED, AND YOU'RE RUNNING FROM SOME-THING--
NO, GRACE, THAT'S WHY I--
YOU JUST KEEP ATTRACTING THIS!
IT'S THE ONLY WAY YOU KNOW HOW TO BURY WHAT'S REALLY GOING ON, ABE!
THERE'S SOMETHING DARK IN YOU, ABE...
...AND I CAN'T BE AROUND IT ANY-MORE...
ABE...
...THE VAN IS JUST OVER HERE ...

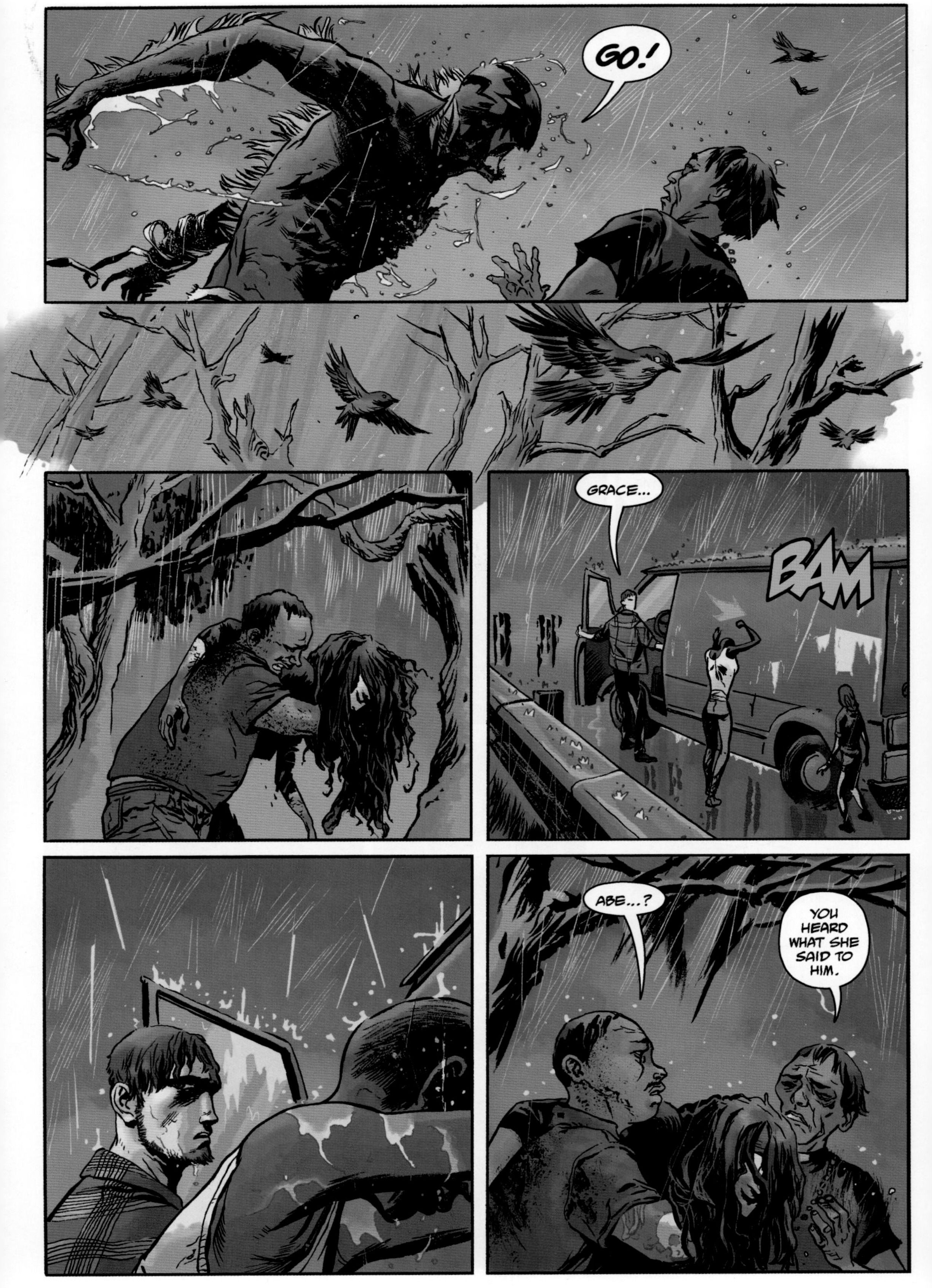
GO!
GRACE...
BAM
ABE...?
YOU HEARD WHAT SHE SAID TO HIM.

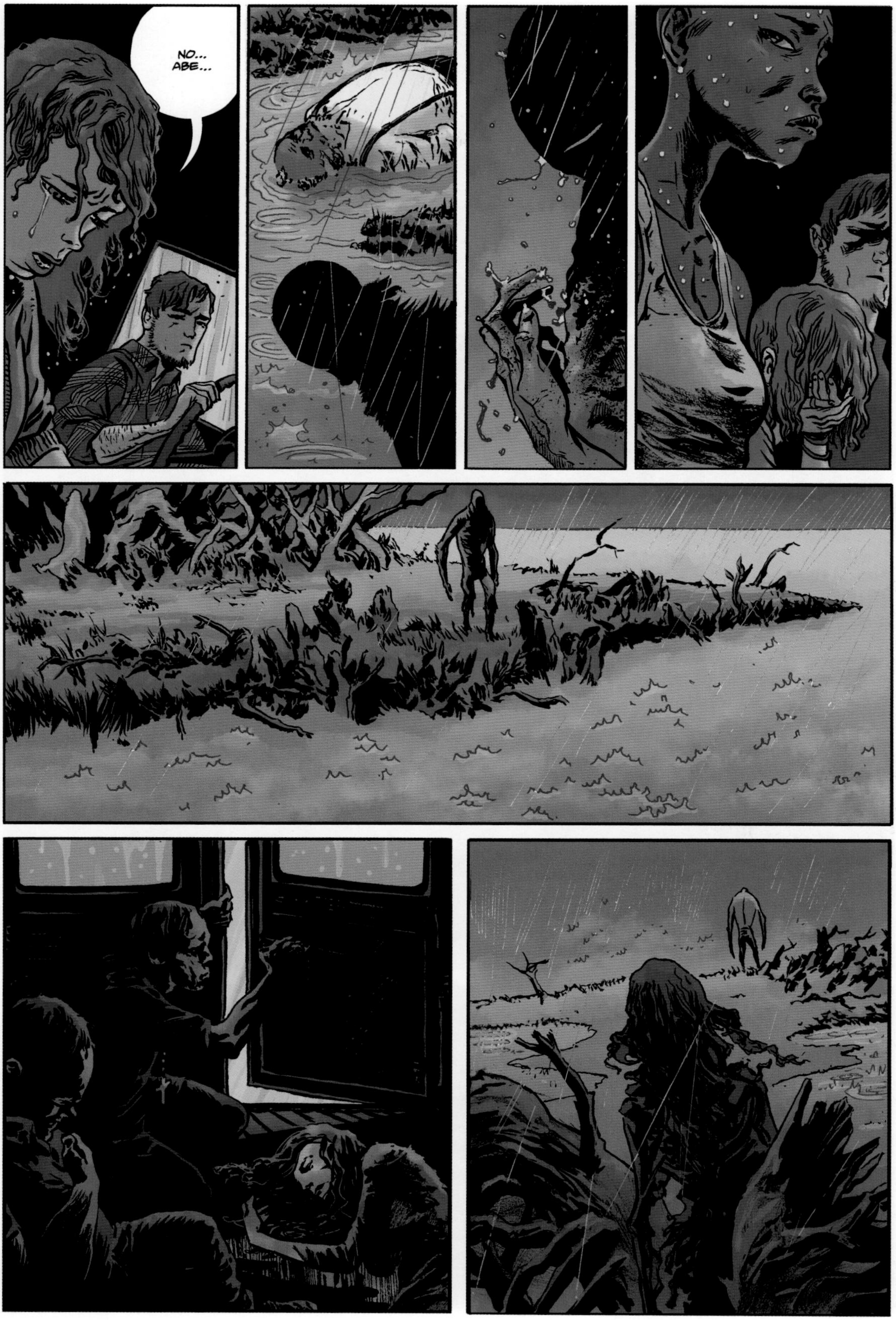
NO... ABE...

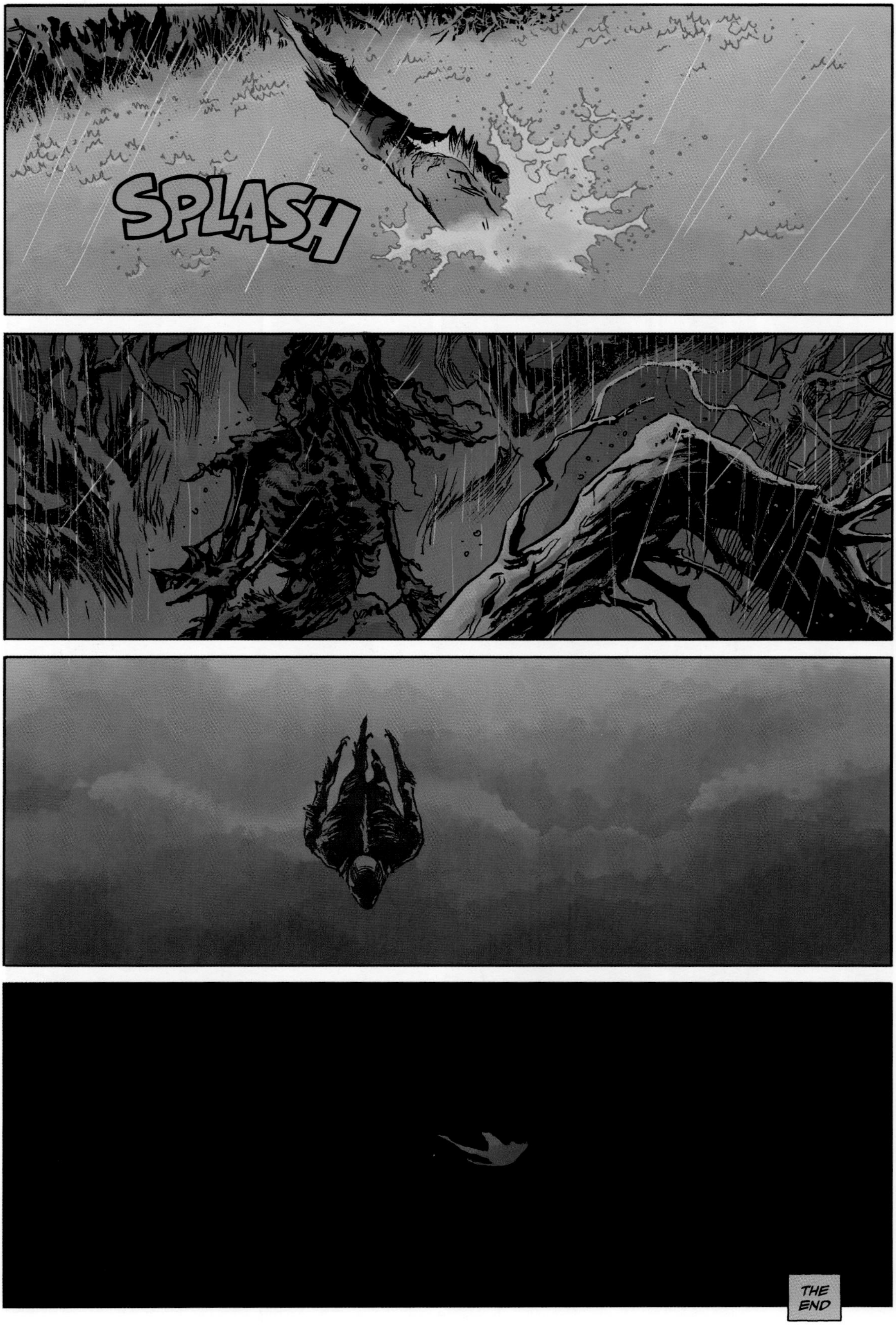
SPLASH
THE END

ABE SAPIEN

Sketchbook

Notes by Scott Allie

ARBOGAST

TONY

Most of the characters were designed in the previous story, *Sacred Places*, except for Arbogast and Tony, drawn here by Sebastián.

Bottom: Height lineup by Sebastián.

GENE   MEGAN   CARMELITA   BATO   DOYANNA   ELIOT   JIMMY   TUCK   DIEGO   GRACE   ABE

ABE SAPIEN
8
DARK HORSE COMICS
$3.50
MIKE MIGNOLA
SCOTT ALLIE
SEBASTIÁN FIUMARA
MAX FIUMARA
DAVE STEWART
FROM THE PAGES OF HELLBOY

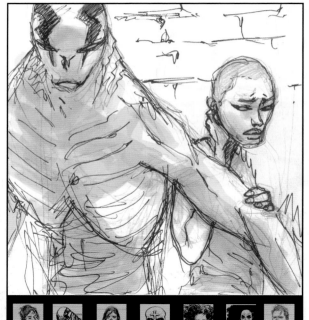

Max took inspiration for these covers from movie posters from the 1970s and '80s, including *The Poseidon Adventure* and *The Swarm*, which feature headshots in the insets.

Sketches and pencils for the first issue's cover.

ABE SAPIEN
8
THE WORLD
DARK HORSE COMICS
The Epic Story Part : 1
MIKE MIGNOLA
SEBASTIÁN FIUMARA
SCOTT ALLIE
MAX FIUMARA
DAVE STEWART
$3.50
FROM THE PAGES OF HELLBOY

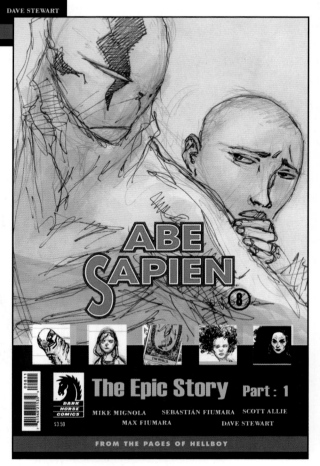

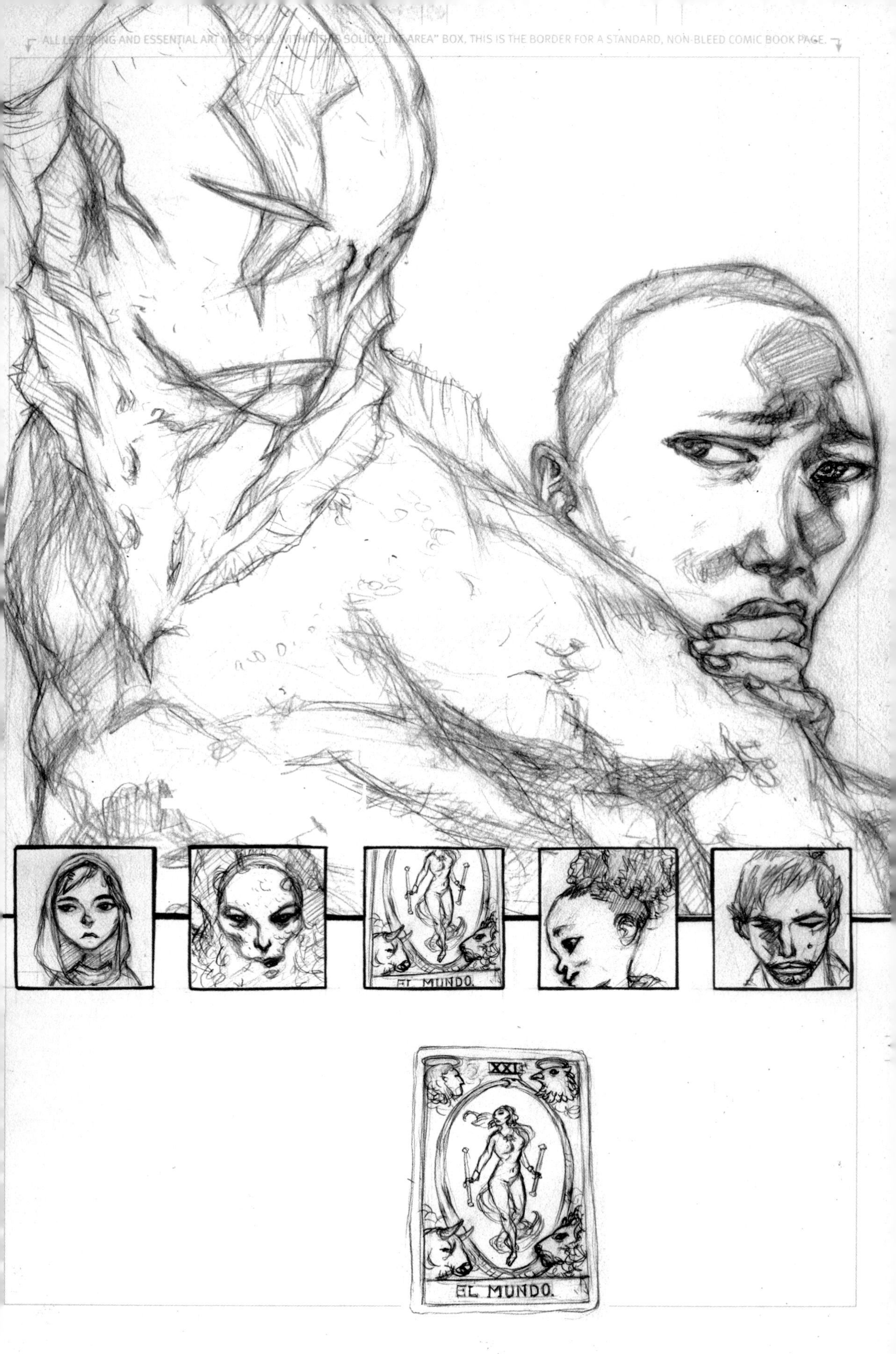
EL MUNDO
XXI
EL MUNDO.

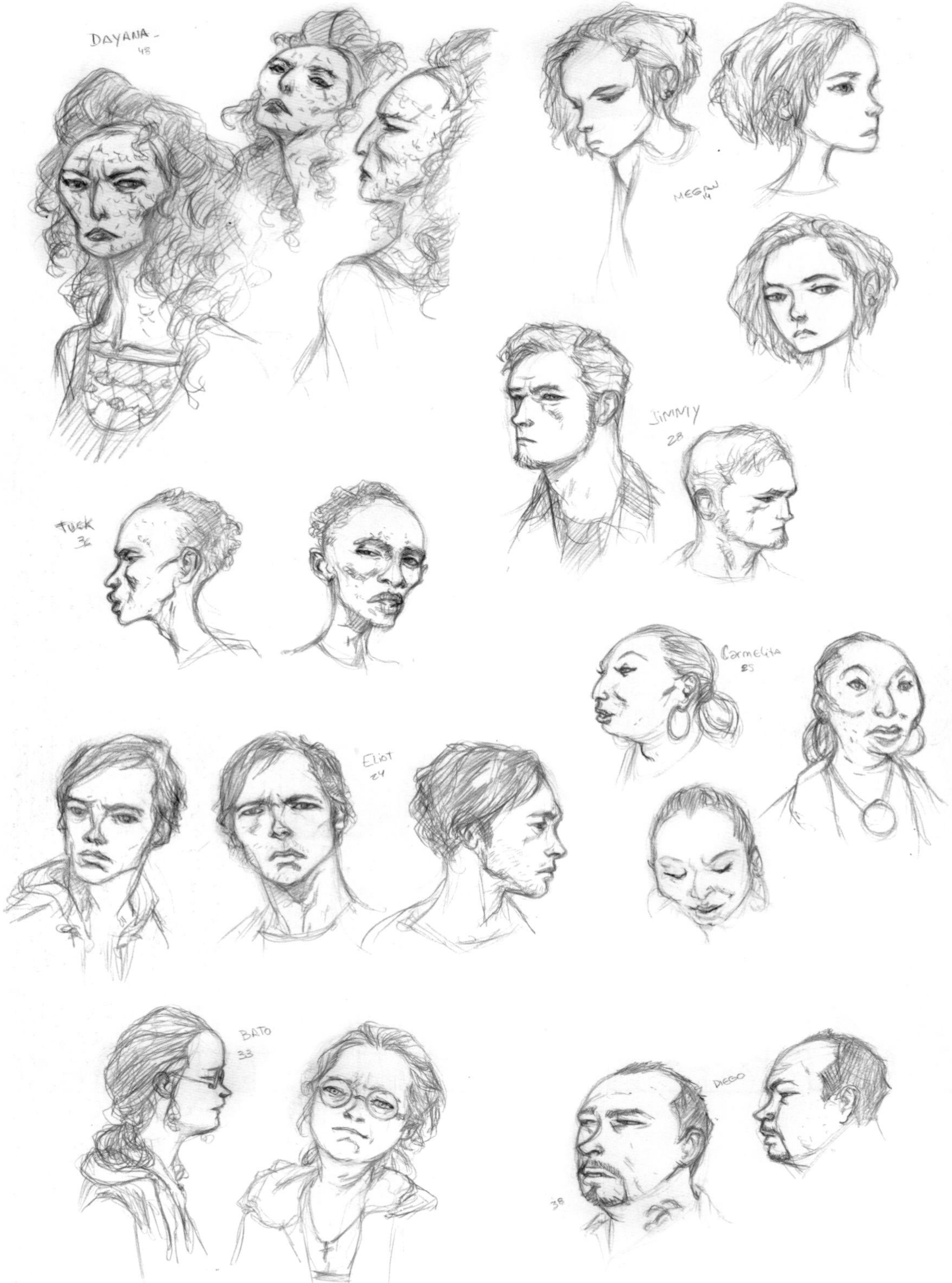
DAYANA
48
MEGAN
14
JIMMY
28
TUCK
36
Carmelita
25
ELIOT
24
BATO
33
DIEGO
38

Seba designed the cult members for the preceding story. Here Max warms up on the characters.

Facing: **Seba's layouts, blue pencils, and inks and Dave's colors for the end of chapter 2.**

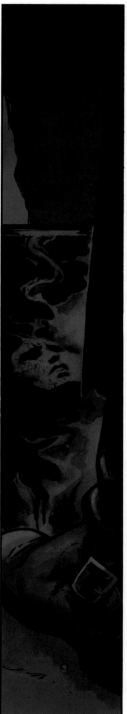

CONTINUED...

The flying monster in chapter 2 was Seba's idea. It was meant to be related to a hammerhead.

***Following:* Raw scans of Seba's inks from chapter 2.**

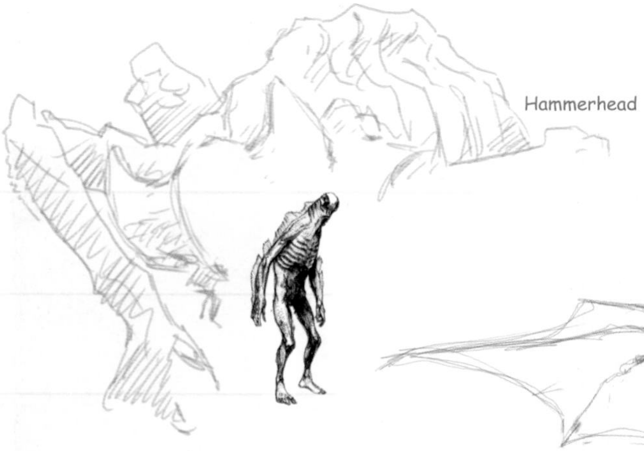
Hammerhead

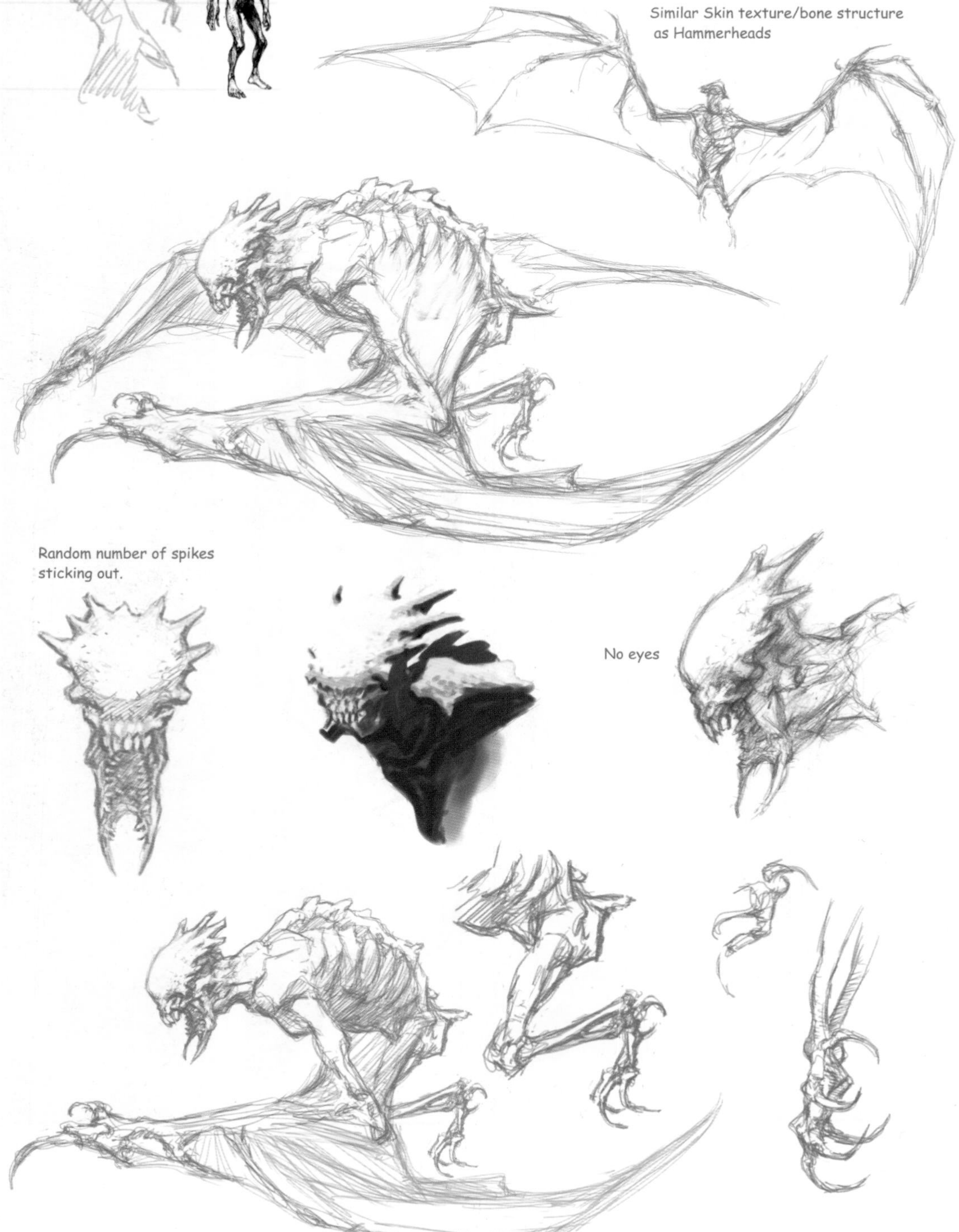
Similar Skin texture/bone structure as Hammerheads
Random number of spikes sticking out.
No eyes

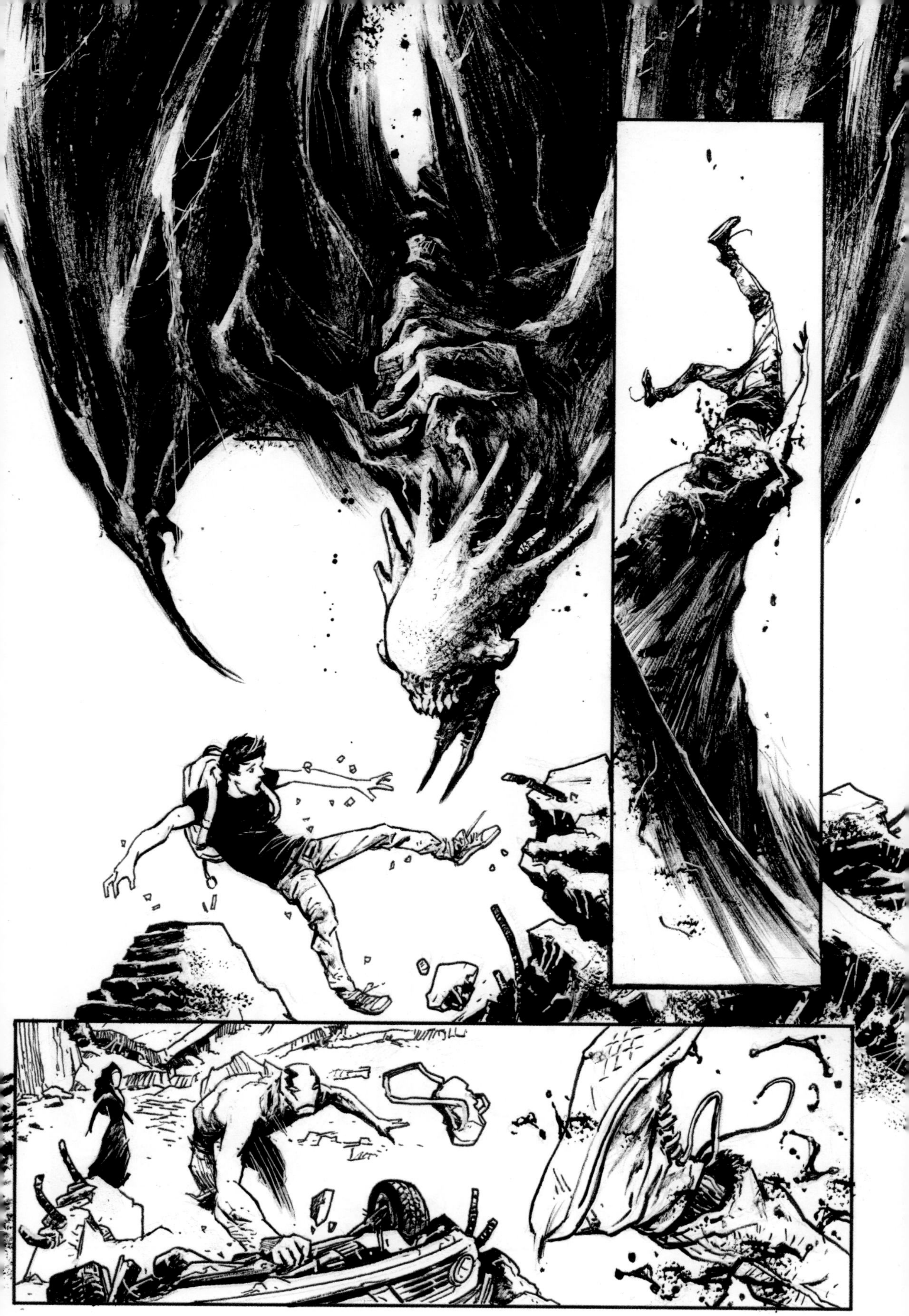

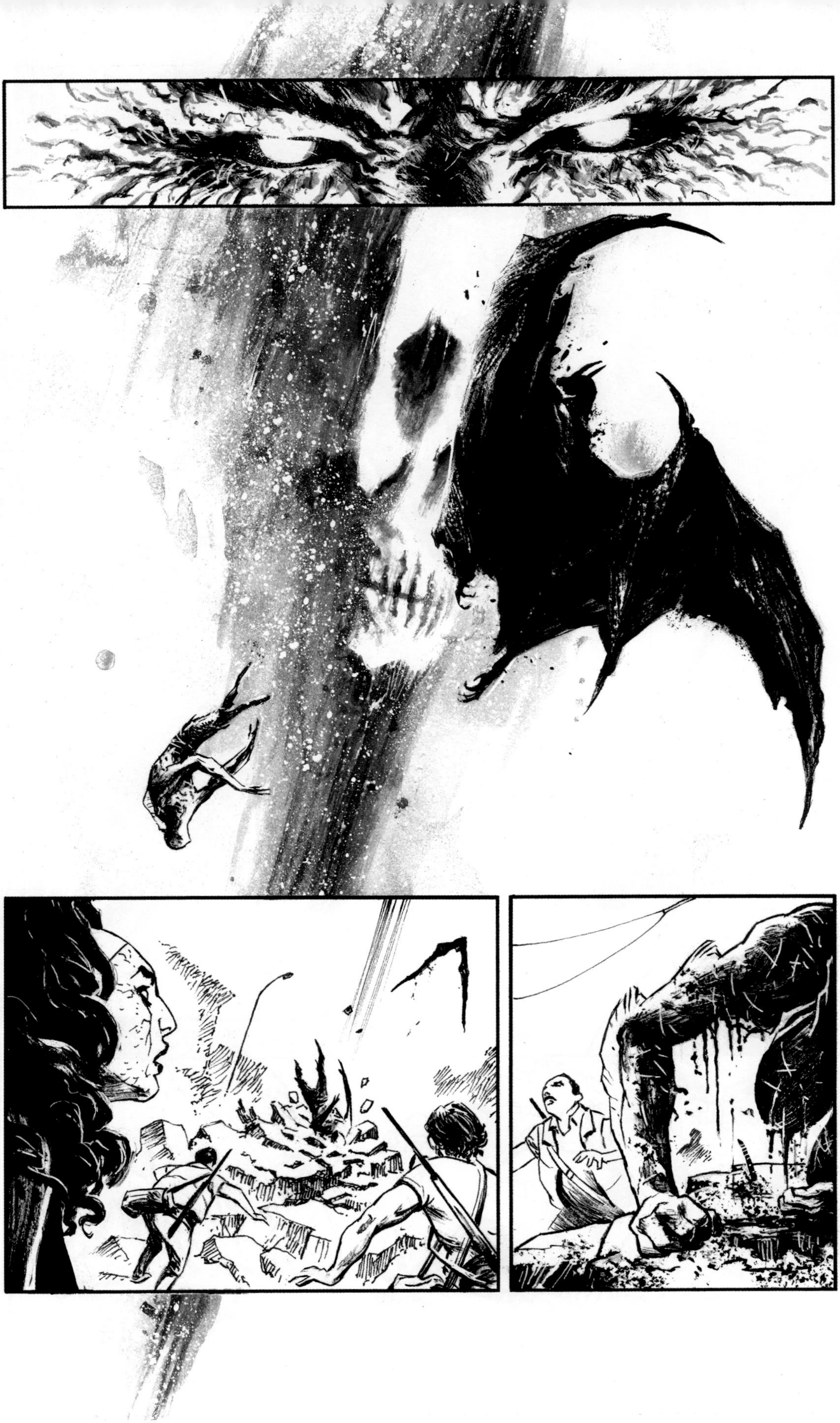

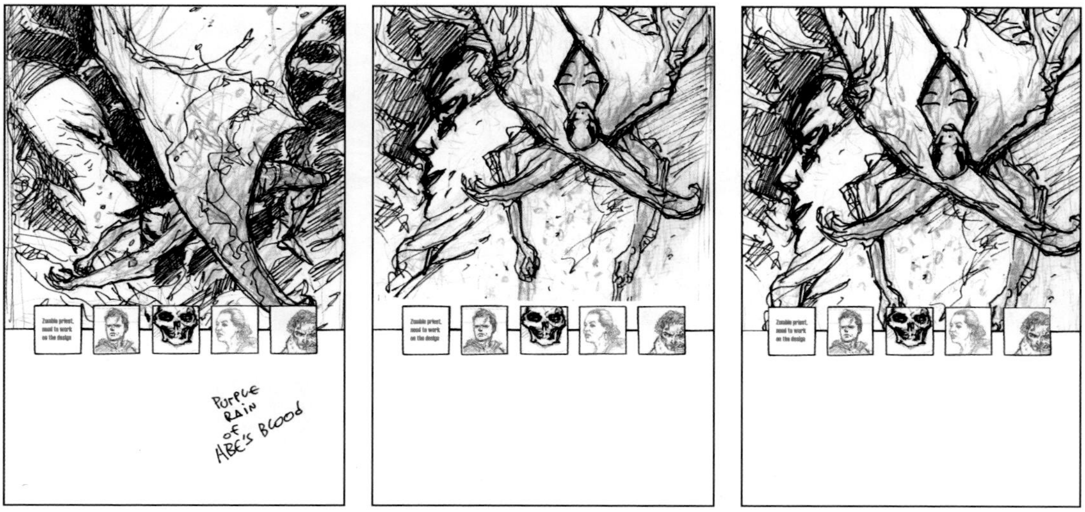

Zombie priest, need to work on the design
PURPLE RAIN OF ABE'S BLOOD

Max's cover sketches for the second issue. He wanted to include Seba's monster without spoiling it.

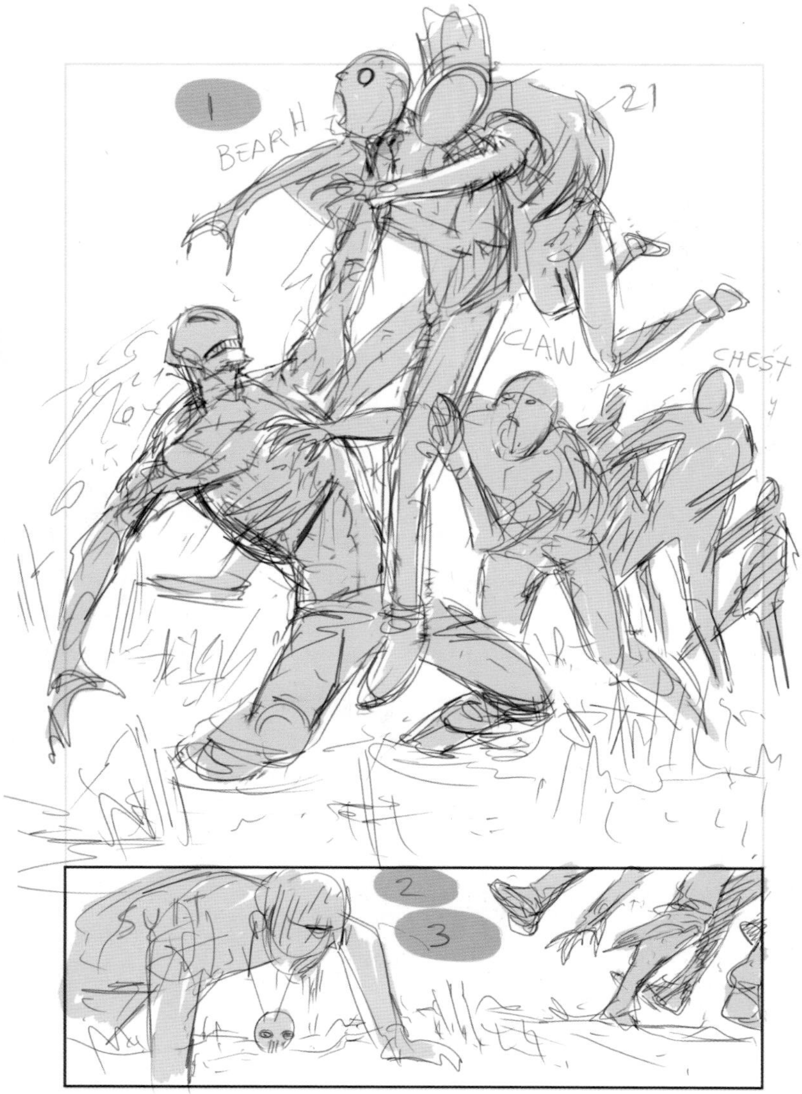

1
21
CLAW
CHEST
2
3

Seba's layout for part of chapter 4's extended zombie fight, which was also his idea.

Following: **Pencils and inks. Note the change to panel 2 from layout to pencil.**

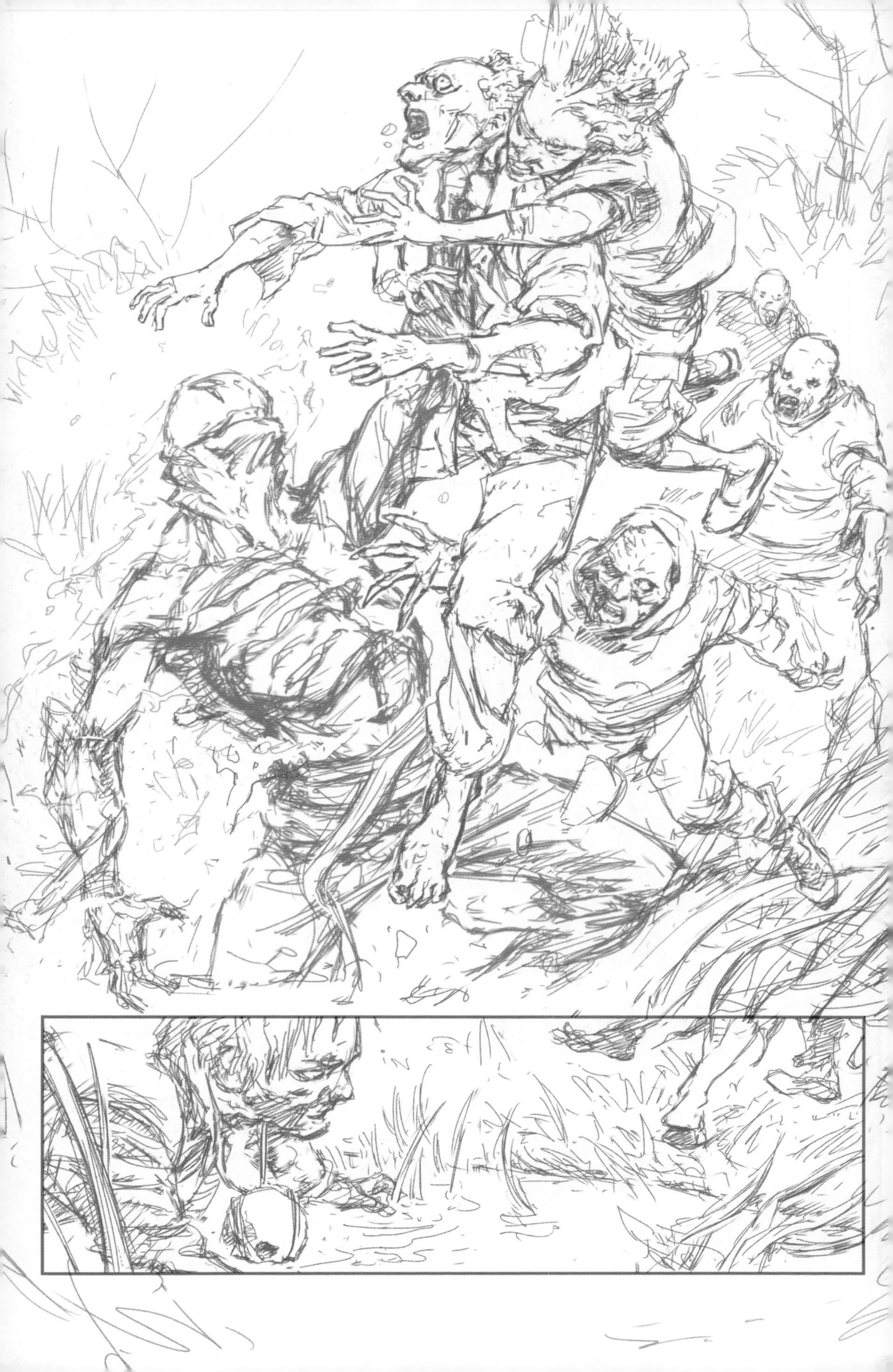

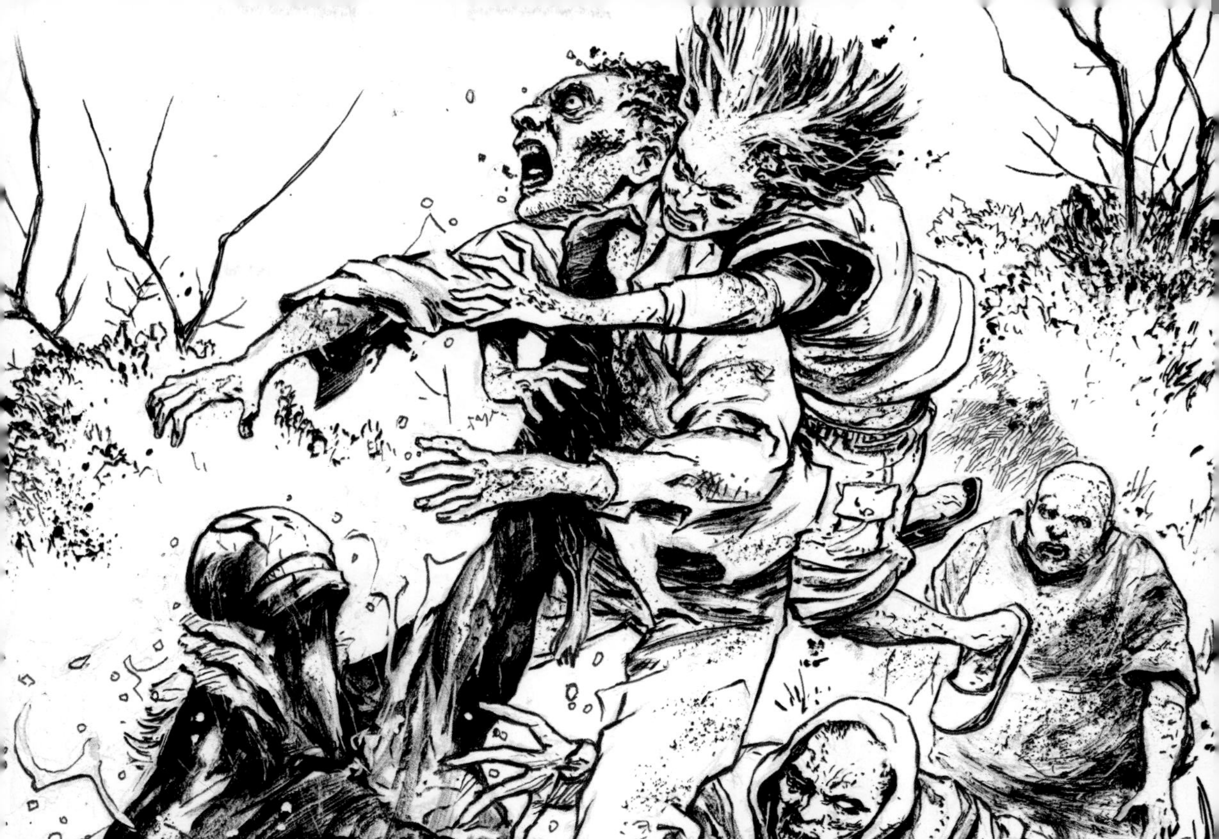

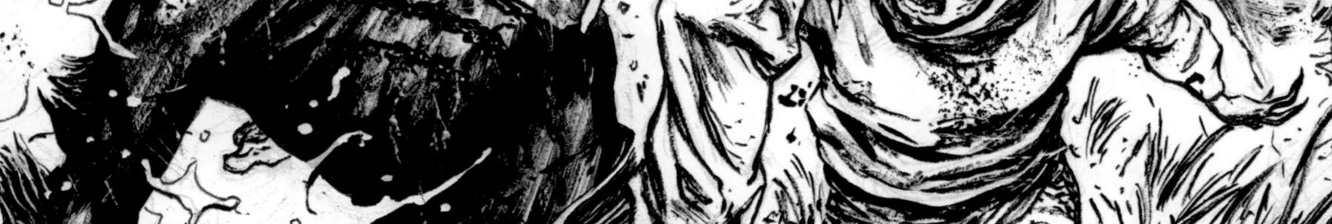

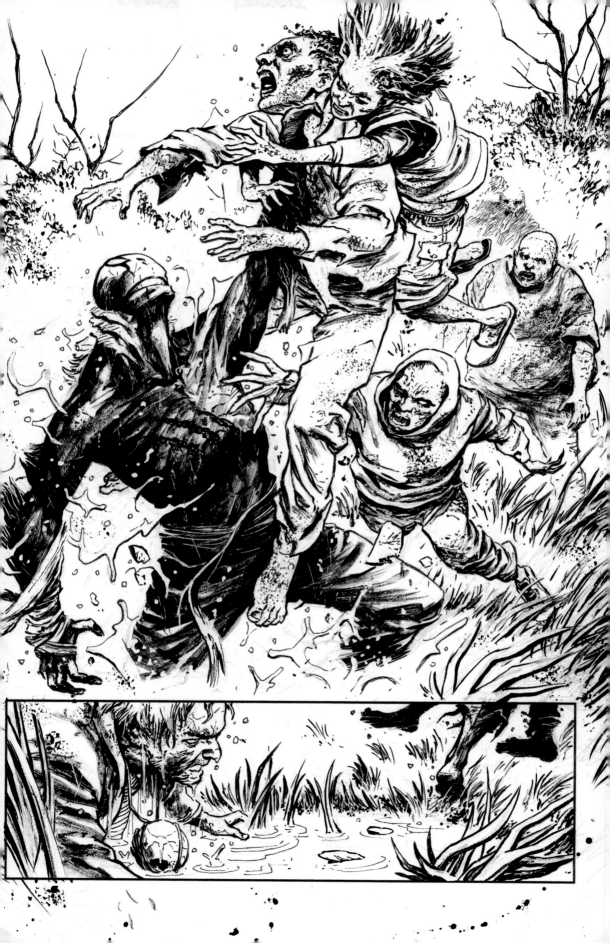

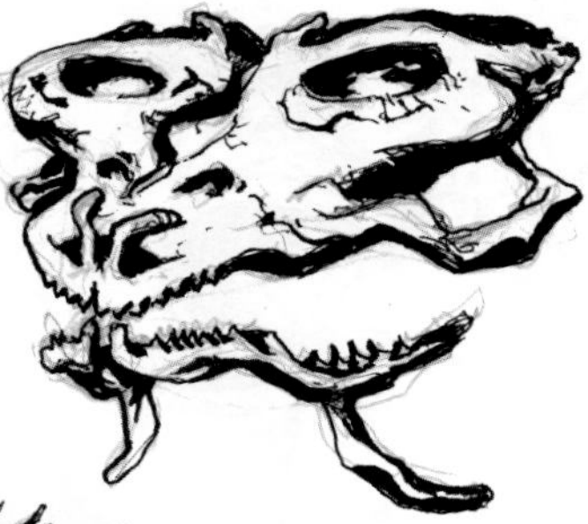

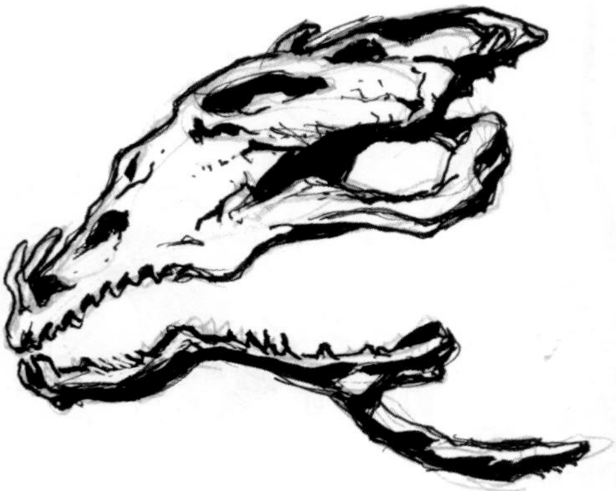

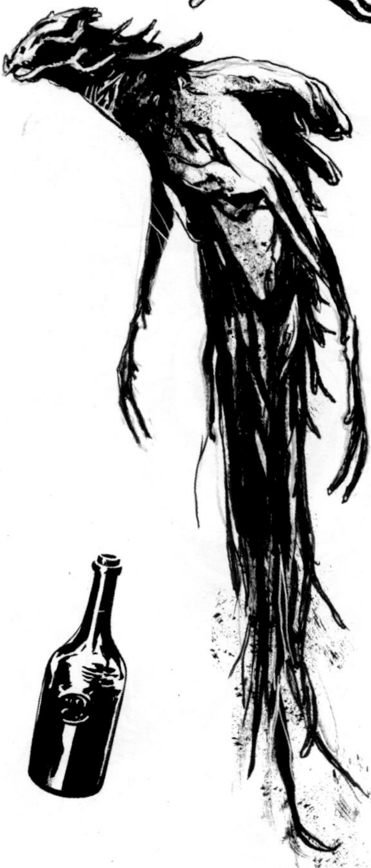

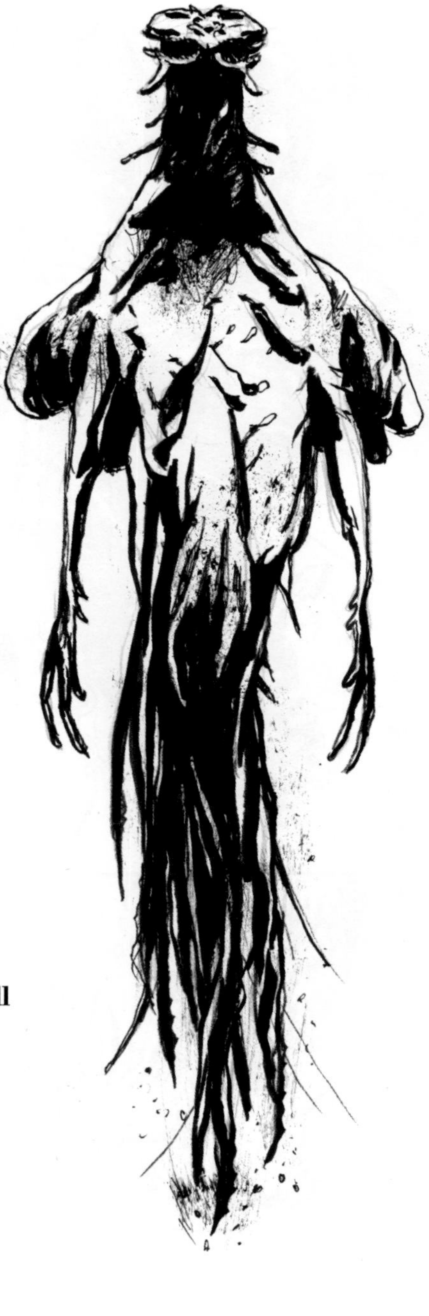

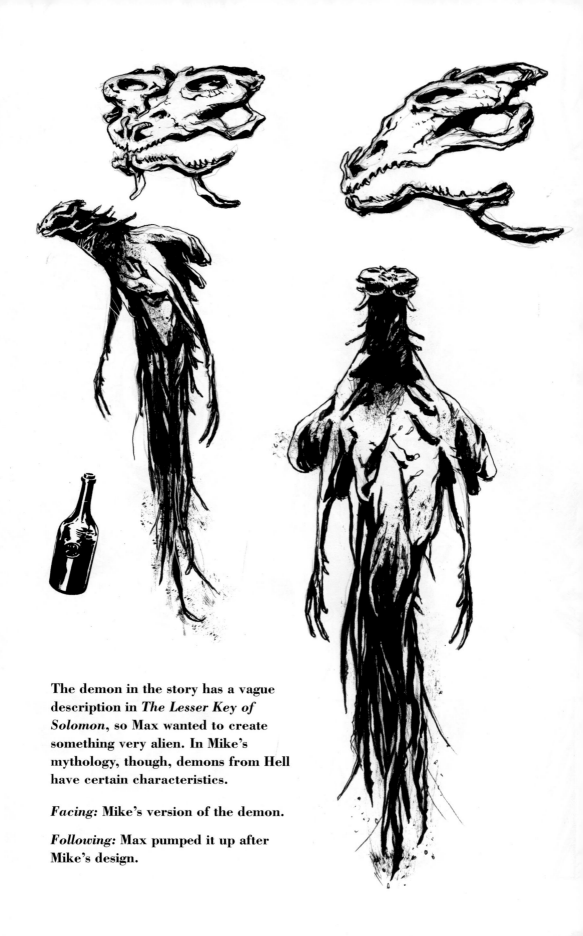

The demon in the story has a vague description in *The Lesser Key of Solomon*, so Max wanted to create something very alien. In Mike's mythology, though, demons from Hell have certain characteristics.

Facing: **Mike's version of the demon.**

Following: **Max pumped it up after Mike's design.**

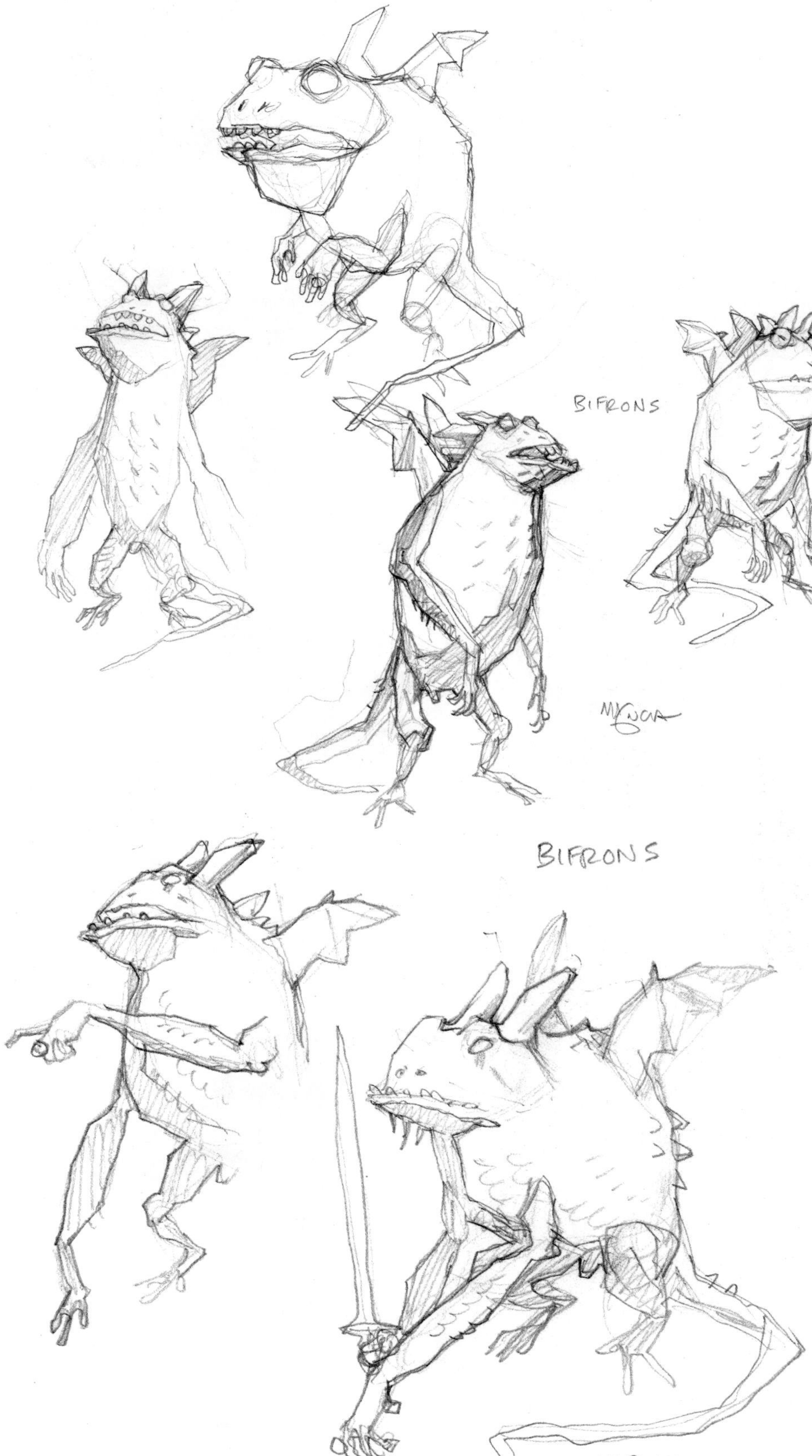
BIFRONS
BIFRONS

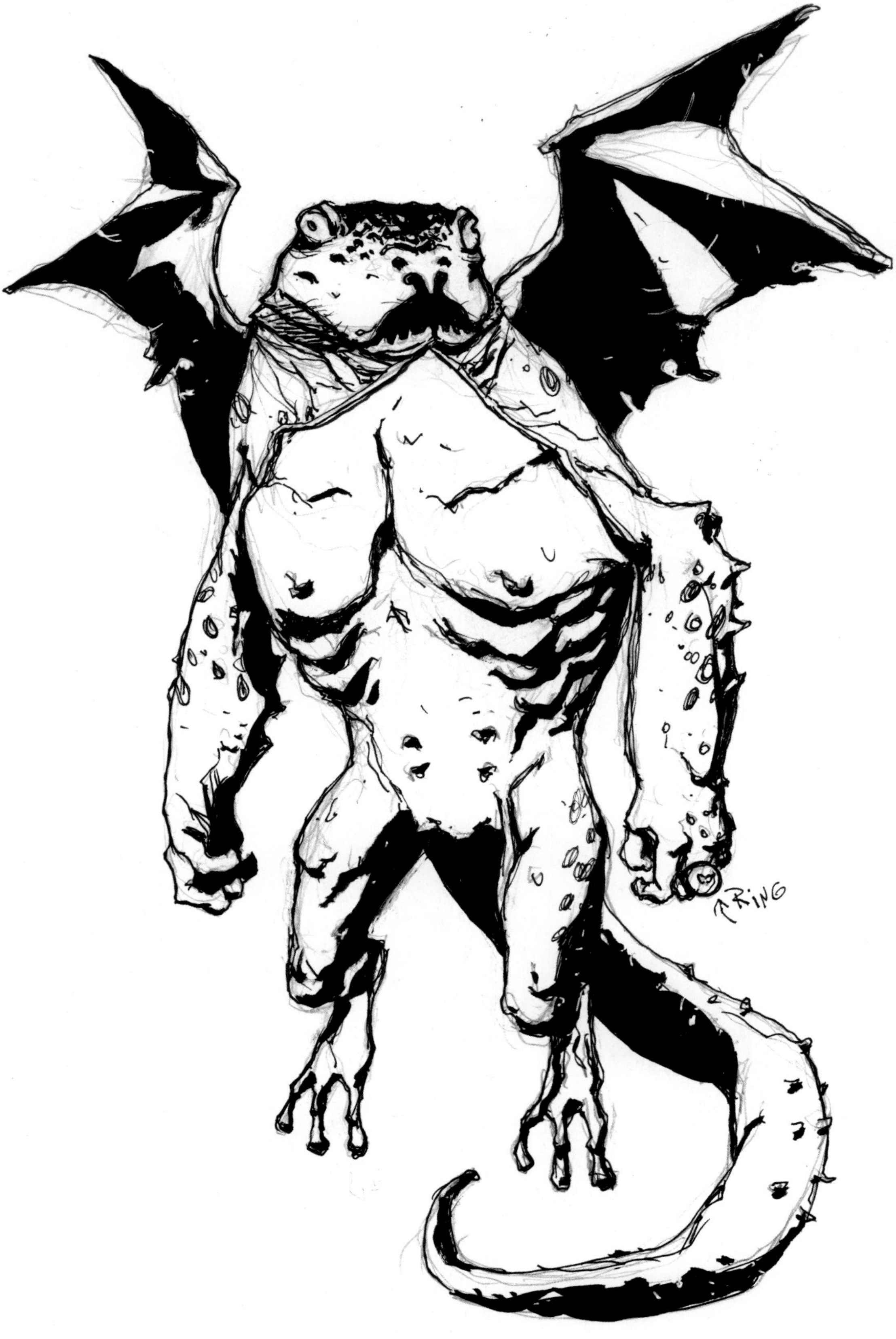
RING

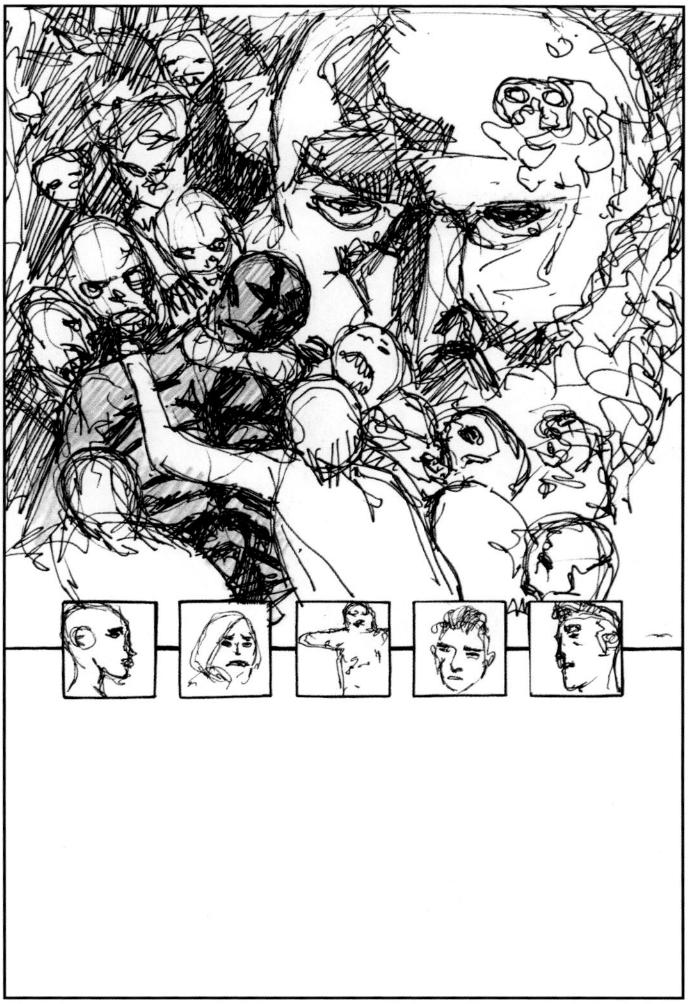

Max's first sketch for the collection didn't include the demon, but we liked the final character design so much we had to add it.

Following: **Pencils and inks for the collection cover.**

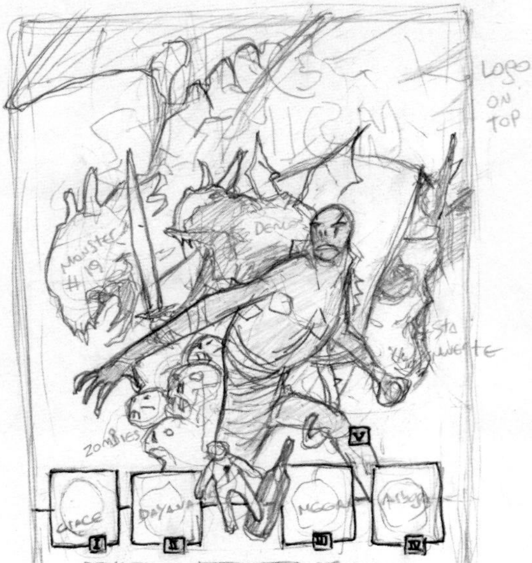
Logo
ON
TOP
MONSTER
#19
ZOMBIES
GRACE
DAYANA

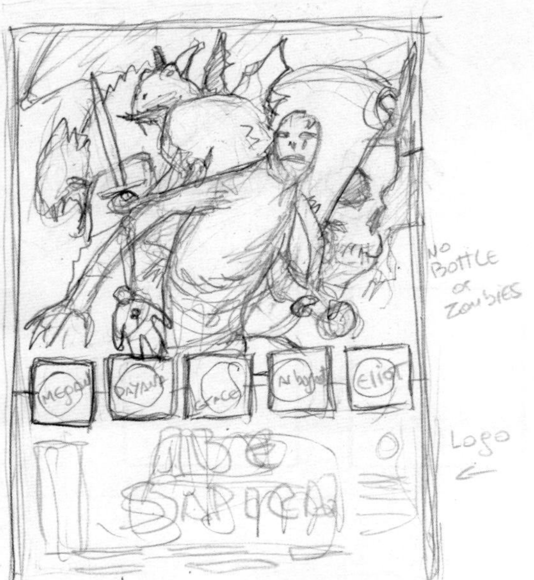
NO
BOTTLE
OR
ZOMBIES
MEGAN
DAYANA
GRACE
ELIOT
Logo

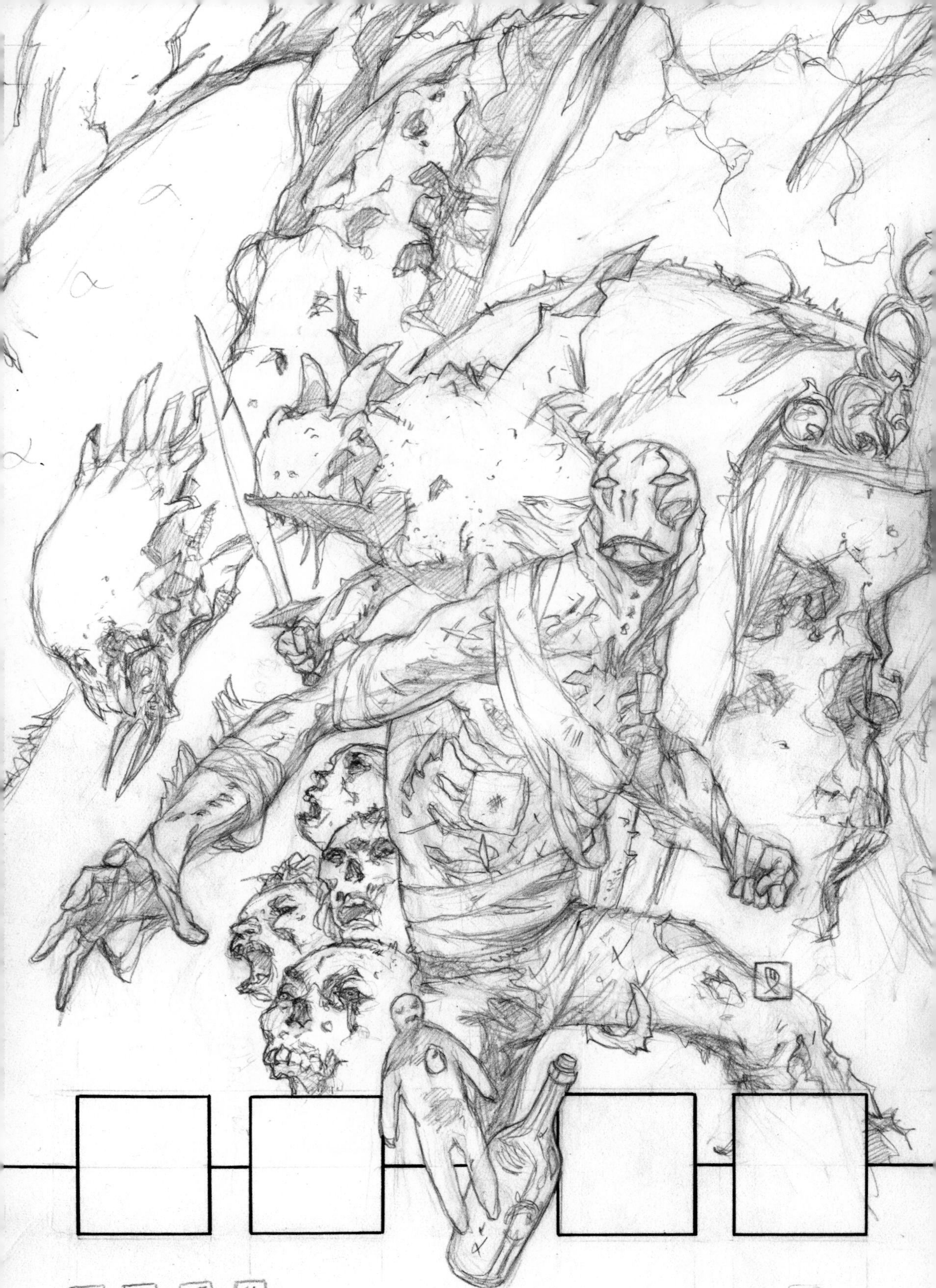

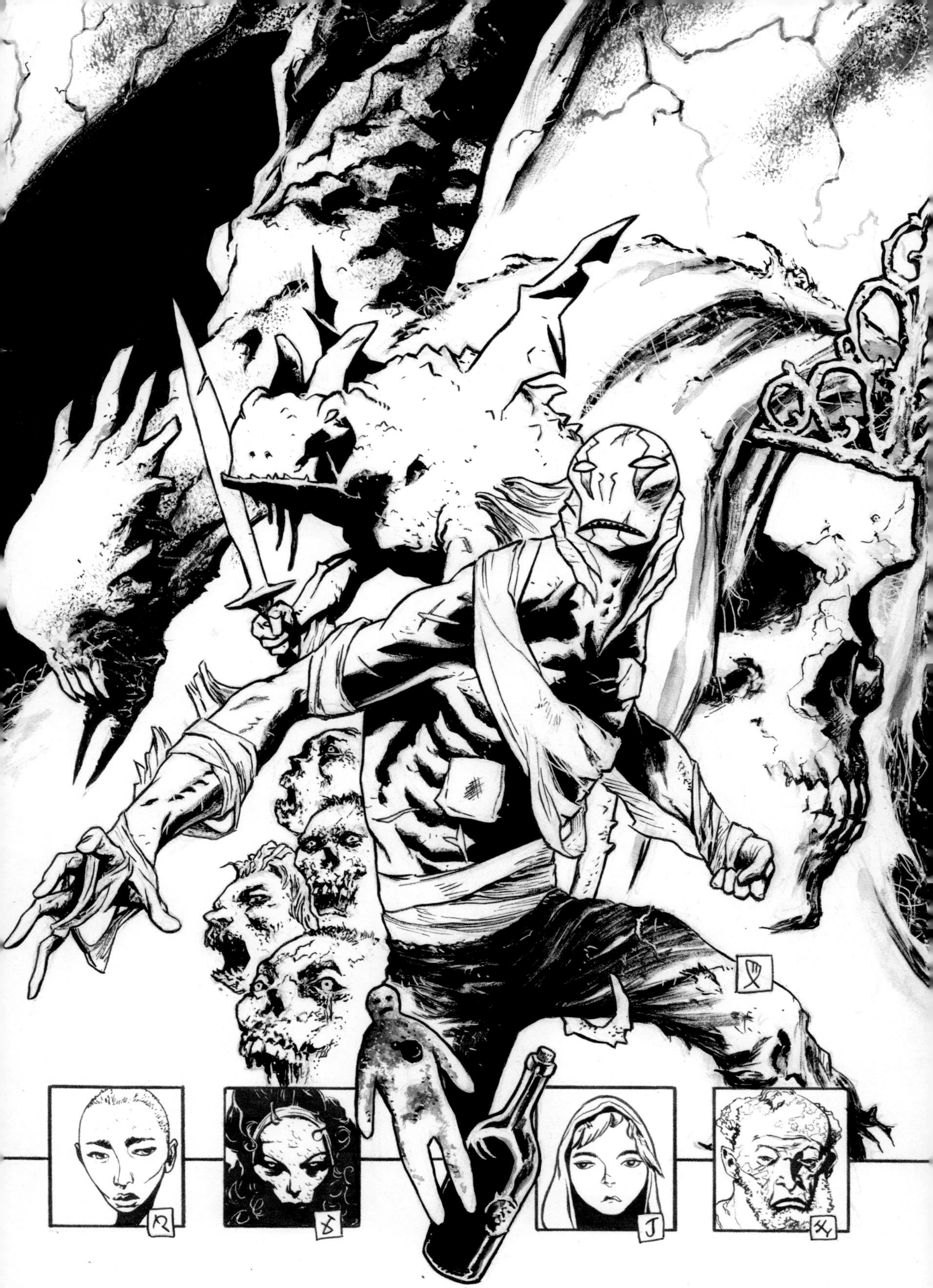

Illustration by Alise Gluškova

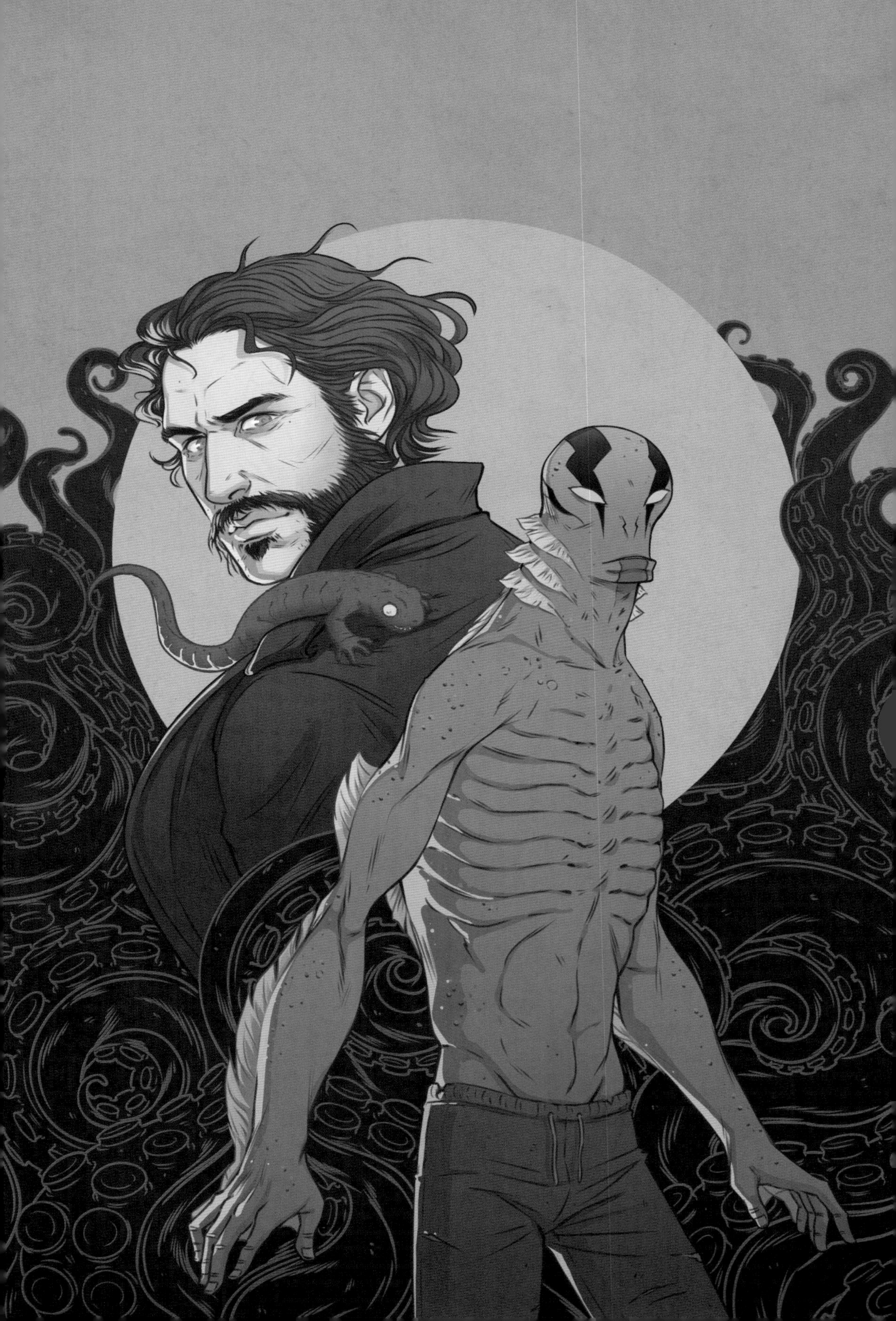

Also by

MIKE MIGNOLA

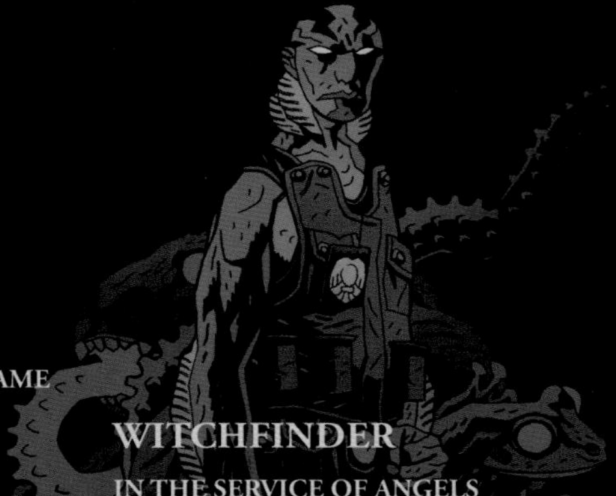

B.P.R.D.

PLAGUE OF FROGS
Volume 1
with Chris Golden, Guy Davis, and others
HC: ISBN 978-1-59582-609-1 | $34.99
TPB: ISBN 978-1-59582-675-6 | $19.99

Volume 2
with John Arcudi, Davis, and others
HC: ISBN 978-1-59582-672-5 | $34.99
TPB: ISBN 978-1-59582-676-3 | $24.99

Volume 3
with Arcudi and Davis
HC: ISBN 978-1-59582-860-6 | $34.99
TPB: ISBN 978-1-61655-622-8 | $24.99

Volume 4
with Arcudi and Davis
HC: ISBN 978-1-59582-974-0 | $34.99
TPB: ISBN 978-1-61655-641-9 | $24.99

1946–1948
with Joshua Dysart, Paul Azaceta, Fábio Moon,
Gabriel Bá, Max Fiumara, and Arcudi
ISBN 978-1-61655-646-4 | $34.99

BEING HUMAN
with Scott Allie, Arcudi, Davis, and others
ISBN 978-1-59582-756-2 | $17.99

VAMPIRE
with Moon and Bá
ISBN 978-1-61655-196-4 | $19.99

B.P.R.D. HELL ON EARTH

NEW WORLD
with Arcudi and Davis
ISBN 978-1-59582-707-4 | $19.99

GODS AND MONSTERS
with Arcudi, Davis, and Tyler Crook
ISBN 978-1-59582-822-4 | $19.99

RUSSIA
with Arcudi, Crook, and Duncan Fegredo
ISBN 978-1-59582-946-7 | $19.9

THE DEVIL'S ENGINE
AND THE LONG DEATH
with Arcudi, Crook, and James Harren
ISBN 978-1-59582-981-8 | $19.99

THE PICKENS COUNTY
HORROR AND OTHERS
with Allie, Jason Latour, Harren,
and Max Fiumara
ISBN 978-1-61655-140-7 | $19.99

THE RETURN OF THE MASTER
with Arcudi and Crook
ISBN 978-1-61655-193-3 | $19.99

A COLD DAY IN HELL
with Arcudi, Peter Snejbjerg, and
Laurence Campbell
ISBN 978-1-61655-199-5 | $19.99

THE REIGN OF THE BLACK FLAME
with Arcudi and Harren
ISBN 978-1-61655-471-2 | $19.99

THE DEVIL'S WINGS
with Arcudi, Campbell, Joe Querio, and Crook
ISBN 978-1-61655-617-4 | $19.99

LAKE OF FIRE
with Arcudi and Crook
ISBN 978-1-61655-402-6 | $19.99

ABE SAPIEN

THE DROWNING
with Jason Shawn Alexander
ISBN 978-1-59582-185-0 | $17.99

THE DEVIL DOES NOT JEST AND
OTHER STORIES
with Arcudi, Harren, and others
ISBN 978-1-59582-925-2 | $17.99

DARK AND TERRIBLE
AND THE NEW RACE OF MAN
with Allie, Arcudi, Sebastián
Fiumara, and Max Fiumara
ISBN 978-1-61655-284-8 | $19.99

THE SHAPE OF THINGS TO COME
with Allie, S. Fiumara, and M. Fiumara
ISBN 978-1-61655-443-9 | $19.99

SACRED PLACES
with Allie, S. Fiumara, and M. Fiumara
ISBN 978-1-61655-515-3 | $19.99

A DARKNESS SO GREAT
with Allie and M. Fiumara
ISBN 978-1-61655-656-3 | $19.99

LOBSTER JOHNSON

THE IRON PROMETHEUS
with Jason Armstrong
ISBN 978-1-59307-975-8 | $17.99

THE BURNING HAND
with Arcudi and Tonci Zonjic
ISBN 978-1-61655-031-8 | $17.99

SATAN SMELLS A RAT
with Arcudi, Fiumara, Querio,
Wilfredo Torres, and Kevin Nowlan
ISBN 978-1-61655-203-9 | $18.99

GET THE LOBSTER
with Arcudi and Zonjic
ISBN 978-1-61655-505-4 | $19.99

WITCHFINDER

IN THE SERVICE OF ANGELS
with Ben Stenbeck
ISBN 978-1-59582-483-7 | $17.99

LOST AND GONE FOREVER
with Arcudi and John Severin
ISBN 978-1-59582-794-4 | $17.99

THE MYSTERIES OF UNLAND
with Kim Newman, Maura McHugh,
and Crook
ISBN 978-1-61655-630-3 | $19.99

THE AMAZING
SCREW-ON HEAD
AND OTHER
CURIOUS OBJECTS
ISBN 978-1-59582-501-8 | $17.99

BALTIMORE

THE PLAGUE SHIPS
with Golden and Stenbeck
ISBN 978-1-59582-677-0 | $24.99

THE CURSE BELLS
with Golden and Stenbeck
ISBN 978-1-59582-674-9 | $24.99

A PASSING STRANGER
AND OTHER STORIES
with Golden and Stenbeck
ISBN 978-1-61655-182-7 | $24.99

CHAPEL OF BONES
with Golden and Stenbeck
ISBN 978-1-61655-328-9 | $24.99

THE APOSTLE AND THE WITCH
OF HARJU
with Golden, Stenbeck, and Peter Bergting
ISBN 978-1-61655-618-1 | $24.99

NOVELS

LOBSTER JOHNSON:
THE SATAN FACTORY
with Thomas E. Sniegoski
ISBN 978-1-59582-203-1 | $12.95

JOE GOLEM AND THE
DROWNING CITY
with Golden
ISBN 978-1-59582-971-9 | $99.99

DARK HORSE BOOKS

DarkHorse.com

AVAILABLE AT YOUR LOCAL COMICS SHOP OR BOOKSTORE! • To find a comics shop in your area, call 1-888-266-4226.
For more information or to order direct visit DarkHorse.com or call 1-800-862-0052 Mon.–Fri. 9 AM to 5 PM Pacific Time.
Prices and availability subject to change without notice.

HELLBOY™

by MIKE MIGNOLA

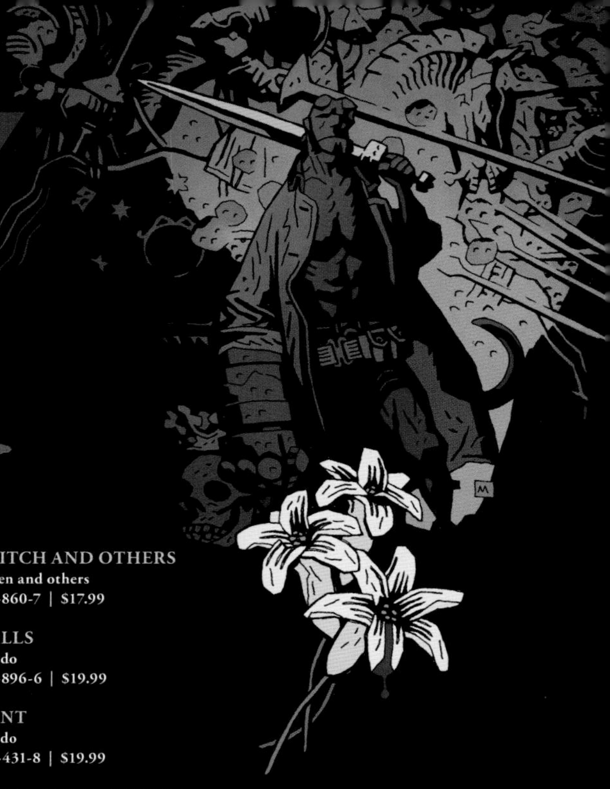

HELLBOY LIBRARY EDITION VOLUME 1:
Seed of Destruction and Wake the Devil
ISBN 978-1-59307-910-9 | $49.99

HELLBOY LIBRARY EDITION VOLUME 2:
The Chained Coffin and The Right Hand of Doom
ISBN 978-1-59307-989-5 | $49.99

HELLBOY LIBRARY EDITION VOLUME 3:
Conqueror Worm and Strange Places
ISBN 978-1-59582-352-6 | $49.99

HELLBOY LIBRARY EDITION VOLUME 4:
The Crooked Man and The Troll Witch
with Richard Corben and others
ISBN 978-1-59582-658-9 | $49.99

HELLBOY LIBRARY EDITION VOLUME 5:
Darkness Calls and the Wild Hunt
with Duncan Fegredo
ISBN 978-1-59582-886-6 | $49.99

HELLBOY LIBRARY EDITION VOLUME 6:
The Storm and the Fury and The Bride of Hell
with Duncan Fegredo, Richard Corben, Kevin Nowlan, and Scott Hampton
ISBN 978-1-61655-133-9 | $49.99

SEED OF DESTRUCTION
with John Byrne
ISBN 978-1-59307-094-6 | $17.99

WAKE THE DEVIL
ISBN 978-1-59307-095-3 | $17.99

THE CHAINED COFFIN AND OTHERS
ISBN 978-1-59307-091-5 | $17.99

THE RIGHT HAND OF DOOM
ISBN 978-1-59307-093-9 | $17.99

CONQUEROR WORM
ISBN 978-1-59307-092-2 | $17.99

STRANGE PLACES
ISBN 978-1-59307-475-3 | $17.99

THE TROLL WITCH AND OTHERS
with Richard Corben and others
ISBN 978-1-59307-860-7 | $17.99

DARKNESS CALLS
with Duncan Fegredo
ISBN 978-1-59307-896-6 | $19.99

THE WILD HUNT
with Duncan Fegredo
ISBN 978-1-59582-431-8 | $19.99

THE CROOKED MAN AND OTHERS
with Richard Corben
ISBN 978-1-59582-477-6 | $17.99

THE BRIDE OF HELL AND OTHERS
with Richard Corben, Kevin Nowlan, and Scott Hampton
ISBN 978-1-59582-740-1 | $19.99

THE STORM AND THE FURY
with Duncan Fegredo
ISBN 978-1-59582-827-9 | $19.99

HOUSE OF THE LIVING DEAD
with Richard Corben
ISBN 978-1-59582-757-9 | $14.99

THE MIDNIGHT CIRCUS
with Duncan Fegredo
ISBN 978-1-61655-238-1 | $14.99

HELLBOY IN HELL VOLUME 1: THE DESCENT
ISBN 978-1-61655-444-6 | $17.99

HELLBOY: THE FIRST 20 YEARS
ISBN 978-1-61655-353-1 | $19.99

THE ART OF HELLBOY
ISBN 978-1-59307-089-2 | $29.99

HELLBOY II: THE ART OF THE MOVIE
ISBN 978-1-59307-964-2 | $24.99

HELLBOY: THE COMPANION
ISBN 978-1-59307-655-9 | $14.99

HELLBOY: WEIRD TALES
ISBN 978-1-61655-510-8 | $24.99

HELLBOY: MASKS AND MONSTERS
with James Robinson and Scott Benefiel
ISBN 978-1-59582-567-4 | $17.99

HELLBOY AND THE B.P.R.D: 1952
with John Arcudi and Alex Maleev
ISBN 978-1-61655-660-0 | $19.99

NOVELS

HELLBOY: EMERALD HELL
By Tom Piccirilli
ISBN 978-1-59582-141-6 | $12.99

HELLBOY: THE ALL-SEEING EYE
By Mark Morris
ISBN 978-1-59582-142-3 | $12.99

HELLBOY: THE FIRE WOLVES
By Tim Lebbon
ISBN 978-1-59582-204-8 | $12.99

HELLBOY: THE ICE WOLVES
By Mark Chadbourn
ISBN 978-1-59582-205-5 | $12.99

SHORT STORIES

Illustrated by Mike Mignola

HELLBOY: ODDER JOBS
By Frank Darabont, Charles de Lint, Guillermo del Toro, and others
ISBN 978-1-59307-226-1 | $14.99

HELLBOY: ODDEST JOBS
By Joe R. Lansdale, China Miéville, and others
ISBN 978-1-59307-944-4 | $14.99

AVAILABLE AT YOUR LOCAL COMICS SHOP OR BOOKSTORE! • To find a comics shop in your area, call 1-888-266-4226.
For more information or to order direct visit DarkHorse.com or call 1-800-862-0052 Mon.–Fri. 9 AM to 5 PM Pacific Time.
Prices and availability subject to change without notice.

DARK HORSE BOOKS
DarkHorse.com